The Social Mobility
of Women

The Social Mobility of Women:

Beyond Male Mobility Models

Edited by

Geoff Payne and Pamela Abbott

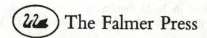 The Falmer Press

(A member of the Taylor & Francis Group)
London • New York • Philadelphia

UK   The Falmer Press, Rankine Road, Basingstoke, Hampshire
RG24 0PR

USA   The Falmer Press, Taylor & Francis Inc., 1900 Frost Road,
Suite 101, Bristol, PA 19007

First published 1990

British Library Cataloguing in Publication Data
The social mobility of women: beyond male mobility models.
  1. Social mobility
  I. Payne, Geoff   II. Abbott, Pamela
  305.513

  ISBN 1-85000-845-0
  ISBN 1-85000-846-9 pbk

Library of Congress Cataloging-in-Publication Data
The Social mobility of women: beyond male mobility models/edited
  by Geoff Payne and Pamela Abbott.
    p.   cm.
  Includes bibliographical references and index.
  ISBN 1-85000-845-0: — ISBN 1-85000-846-9 (pbk.):
  1. Women — Great Britain — Social conditions.   2. Social
  mobility — Great Britain.   3. Occupational mobility — Great
  Britain.
  I. Payne, Geoff.   II. Abbott, Pamela.
  HQ1593.S63   1990
  305.5 ′3—dc20   90-42872
                                                             CIP

Jacket design by Benedict Evans

Typeset in 11/13 Bembo by
Chapterhouse, The Cloisters, Formby L37 3PX

*Printed in Great Britain by Burgess Science Press, Basingstoke
on paper which has a specified pH value on final paper
manufacture of not less than 7.5 and is therefore 'acid free'.*

Contents

List of Figures and Tables		vi
Preface		ix
Chapter 1	Introduction: Origins and Destinations	
	Geoff Payne and Pamela Abbott	1
Chapter 2	Women's Social Mobility:	
	The Conventional Wisdom Reconsidered	
	Pamela Abbott and Geoff Payne	12
Chapter 3	The Mobility of Women and Men	
	Tony Chapman	25
Chapter 4	A Re-examination of 'Three Theses Re-examined'	
	Pamela Abbott	37
Chapter 5	The Changing Pattern of Early Career Mobility	
	Geoff Payne, Judy Payne and Tony Chapman	47
Chapter 6	Gender and Intergenerational Mobility	
	Robert L. Miller and Bernadette C. Hayes	61
Chapter 7	The Career Mobility of Women and Men	
	Tony Chapman	73
Chapter 8	Credentials and Careers	
	Rosemary Crompton and Kay Sanderson	83
Chapter 9	Marriage Partners and their Class Trajectories	
	Gill Jones	101
Chapter 10	Occupational Mobility over Women's Lifetime	
	Shirley Dex	121
Chapter 11	Stratification over the Life-course:	
	Gender Differences within the Household	
	Angela Dale	139
Chapter 12	Beyond Male Mobility Models	
	Geoff Payne and Pamela Abbott	159
	Bibliography	175
	Notes on Contributors	185
	Subject Index	187
	Author Index	191

List of Figures and Tables

Chapter 2

Table 2.1:	Labour market distribution by gender in the UK in 1981	16
Table 2.2:	Market and work situations of men and women in full-time employment	18
Table 2.3:	Gross mobility rates by gender in the Scottish Mobility Study	18
Table 2.4:	Current class and class of origin, percentaged by current class (Inflow %)	19
Table 2.5:	Current class and class of origin, percentaged by class of origin (Outflow %)	20
Table 2.6:	Changes in labour market structure, 1921–1971	23

Chapter 3

Figure 3.1:	Payne's seven category occupational status scale	26
Table 3.1:	Occupational mobility of men and women, by their father's job when respondent aged fourteen	27
Table 3.2:	Rates of occupational mobility over seven occupational categories and two occupational categories.	28
Table 3.3:	Occupational distribution of men and women by class of father when respondent was aged fourteen: percentage by row	30
Table 3.4:	Occupational composition of men and women by class of father when respondent was aged fourteen: percentage by column	31
Table 3.5:	Rates of intergenerational mobility for men and women assuming perfect symmetry.	33
Table 3.6:	Rates of occupational mobility over seven occupational categories and two occupational categories for asymmetrical and symmetrical mobility tables	34
Table 3.7:	Occupational distribution of men and women compared with that of their fathers	35

Chapter 4

Table 4.1:   The social mobility of women, by class of origin (Outflow %)   40
Table 4.2:   The social mobility of women, by destination class (Inflow %)   40
Table 4.3:   The education, backgrouund and occupation of women:
                 percentage with 2+ years of post-compulsory schooling   42

Chapter 5

Figure 5.1:   Five-year moving averages for non-manual employment and
                 mobility on first entry to the labour market   50
Figure 5.2:   Proportions of upward mobility in three industrial sectors (five-
                 year moving average for first job)   55

Chapter 6

Table 6.1:   Determinants of respondents' occupational and educational
                 level, standardized regression coefficients   67
Table 6.2:   Occupation by gender for matched sibling pairs   69

Chapter 7

Figure 7.1:   Three point occupational mobility patterns: flows representing
                 three per cent or more of all in class of origin, men and women
                 aged 35 and over   75
Figure 7.2:   Three point occupational mobility patterns — flows
                 representing three per cent or more of all in class of origin,
                 men and women: 1910–1929 and 1930–1949   76
Figure 7.3:   Occupational distribution of men and women over seven
                 occupational categories by year of entry into the labour market:
                 five year moving averages   79

Chapter 8

Figure 8.1:   Employment careers, qualifications and gender   92
Table 8.1:   Trends in women studying and qualifying: various professions   94
Table 8.2:   Pharmacists: membership by sex and principal occupation   96
Table 8.3:   Pharmacists: membership by sex and normal extent of
                 occupation   97

Chapter 9

Table 9.1:   Derivation of occupational class schema   105
Table 9.2:   Class Endogamy   106
Table 9.3:   Class Endogamy — men 16–29 years   108
Table 9.4:   Class Endogamy — women 16–29 years   110
Table 9.5:   Elements of endogamy   112

Table 9.6:	Youth class in the GHS	*114*
Table 9.7:	Class trajectories of marriage partners (%)	*115*
Table 9.8:	Class trajectories of marriage partners	*116*

Chapter 10

Table 10.1:	Occupations of employed women in WES in 1980	*124*
Table 10.2:	Proportions of full and part-time employed women in different occupation groups according to whether only women do same work	*125*
Table 10.3:	Downward occupational mobility	*127*
Table 10.4:	Upward occupational mobility	*128*
Table 10.5:	Timing of occupational mobility for women aged 20–59, with children	*130*
Table 10.6:	Occupational transitions between last job before childbirth and first job after	*132*
Table 10.7:	Downward occupational mobility over childbirth and status recovery for women aged 40–59	*133*
Figure 10.1:	Labour market segmentation and women's employment	*134*

Chapter 11

Figure 11.1:	Levels of owner occupation: 1973 to 1982	*142*
Table 11.1:	Number of people in paid work by type of household	*143*
Table 11.2:	Median net weekly income of household, for selected household types, by employment status of spouses	*144*
Table 11.3:	Relationship between husband's income from main job and wife's employment status and income	*145*
Table 11.4:	Contribution to an occupational pension scheme among those in paid employment, 1984	*147*
Table 11.5:	Occupational distribution by life-cycle and sex	*149*
Table 11.6:	Full and part-time work among women aged 20–64 (%)	*151*
Table 11.7:	Current net weekly income for male and female headed households of selected types	*153*
Table 11.8:	Marital history of women aged 18–49 (or 16–49 if married)	*154*

Chapter 12

Figure 12.1:	Female mobility profiles	*165*
Table 12.1:	Class of marriage partners and class-relevant behaviour	*167*
Table 12.2:	Changes in occupational mobility, 1921–1971	*170*

Preface

We have both been writing about class, mobility and women for a long time, so long that it is now difficult to remember exactly when the idea of a collection on the social mobility of women first arose. It was probably in the early 1980s, when criticisms of the Nuffield Study began to appear, and the issues of gender and stratification were brought to the fore by the 1982 Annual Conference of the British Sociological Association at Manchester, and by the exchanges on the class of women in *Sociology*. Certainly it was as long ago as 1986, when we had both just separately completed books on closely related subjects, that we took the first steps of serious editorial work on this book. Our contributors were remarkably patient as we slowly gathered together our final list: the project, like many a joint publishing venture encountered a number of checks before we could deliver the manuscript, so that our thanks are due to them for their co-operation and tolerance during the run-up to publication.

The initial task was to convert a hunch, that there was good material around, into a concrete selection of chapters. The hunch proved to be right, although some of the work was well hidden among other topics, such as careers, labour markets, marriage, household studies and the gender/class debate. Social mobility is like that: once one moves away from a narrow concentration on class mobility in the traditional sense, it pervades a wide range of fields of sociological interest. That is one of its attractions, and of course, one of its difficulties.

The process of selection itself helped us to clarify our own ideas. There is a coherence which emerged from the final choice, and the emphasis we placed on certain common themes, that helps to draw the range of material together. This book is wide ranging, but it does approach its subject from a specific perspective, which we spell out in the first chapter.

We chose mainly from work which was unpublished, often by well-known figures whose main focus of interest had, almost it sometimes seemed by accident, produced an interesting perspective on female social mobility as a by-product. In the end, we had to exclude a number of pieces on grounds of their not quite fitting our basic themes. For example, we have concentrated on Britain, and so left the comparative aspects relatively unexplored, at least as far as an empirical treatment is concerned. Chapter 5 is based on a re-working of 'Trends in Female Social Mobility' from the 1982 BSA Conference Volume (edited by Eva Gamarnikow *et al.*), and Chapter 8 first appeared in a slightly different form in *Sociology*, Volume 20. We are grateful to the Editors, BSA and Publishers for their permissions to include this material.

The preparation of the manuscript was dependent on the support of our respective partners, the encouragement and advice of Christine Cox and Jacinta Evans at Falmer Press, and in particular the assistance of colleagues at Polytechnic South West. Mae Lowe and her team as always helped to shift the burdens of administrative duties, while first Dawn Cole, and then to an even greater extent Marilyn Darch, organized, typed and prepared the final version. To do this kind of thing so efficiently is no mean task: that they do it with such cheerfulness and goodwill is a constant source of amazement to us.

The final shape and focus of the book, of course, remains the responsibility of the editors. We hope that all our collaborators and our readers will feel that the result is valuable. To the extent that we have placed some sociological stones in the gap of ignorance about female mobility, and more importantly, moved the underlying social mobility paradigm forward, we will have achieved our editorial goals.

Geoff Payne and Pamela Abbott
Polytechnic South West,
Plymouth,
June 1990

Chapter 1

Introduction: Origins and Destinations

Geoff Payne and Pamela Abbott

This book will probably attract three main types of reader. One kind will consist of feminists, who are primarily interested in learning more about women's lives, in this case about women's opportunities — or lack of opportunities — for occupational achievement and movement between social classes. For this readership, the significance of the book will be its attempt to provide the first comprehensible description of female social mobility. A second, smaller audience will be those sociologists with a specialist knowledge of the sociology of social class and mobility. In a sense, they will be the reverse of the first audience, because their interest will be in mobility itself, here reported almost coincidentally about women. They will find, none the less, that conventional frameworks for mobility analysis are sharply tested when they are applied to female experiences. Our third readership will be drawn from the broader constituency of sociology and social science in general, with an equal curiosity about both women and social mobility. This group is likely to have less detailed background knowledge about these topics than the first two audiences do about one or the other subject.

In putting together this collection, we therefore had to take into account the levels of prior knowledge that each of the three types of reader would have. We hope that all three readerships will find something to satisfy them, not only because of the intrinsic interest and importance of female social mobility, but also because we have tried to select a range of treatments and topics from the introductory to the more advanced. Inevitably, those with a specialist background will find some parts a little basic, while others may feel at times unsure of the assumptions, terminology and cross-references.

The papers chosen do, on the whole, keep technicalities to a minimum. The processes used to explore and reveal patterns of mobility are carefully explained. If anyone is new to the field of social mobility, they may find it useful to look at a short, non-technical introduction to the subject (Payne, 1989a), or at more length, Heath (1981). Of course, as a cursory glance ahead will show, there are still plenty of tables and arguments built on a variety of measures. The less numerically-inclined should not be put off, however, because they will find key conclusions restated in the narrative (so that they can always resort to the time-honoured practice of skipping over some of the numerical detail!). The outcome is likely to be worthwhile, because the picture of the social mobility of women that emerges is a fascinating one.

Women and Mobility

This could hardly be otherwise, because mobility is such a central process in modern society. We have already learned a great deal from its study, both about people's life chances, and about the underlying structures of our society. When we compare the social circumstances of a person's early life with the social and occupational positions that are currently held, we see how, in everyday parlance, that person has 'got on in life'. When we examine career paths through education, first job, and subsequent employment, we discover routes, blockages, successes and failures which are patterned and systematic. They therefore need to be understood as shared experiences and as the outcome of social processes, as well as of individual talents and achievements. Social mobility combines the study of paid employment, labour markets, occupational change — work in general — with the analysis of structured inequalities and social classes. Not only is social mobility a central topic in sociology as a subject, it is also a topic that lies at the heart of our experience of our own lives.

It is not surprising, then, that when feminist sociologists began to draw attention to the invisibility of women in most sociological studies, they identified social mobility as one of the key areas of shortcoming. Indeed, if one re-examines the previous paragraph and masculinizes its terminology, one would have a more accurate statement of the contribution of social mobility to our knowledge, from the end of the Second World War through to the start of the last decade. However, it would equally be wrong to claim that we know nothing about female mobility, or to reject everything we know about mobility from the study of men, just because it is incomplete.

For a start, as this collection demonstrates, there *has* been research into the social mobility of women. It is true that much of it has not been published, or received the attention that it arguably deserves. When it is drawn together, on the other hand, it presents a surprisingly extensive set of information which at the very least outlines the basic patterns of contemporary female mobility. The apparent absence of women from mobility analysis can be largely attributed to their absence from the main published reports of three of the four most extensive empirical studies of social mobility in this country (Glass, 1954; Goldthorpe, 1980; Payne, 1987a and the exception, Marshall *et al.*, 1988). There is little point regretting that past opportunities were missed: until such time as a new major study can be implemented, we must make the most of the results that we already have. At times, the discussion of these results will be frustrated by gaps in our knowledge, limitations to the data, and inadequacy of conceptual frameworks that were developed to handle the mobility of men. But the study of *male* mobility is to a large extent also bedevilled by many of these same problems, and the number of substantial studies of men has also been very small (Payne, 1989b).

Two things follow from this observation. If our knowledge base is restricted, and likely for the time being to remain so, it would be as well to maximize usage of the knowledge we do have. This will include concepts and data relating to male mobility. Second, given the contestation over concepts, measures and perspectives, there are advantages in starting with current debates. Many of the operationalizations and questions in the following chapters are borrowed from previous literature on male mobility, although often with the ultimate intention of turning them back on themselves by showing how uneasily they contain the female dimension.

The view of mobility analysis that lies behind this collection of papers is that mobility cannot be fully comprehended as solely a male, or solely a female, process. At this stage of our understanding, and typically for ease of exposition, one may need to talk about one or the other: the goal to which we are working is to account for the interaction of the two. This applies equally well to the two main schools of thought in current mobility research (Payne, 1990). The more traditional position, exemplified by John Goldthorpe, sees mobility as movement between social classes, and of interest because of the way it may modify class behaviour. However, even if the class behaviour of married women does resemble that of their husbands, there is still the question of why this should be so. An answer cannot be provided without looking at both men and women, and their interaction through mate-selection, class endogamy, and subsequent household roles. It is not sufficient to point to evidence of similarities between marital partners as a reason for continued concentration on the male half of the population.

The case can be put more starkly for the alternative perspective, to be found for example in the work of the Scottish Mobility Study. This approach stresses that mobility is measured between groupings based on occupational categories, and that mobility has therefore to be understood as an outcome of labour market processes. As men and women are at least notionally in competition with each other for the same jobs, it follows from this view that occupational mobility must take account of all players in the labour market. The fact that labour markets are predominantly gender-segregated creates different mobility chances for men and women: their relative chances are dependent upon the nature of that segregation. The mobility of each gender depends on the totality of the labour market.

It follows that a new female mobility analysis without a comparable male analysis would be little improvement on what we already have. At our present stage of development, the understanding of the interactions between the two mobilities is rudimentary. The exposition of a social mobility of women is a necessary step towards the destination of an integrated explanation.

Approaches to Mobility

The prime task of this collection is then to present for the first time a representative picture of female social mobility in Britain, and to connect this to our knowledge of male mobility. Such a picture naturally reflects the sociological perspectives of the editors and the contributors with whom they have collaborated. Not all writings can be included (although most are, we believe, reported and discussed below): for example Goldthorpe and Payne's 1986 article is sufficiently familiar not to require republication, while the key findings of the Essex Class Study are discussed in Chapter 12. Equally, the competing paradigms for mobility analysis do not receive even-handed treatment. The most important case of this is that patterns of social mobility for both women and men are seen by the editors as owing more to *occupational* processes than to *class* processes. The term 'class mobility', employed extensively by the Nuffield team, is not one that is normally used here. Instead, mobility is more frequently called 'occupational mobility', and seen as movements between occupational groupings which may or may not be social classes, and may or may not be related to other aspects of class analysis. This is not to replace 'mobility' with the idea of 'career', but rather to leave open the question of exactly how movements in the occupational dimension relate to movements in the class dimension. Origins and destinations are not just jobs, but complex social positions that have coherence and are differently placed in the competition for resources and power. These social positions may be *occupational classes*, but they are not necessarily social classes in the wider sense (see Crompton, 1989). Mobility's contribution to class structuration must as yet be seen as more problematic than Giddens (1973) or Parkin (1972) have assumed.

It follows from this view of mobility as an occupational process that the most appropriate unit of analysis for present purposes is taken to be the individual, and not the household (see Abbott and Sapsford, 1987, for a discussion of the alternatives). To be more specific, a woman's class position and her occupational identity are best given by her own current or most recent paid employment. This applies to both single and married women. The choice of 'own occupation' is not without its drawbacks, as Chapter 2 explains, but for the purposes of analyzing mobility when the latter is conceived of as primarily occupational, the advantages outweigh the disadvantages. This approach runs through all of the chapters, although as Abbott and Payne observe in their chapter, the question of what is a women's social class is a central one. The difficulty in resolving it has been a major reason for omitting women from earlier studies of social mobility.

In saying that the unit of mobility analysis is the individual, the focus of attention is on movement and destination. The *origin* from which the person moves is on the other hand in most cases taken as a household identity (at least when one talks about intergenerational mobility). Origin positions for both men and women are normally defined by the occupational class of the head of household when the respondent was aged 14. The head of the household is most commonly male, although both the Nuffield and Aberdeen studies recorded a female household head when there was no male 'breadwinner'. The more recent Essex Class Study used 'Chief Childhood Supporter' in an effort to restrict any gender bias.

The obvious limitation of such an operationalization is that the influence of the mother is usually disregarded. As Robert Miller and Bernadette Hayes show in Chapter 6, this is to restrict our understanding of parental influences. The Irish Mobility Study data reveal that the mother's occupation and her education affect the offspring's occupational achievement, most notably in the case of daughters. Unfortunately, the other data-sets have restricted information on these subjects. In the past, it could be argued that few women worked after marriage, and few had post-elementary education. In today's world, this sharp distinction and minority status have been replaced by universal secondary schooling and greatly extended labour market participation (some consequences of which are discussed by Shirley Dex in Chapter 10). The new picture is likely to be more complicated, and worthy of more extended treatment.

This brief statement of the individual/household unit question serves to show how the two elements of mobility — origin and destination — contain a distinctive female dimension. We cannot fully explain the mobility of one generation without the inclusion of *both* parents from the previous generation. And we cannot claim to have described mobility in the present generation without including the half of the population who are women.

A Basic Picture of Mobility

The collection is organized around the idea that there are a series of basic markers of mobility, for which evidence about men is generally known whereas it is not so for women. As the book develops, this is broadened to address features of female mobility that can be less well contained in a framework that was developed for the more limited task of conceptualizing male mobility. This latter theme follows the conventional life-course events of early career, marriage and re-entry to the labour market. The collection is 'top and tailed' by two editorial chapters setting the context, and drawing conclusions for mobility analysis from the core chapters.

In Chapter 2, the editors reflect on the conventional wisdom that women have been left out of mobility research, exploring some reasons for this, and some of the consequences of the omission for the way mobility has been conceived. Central to this is the narrowness of definitions and the restricted focus on class, with its attendant problems for locating women in a system of social stratification. As a consideration of gender and labour markets, and the changing roles played by women in society show, the basic experience of mobility must on average and in detail be different from men.

The distinctive employment patterns mean that routes and opportunities are also gender specific, so that they require study in their own right. This view contrasts with that of Goldthorpe, who has argued that the mobility regime for both genders is essentially the same in class terms, once allowance for occupational differences has been made. Building on data from the Essex and Aberdeen Studies, the authors show how the work situations, concentrated in certain occupational classes, give a character to mobility that depends on the rules of access to employment. This character, in terms of rewards, autonomy and power at work, provides a bridge to class experiences, and to the typical self-experiences of women as under-esteemed. It thus connects both to class analysis and to the direct concrete experiences of women in contemporary Britain.

In what is the first systematic analysis of the data on women from the Scottish Mobility Study, Tony Chapman shows how occupational distributions amd mobility experience are connected (Chapter 3). At one level, this can be read as a series of basic statements about overall mobility, inflow rates (looking at women's *present* classes, and asking from which origins did they 'flow in') and outflow rates (looking at *origins*, and comparing chances of 'flowing out' to different destinations). Chapman is in this work providing some of the fundamental building blocks of knowledge about intergenerational female social mobility, of the kind that have for a long time been available about male mobility. Although, as he stresses, these data are drawn from the partners of the men in the study's sample, and so cannot encompass the never-married women, his chapter provides a solid starting point for understanding the core patterns.

At a second level, however, Chapman goes beyond telling us that 32 per cent of women are upwardly mobile, compared with 42 per cent of men, or that men and women presently in the service class are recruited from broadly similar backgrounds. He shows that particular measures of mobility may contain variation in thier components: female upward mobility is concentrated into movements into semi-skilled, routine non-manual, and lower professional occupations, because these are the jobs that women rather than men do. Even if overall rates of mobility are similar, their components (and their explanations) will differ. When we include women in our data, we begin to realize how male oriented are our analytical techniques.

Chapman is asking two points here. One is about female social mobility *per se*, while the other is about methods of analysis inherited from the study of male mobility. Equally, more sophisticated techniques, such as manipulating the distributions of the mobility table in order to separate out 'real' mobility from changes in occupational structures, may not be very fruitful. Whereas in male mobility, such an adjustment is to fathers and sons, in female mobility it is to fathers and daughters. This is akin to saying that had daughters been sons, the experience of employment would have been different. It leads both to an impression that women could have been more mobile than in real life, and to exaggerating the connections between origins (the father) and actual destinations.

On the other hand, applying the basic tools of mobility analysis to data on women is a useful exercise in itself, as well as reminding us that women form a significant part of the class structure. In Chapter 4, Pamela Abbott re-examines the theses of 'closure', 'buffer-zone' and 'counter-mobility', which were rejected by Goldthorpe and Payne on the basis of male data. The relative absence of women among the upper segment of the service class means that parents in that class cannot guarantee to protect the class position of their female offspring. However, the same fact implies that some process of closure is operating, against women if not against would-be entrants from lower classes. Similarly, the heavy concentration of women in routine non-manual jobs creates a buffer-zone which was not evident to Goldthorpe in his study of men. The picture for countermobility is more complicated, not only because women do not have work careers in the same way as men, but because possession of educational qualifications carries more weight in female occupational achievement. Women are certainly less likely to be promoted in their work careers, so that all three theses find considerable support from the evidence on female workers.

It would be wrong, however, to give the impression that male and female experiences are totally different. As Chapter 5 shows, the differences may be more one of degree rather than kind. The examination of trends in mobility at entry to work reveals a broadly congruent picture of young men and women between 1920 and 1970, as we might expect from the historical pattern of macro-sociological changes. After all, the Depression, the Second World War, the 1944 Education Act, and the underlying processes of industrial and occupational transition provide a common context. As the authors argue, the historical profiles of manual/non-manual upward mobility differ only in as far as the same process — the shift of new job creation increasingly into the service sector of industry — has somewhat different consequences for men and women. For men, the dominance of tertiary industry came later, in the 1970s, whereas for women, this sector has been significant since the First World War while manufacturing industry has not contracted so sharply. These structural factors suggest that it is the demand side of the labour market that is worth more attention in explaining mobility, rather than such supply side factors as educational qualifications.

It can be seen from these conclusions that the opening chapters do two things. First, they draw together a clear description of intergenerational mobility rates. Second, they begin to stretch the conceptual model of mobility that has been inherited from studies of men. The remaining chapters begin to stretch that model more directly, by examining the impact of mothers and the distinctive features of female 'careers' in greater detail.

Developing New Models of Mobility

The question of parent-child connections is central to Chapter 6. Robert Miller and Bernadette Hayes use data from the Irish Mobility Study to explore the role of mothers in the subsequent occupational achievement of their off-spring. They do this in a novel way, selecting from the original sample only those families in which both parents, and a pair of brothers and sisters, have been in paid employment. This 'twenty-first century' sample of people over 27 is a surrogate for a society in which female activity rates are universally high, thus eliminating the historical effect of women (mothers) who were never employed. Using path analysis, the authors show that in contrast to American results, there are only modest Mother-Daughter and Father-Son patterns of association, suggestive of a role-model or socialization interpretation. Rather, the relationships are a little more complicated than this. Mothers' educational and occupational attainment exert independent effects on both daughters' *and* sons' occupations, both directly, and indirectly through their educational levels. Daughters have lower occupational achievement than sons, irrespective of the attainment of both parents: this indicates a further distinctive gender effect. Although some of the detail of the results reflects the concrete historical, educational and religious context of Northern Ireland, the broad patterns are unlikely to be restricted to that society. Even if, as Goldthorpe has argued, married women display certain class attitudes and behaviour which is very similar to that of their husbands, Miller and Hayes establish that women's own experience of schooling and work have an influence on their children's education and employment, which is separate from the fathers'. Even if we were to be concerned with the mobility of men, we should in future need to include women as mothers in the treatment of origins.

This view of destinations can be put alongside Tony Chapman's analysis of career — or *intra*generational — mobility in Chapter 7. He shows how movements between first and latest occupational class are different for men and women, again relating this back to the changing employment structure of each gender. Among those with professional and managerial family backgrounds, whose initial mobility was downward, men were three times more likely than women to regain a higher career mobility. Among those from intermediate class backgrounds, the differential was more than four times in favour of the men. Over time (i.e. using a cohort analysis) it appears that *inter*generational upward mobility increases for both males and females, but whereas *career* mobility decreases slightly for men, it increases slightly for women, so that the gender differential is reduced among the younger workers. However, its relative importance is less, because intergenerational mobility becomes comparatively the greater route of movement. All of the ten flows that mark upward mobility or maintenance of advantageous position in the two 'three by three' mobility tables for men and women show this pattern.

Chapman links this to the changes in first employment. This demonstrates a marked reduction in manual work, with women increasingly entering routine non-manual jobs. Breaking the three main categories into seven reveals, once again, the concentration of female employment in the less attractive sub-sectors of the larger classes. Despite more recent trends of increasing female recruitment into the professions and more skilled occupations, the long term prognosis is still a pessimistic one for significant female advancement.

This view that an increase in the qualification levels of women will not translate into male-like patterns of mobility is developed by Rosemary Crompton and Kay Sanderson in Chapter 8. Drawing together a range of sources, they show that while women have traditionally had lower levels of post-school qualifications (and these concentrated in the clerical and commercial fields), younger women have a higher participation rate in Further and Higher Education, and show substantial increases in training for the medical professions, accountancy, public finance, law and even banking. Regarded from a 'human capital' viewpoint, this is evidence that the quality of the 'supply' of female labour is improving: women are investing in their own education, and might be expected therefore to occupy new positions in employment.

However, women do not have 'linear' careers like men: the typical work experience is one of breaks in paid employment for child-bearing, or even an absence of any planned 'career'. Crompton and Sanderson examine several professions, using a modified typology based on Brown's idea of entrepreneurial, organizational and occupational career strategies, showing how the structure of employment (bureaucratic or de-centralized) interacts with women's employment needs for flexibility. Women are more likely to be qualified 'practitioners' rather than 'careerists', fitting into particular segments of the labour market in each profession. The class of professionals needs to be sub-divided to reveal the different labour markets that it contains as a result of the various structures of organization, its qualifications regime, and the people working as professionals. It is these factors that determine women's experience of mobility.

Indeed, these factors determine both women *and* men's experiences, as Gill Jones emphasizes in her discussion of cross-class marriages. Just as a women's paid work expands her class situation beyond what is implied by the class of her husband or father, so a man's domestic situation (his marriage partner's class) expands his class situation as defined by his employment. In Chapter 9, she uses a sample of young married people from the General Household Survey to explore how choice of partner (i.e. the class of the partner) relates to origins, current early career destinations and mobility experience *per se*. Her question is not whether marriage is an alternative mobility route for women (the traditional perspective), nor the effects of marriage on career. Instead, she asks whether choice of partner confirms other aspects of the class process: do the upwardly mobile (both men and women) marry into the class that they have entered, so confirming their new position, or do they choose other aspirant mobiles, or partners whose origins they share?

Her findings demonstrate the complexity of mate selection. People who are currently in the same class as their family of origin are likely to marry each other. On the other hand, the upwardly mobile, particularly if education has been an important part of their career achievement, tend to marry into the class that they have entered, so confirming their new identity. This marrying into the new class is also present among men who have been downwardly mobile, but there is more evidence of downwardly mobile women marrying 'back up', i.e. possibly using marriage as a counter-mobility route.

Two general lessons can be learned from Jones's analysis. First, if we wish to explain class endogamy and exogamy (marrying within, or outside of, one's class) then young people's own education, and their occupations at time of marriage, are more significant than their classes of origin. Implied in this, and running throughout her chapter, is the point that we need to see class situation as a process: a longitudinal view enables us to identify typical 'trajectories' through a series of class experiences.

As Shirley Dex also argues, 'an understanding of women's lifetime and life-cycle mobility is a necessary foundation of the conceptual developments' needed to grasp women's place in class analysis (Chapter 10, p. 121). Her analysis of the Women and Employment Survey data shows how women move between a range of key employments in a way that helps to create female labour markets which are congruent with women's domestic commitments. Their occupational class at one time owes as much to their non-work circumstances — recency of childbirth, for example — as it does to their class of origin or qualifications.

Seen from the demand side of the market, women can occupy one of three main sectors. They may be in the Primary Non-Manual Sector, alongside men, where they will enjoy higher pay, lower turnover, and the benefits of an internal labour market. The key occupation here is teaching. The largest sector, however, is a Women's Primary Sector, consisting of nursing, clerical and intermediate non-manual jobs, and factory work with some level of skill. This sector consists of full-time employment, with little movement between its occupational sub-groups. The third sector is the Women's Secondary Sector which is comprised largely of part-time work, most of it semi-skilled, and with lower pay, worse conditions of service and fewer benefits.

However, turnover among the part-time jobs is not necessarily higher. Initially, these jobs suit women whose former employment in the Women's Primary Sector has been interrupted by childbirth and child care commitments. Some will return to their former sector in due course, although by no means all follow this route. Their new circumstances dovetail neatly into the demands of the labour market, so that the 'occupational profiles' of women are different from men. To measure mobility by a cross-sectional analysis would be to miss the transitional nature of many women's positions at the time of such a survey. Mobility cannot be modelled simply as an occupational process, just as it cannot be modelled simply as a class process which is both gender- and occupation-blind.

Angela Dale expands on this idea in Chapter 11, showing how the dynamics of the household — including its dissolution in divorce — create a changing complex of successive material states for its members. Drawing together a wide range of studies, she sets out the case for an approach to stratification and mobility analysis in which 'the individual within the household', rather than the individual, or the household, is the central focus. On the one hand, life-course studies and the Women and Employment Survey show households evolve through stages ranging from those in which both partners (and even adult children) may be in paid employment, to those in which the women may be out of the labour market due to childbirth, or both partners are retired. Not only do people's responses to the labour market change according to their domestic circumstances, but their sense of material well-being must also change, and this is related to their subjective experience of mobility: to feel better or worse off is probably to 'feel' upward or downward mobility (and as the 1980s showed, tends to be translated into voting behaviour, traditionally one of the key tests of class behaviour).

On the other hand, research on household economies and the way types of employment generate both cash and fringe benefit income, shows how 'partners' do not share equally in terms of consumption. For example, the participation of women in the part-time labour market usually deprives them of the superior conditions of employment — not least occupational pensions — to which full-time (male) workers are normally entitled. In the event of marriage breakdown, and the even more common experiences of retirement and longer survivial as a widow, a woman's financial position is much worse than that of a divorced man or widower, and depresses their joint pension income during retirement. Even without dealing with the question of power within the household, we have here a further dimension to mobility which is generated over time by the interaction between household structures and the labour market.

Dale's chapter, although not originally addressed to mobility, demonstrates how the starting paradigm derived from an analysis of male class mobility is now in need of reconstruction. The final chapter attempts to delineate some of the steps involved in this, as the editors draw on the contributions of the volume to go 'beyond male mobility models'. Our purpose is not only to create a better understanding of the social mobility of women, but also a better understanding of mobility itself, whatever the gender of the mobile people involved.

The central messages of the collection are, then, first that women experience distinctive kinds of mobility. This has relevance both for their lives, and for stratification analysis. If women *do* behave as if they occupy a derived status, as the traditional approach has claimed, then this will in itself be a surprising outcome: different routes will have led to the same point. It will be apparent that the editors do not, in fact, believe this. The second of the core messages is that the traditional framework simply cannot accommodate female social mobility. This is an argument for a new paradigm for mobility research, even to the extent of new operationalizations. We assert that, had women been included from the outset, the conventional concepts and measures of social mobility would not have survived into the 1960s, let alone the 1990s.

Chapter 2

Women's Social Mobility: The Conventional Wisdom Reconsidered[1]

Pamela Abbott and Geoff Payne

Despite the common view, it is an exaggeration to say that women have been excluded from mobility studies; the real picture is more complicated. It is true that David Glass's paradigm-setting LSE study (1954) had hardly a word to say about women's social mobility: women were omitted from consideration in the analysis, and this study stood as the main or only empirical data on which arguments about social mobility were based for a period of twenty years. However it is often forgotten that the original British study by Glass did in fact collect data on women, but no analysis was published before the original questionnaires were routinely destroyed as part of normal civil service practice. One of the few contributions during the 1960s was the Labour Mobility Study, which did include women (Harris and Clausen, 1967), but the female data from this have largely been ignored by feminists and non-feminists alike. On the other hand, the main Nuffield study of England and Wales did not include women, and John Goldthorpe, one of the leading figures in the study, followed this by engaging in active debate to justify his position in not sampling women in the 1972 Nuffield Study. His defence can be regarded as having two parts: the informal response in 1973/4 when the Scottish Mobility Study research team proposed the partial inclusion of women, and the more considered response in recent years.

At the time, members of the Nuffield team advanced two arguments (in personal communications): that the Hope-Goldthorpe Scale was a male-only scale and could not be applied to women's jobs; and that most women did not work after marriage. The first objection is easily disposed of. Not only is the gender specificity of the scale not directly addressed in *The Social Grading of Occupations* (Hope and Goldthorpe, 1974), but Goldthorpe himself has since used a version of his class scale in examining female mobility (Goldthorpe and Payne, 1986). While the second objection may have been true in the past it is no longer true today (see also Martin and Roberts, 1984).

We can contrast this resistance with the partial inclusion of women in the Scottish Mobility Study, which was directed by one of the present authors. The device of interviewing the wives of a random sample of men was adopted for purely pragmatic reasons. The research budget could obtain about 5,000 interviews: if these had been split between men and women, this would have yielded about 2,500 cases in each gender, too few cases of each gender for detailed statistical analysis. (This argument about sample size is also advanced in Goldthorpe (1980, p. 287) in defence of the male-only sample in the English study.) The exclusion of women was avoided in the Scottish study by interviewing the wives about their family backgrounds and careers — which, while not a perfect solution, did provide some usable data. (However, about 90 per cent of the published analysis of the Scottish study is about men, so perhaps creating a distorted impression.)

Again, the Irish study (e.g. Robert Miller and Bernadette Hayes, Chapter 6 of this volume) included full employment histories for both men and women. Abbott and Sapsford (1987) have produced information from the Open University *People in Society Survey*, Goldthorpe and Payne (1986) have extracted relevant data from the British Election Survey; Arber, Dale and Gilbert (1984) have analyzed short-term shifts and female classifications using the General Household Survey and the Labour Force Survey, and Marshall and his colleagues, most comprehensively of all, drew a random sample of men *and* women for the Essex Class Project (1988). The UK Office of Population Censuses and Surveys has also carried out a very comprehensive study of women's *intra*generational mobility — see Martin and Roberts, 1984; Dex, 1987. Clearly, mobility among women *has* been studied. The problem is that this growing body of work has not yet been taken up by sociologists in general, who understandably have been influenced by the fact that most of the actual work has been focused largely on men. Even when results for women were presented in these works, the bulk of the texts concentrated on discussion of male mobility, so preserving the impression that we knew little about female mobility. We might add, following Delamont's observation about male mobility (Delamont, 1989), that there has been a curious reluctance on the part of British sociologists to cite parallel studies (about men *or* women), so that there has been no codification or cumulation of knowledge.

Reasons for the Exclusion of Women in Mobility Studies

The conventional view justifies the non-inclusion of women in mobility studies in two main ways. First, mobility has generally been conceived as being about social class, and the conventional view is that social class is based on the occupation of the head of household, which means in practice that most women have a derived class position — that is, their class is determined by the occupation of their husbands (or fathers). If they have no independent class position, women cannot be class mobile, so that some sociologists — such as Goldthorpe, especially in his earlier writing — have, indeed, argued that there is no need to study the movement of women. A modified form of the household position has been suggested: that the class of the household should be computed from characteristics (generally occupation) of husband *and* wife (see for example, Britten and Heath, 1983; Erikson, 1984; Pahl and Wallace, 1985). The alternative position is to base class on a person's own occupation. While this poses problems, most notably for the assignation of a class position to those not in paid employment, nevertheless it is increasingly seen as the most viable position (see Heath *et al.*, 1985; Abbott and Sapsford, 1987; Crompton and Mann, 1986; Marshall *et al.*, 1988). Until a theory of class is developed that properly includes women, it is not possible to account for the movement of women between class positions.

The second reason for women's invisibility is that mobility, more than most topics, requires careful operationalization of occupation, occupational classification, and class modelling, so that the enterprise of studying women's mobility is held back by methodological difficulties. In his more systematic account, Goldthorpe has based his arguments on both empirical and conceptual grounds, the former being much the weaker. In his debate with those who have argued against his position, he claims (Goldthorpe, 1983, 1984) that

(a) women have a low economic participation rate and therefore have no measuring points (jobs) for the calculation of class mobility,

(b) the apparent rise in participation rate is largely due to part-time employment, and therefore women's employment is less salient than men's permanent and full-time work,

(c) there are relatively few cross-class marriages, and

(d) whether a woman works is largely dependent on her husband's position.

Subsequent empirical research throws doubt on these claims. While it is true that in 1931 only about 10 per cent of married women were in paid employment (Westergaard and Resler, 1975), this figure rose to over 40 per cent in the 1960s and stands currently at over 70 per cent (Marshall *et al.*, 1988). Current research demonstrates that the majority of women are fully committed to the labour market and work for the majority of their employable lives (Martin and Roberts, 1984). Secondly, Abbott and Sapsford (1987) looked separately at women in full-time and in part-time employment, and within these broad groups at married and single women separately. They found similar patterns across all groups, which suggest that female patterns of intergenerational mobility are consistently different from those of men, even controlling for marriage and hours worked.

Goldthorpe's third contention, that there are very few cross-class marriages, is equally suspect. On a three-class model (service class, intermediate class, and working class) the Scottish Mobility Study found that 46 per cent of marriages could be described as cross-class (Payne *et al.*, 1981). Marshall *et al.* (1988) report a similar figure, 50 per cent. We therefore see that the empirical grounds for not including women 'because they get married' are not sustained. Neither do empirical data support his fourth contention, that wives' employment is conditioned by their husbands' class.

(For a critique of Goldthorpe's contention that women's patterns of employment are determined by those of their husbands or that contemporary marriages are largely homogeneous with respect to class, based on a re-analysis of his own data, see Stanworth, 1984). More recently, Goldthorpe and Payne have rejected the need for consideration of the class mobility of women, as the result of conclusions they draw from an analysis of the mobility data from women and men in the British General Election Survey (Goldthorpe and Payne, 1986). In their analysis they ask what difference it would make to our conceptualization of class mobility if three competing conceptual stances incorporating women were taken.

The first of these stances, the conventional approach, assumes that a women's class (i.e. the class of the family) is determined by the occupation of her husband or father. Goldthorpe and Payne incorporate women by examining marital mobility. An analysis of the marital mobility — i.e. comparing the classes of father-in-law and son-in-law — for the female sample in the British General Election Survey, considering both absolute and relative mobility rates, suggests that no serious revision is required to the understanding of class mobility developed from studies of male-only samples.

Second, the dominance approach, takes as the determinant of the family class of a marital couple the occupation of the partner with the highest class position, provided that he or she has full-time, permanent employment. Women without a male partner are included on the basis of their own occupation. Goldthorpe and Payne conclude that it adds little to the understanding of patterns of relative mobility. However, they argue that this approach does enable information to be included on the experiences of women who are unattached or who are family heads.

Third, they take the individualistic approach, which assumes that an individual's class is determined by his or her *own* occupation. They examine the absolute and relative mobility rates for women and compare them with those for men. They conclude that absolute mobility rates for men and women are very different. However, under the conditions in which they compare relative mobility rates, they conclude that the mobility chances of women in relation to other women are the same as the mobility chances of men in relation to other men. In particular, they say that if the distribution of female occupations was the same as that of male occupations, then the mobility patterns of men and women would be the same. The entirety of the difference in class mobility is accounted for by the gendered nature of the labour market. (We should point out, however, that this merely underlines the fact that British society is closed against upward mobility for women, relative to men, which is in itself a statement about the class structure of Britain as well as the gender structure.)

The major conclusion that they draw from these three analyses is that it is necessary to take account of women's experiences in order to understand their occupational mobility, but *not* in order to understand intergenerational class mobility. However, this conclusion is based on the *assumption* that class mobility is essentially separate from occupational mobility and that while a man's occupation determines his class position, a woman's does not — which is what they set out to prove. It also ignores absolute mobility rates, which as Saunders (1990) has recently pointed out ignores the real mobility experiences of many people. More fundamentally, by using relative mobility rates Goldthorpe ignores the ways in which class and gender *interact* to influence the class mobility patterns of men and women.

Gender Segregation in the Labour Market

One of us has argued at length elsewhere in contradiction to Goldthorpe (Payne, 1987) that studies of 'class mobility' are in fact studies of occupational mobility, because class is operationalized in terms of occupation. It follows that our starting point has to be the female occupational distribution, which an increasing body of research has shown to be different from that of males (e.g. Hakim, 1979; Payne, 1981; Martin and Roberts, 1984). Briefly stated, women are much more likely to be found in semi-professions (teacher, nurse, librarian) than professions (doctor, lawyer, chartered

Table 2.1 Labour market distribution by gender in the UK in 1981

Socio-economic group	Men %	Women %
Employers and managers		
large establishments	5.6	2.1
small establishments	9.4	4.7
professional workers		
self-employed	1.0	0.1
employees	4.7	0.8
Other non-manual		
intermediate	7.6	14.9
junior	9.9	39.1
personal service	1.2	12.5
Manual workers		
formen/supervisors	3.7	0.7
skilled	27.0	4.1
semi-skilled	14.0	10.9
unskilled	5.9	6.9
own account	5.8	2.0
Farming		
employers/managers	0.7	0.1
own account	0.7	0.1
labourers	1.2	0.7
Armed Forces	1.6	0.2

Note: cases recorded as inadquately described are excluded.
Source: Abbot and Sapsford (1987), Table 71, p. 182.

accountant); are concentrated in routine office work and shop work; but are less likely to be found in skilled manual work than men. Table 2.1, from the 1981 UK Census, illustrates this imbalance in distribution. It will be seen that over a quarter of the men are described as in skilled manual work, compared with 4 per cent of the women, and conversely that nearly two-thirds of women are in the 'other non-manual' category (nearly 40 per cent of them in the 'junior' category — routine office work and the like), compared with less than 20 per cent of the men. Within the 'other non-manual' category the differences become more extreme as we go down the scale: for 'intermediate' positions the figure for women is twice that for men, for 'junior' positions it is four times as large, and for personal service work it is twelve times as large.

Also of interest is the segment *within* a class into which women as opposed to men fall. Again, from labour market studies we know that women are more likely than men to occupy the lower status positions with occupations — to be teachers rather than school heads, lecturers rather than professors — and that women's work is less likely than men's to be classed as skilled in the manual sector (see Abbott and Wallace, 1990). There is also some evidence not only that women are less likely to be seen as promotable but that they are recruited on the specific assumption that they will not seek promotion. The Essex survey provides more information on this by examining the market and work situations of women and men in each Hope-Goldthorpe category.[2] Table 2.2. shows the average gross annual pay, percentage on a career ladder, and average scores for autonomy, decision-making and supervision. These data clearly indicate that men score higher than women on virtually every item within each class. Importantly, as Marshall *et al.* indicate, they clearly show the differences between women and men in routine non-manual work (where women predominate), indicating that men in such work earn on average considerably more than women and are much more likely to be on a career ladder.

Labour market segmentation is also an important factor in understanding female intergenerational mobility, as has been shown by all the British studies into it, and also by American and European studies (see Abbott and Sapsford, 1987, for a review). For example, Table 2.3, from the Scottish Mobility Study, shows clearly that the 'track' of upward mobility is differently distributed, with female mobility being associated with the semi-professions and routine office work (SMS Classes II and IV), and male mobility into the non-manual sector concentrated in the professional/managerial and supervisory/technical classes (SMS Classes I and III), where men predominate. Marshall *et al.* have also identified characteristic female mobility tracks. They argue that the limited availability of service positions for women creates a downflow of the daughters of service class men into Hope-Goldthorpe (HG) Class III (office/sales work) whereas the comparable sons are, first, less likely to be downwardly mobile and, second, more likely if they are downwardly mobile to move into manual work. The flows in the reverse direction are correspondingly greater for men than for women,

Table 2.2 Market and work situations of men and women in full-time employment

Social class		Mean wage (pounds)	Career (% affirmative)	Autonomy (mean score)	Decision-making (mean score)	Supervision (mean score)
I	M	14,130	80	5.1	3.7	4.5
	F	9,357	77	4.7	2.2	3.0
II	M	11,017	75	4.4	2.4	3.1
	F	7,011	72	3.8	1.5	2.5
III	M	7,238	60	3.5	0.7	0.4
	F	4,859	43	2.7	0.4	0.4
V	M	8,567	72	3.0	1.6	3.3
	F	3,611	56	3.5	1.3	2.8
VI	M	7,024	36	1.9	0.4	0.2
	F	4,395	35	1.7	0.3	0.1
VII	M	6,604	26	1.9	0.2	0.2
	F	4,558	11	1.4	0.0	0.0

Notes:
1 Full time is defined as 30 + hours per week.
2 Class IV (self-employed) is excluded.
3 The mean scores refer to composites of questionnaire items and can score from 0 (low) to 6 (high).
Source: Marshall *et al.*, 1988, Table 4.9, p. 78.

Table 2.3 Gross mobility rates by gender in the Scottish Mobility Study

Gender	Mobility (%)			% upwardly mobile found in	
	Upward	Static	Downward	Classes I or III	Classes II or IV
Men	42.5	27.4	30.4	44	29
Women	32.2	19.9	48.8	6	67

and for the latter typically consist of entry to the cadet branch of the service class (e.g. HG Class II), not the senior branch (similar results are reported by Abbott and Sapsford, 1987). Compared with men, when women experience downward mobility into the working class, it is more likely to be to semi- or unskilled manual work than to the skilled manual class. Thus the distributions within and between occupational classes are not just different; the terms 'upward' and 'downward', of gross mobility, cover different types of movement for men than for women. We can also observe that brothers and sisters are likely to experience different mobility chances, despite sharing a father, so that the 'destination effect' interacts with the 'origin effect'. These points can be made equally strongly in more detail from the full mobility tables of the Essex

Table 2.4 Current class and class of origin, percentaged by current class ('Inflow' %)

Class of origin	Current class													
	I		II		III		IV		V		VI		VII	
	M	F	M	F	M	F	M	F	M	F	M	F	M	F
I	14.1	20.0	13.8	8.9	15.8	8.6	4.1	4.3	3.0	0.0	4.6	0.0	2.1	2.1
II	12.0	20.1	19.3	13.3	5.3	5.6	8.2	0.0	1.5	0.0	6.4	0.0	3.4	3.2
III	8.7	5.0	6.4	10.0	0.0	5.6	2.7	4.3	4.5	0.0	9.2	4.8	1.4	3.2
IV	14.1	25.0	12.8	15.6	13.2	10.5	35.6	21.7	13.6	13.3	9.2	4.8	9.0	11.7
V	17.4	0.0	19.3	24.4	13.2	21.0	11.0	21.7	22.7	6.7	13.8	23.8	21.4	13.8
VI	13.0	20.0	16.5	18.9	34.2	30.2	12.3	13.0	30.3	40.0	29.4	42.9	24.1	24.5
VII	20.7	10.0	11.9	8.9	18.4	18.5	26.0	34.8	24.2	40.0	27.5	23.8	38.6	41.5
N =	92	20	109	90	38	162	73	23	66	15	109	21	145	94

Source: Adapted from Marshall et al., 1988, Table 4.7, p. 76.

Table 2.5 Current class and class of origin, percentaged by class of origin ('Outflow' %)

Class of origin		Current class I	II	III	IV	V	VI	VII	N=
I	M	27.7	31.9	12.8	6.4	4.3	10.6	6.4	47
	F	13.8	27.6	48.3	3.4	0.0	0.0	6.9	29
II	M	20.8	39.6	3.8	11.3	1.9	13.2	9.4	53
	F	14.3	42.9	32.1	0.0	0.0	0.0	10.7	28
III	M	25.0	21.9	0.0	6.3	9.4	31.3	6.3	32
	F	4.2	37.5	37.5	4.2	0.0	4.2	12.5	24
IV	M	14.4	15.6	5.6	28.9	10.0	11.1	14.4	90
	F	9.1	25.5	30.9	9.1	3.6	1.8	20.0	55
V	M	14.4	18.9	4.5	7.2	13.5	13.5	27.9	111
	F	0.0	27.5	42.5	6.3	1.3	6.3	16.3	80
VI	M	8.0	12.4	9.5	6.6	14.6	23.4	25.5	139
	F	3.6	15.3	44.1	2.7	5.4	8.1	20.7	111
VII	M	11.9	8.1	4.4	11.9	10.0	18.8	35.0	160
	F	2.0	8.2	30.6	8.2	6.1	5.1	39.8	98

Source: adapted from Marshall *et al.*, (1988), Table 4.8, p. 77

study (Marshall *et al.*, 1988). Of men in Class I (see Table 2.4), 26 per cent came from Class I or II origins, 40 per cent from Classes III-V, and 34 per cent from Classes VI or VII (manual occupations). The comparable figures for women are 40 per cent from Classes I and II, 30 per cent from Classes III-V, and 30 per cent from Classes VI ot VII. Looking specifically at the highest class, Class I, we can see that 14 per cent of the men now in it come from Class I origins, and 20 per cent of women (Table 2.4), but that almost 28 per cent of men with Class I fathers finished up in Class I but only 14 per cent of women with Class I fathers (Table 2.5). What we are looking at, therefore, is not so much the relative power of high-class fathers to transmit their status to their children, but rather the dearth of occupational places in Class I which are open to women, meaning that upward mobility into that class is far less of a realistic possibility for women than for men. Women's mobility from Class I origins is partly into Class II, but more into Class III, where there are vastly more women than men. Similarly, a few women of Class II origins finish up in Class I, but most either remain in Class II or fall to Class III; a third of women with Class II fathers are themselves in Class III jobs (and nearly half the women with Class I fathers) — see Table 2.5. Long-range upward mobility is also more common among men than women: 21 per cent of men from working-class origins are currently in Class I and II occupations, but only 15 per cent of women. Whatever their class origins, women are very much more likely to finish up in Class III than are men. Men are also more likely than women to be upwardly mobile into self-employment (Class IV) or supervisory positions (Class V). If women are mobile into the 'service class' (Classes I and II), they are more likely to finish up in II than I. Within the working class (Classes VI and VII), men are far more likely than women to achieve the higher of the two classes.

Problems in Mobility Rate Analysis

The figures show that to engage, for example, in the testing of the openness of society — the major interest of the 'second generation' studies in Britain — and to assume that women's social mobility is of no relevance to the central question of mobility studies would seem not just sexist but positively naïve. Indeed, they serve to highlight the problems of analyzing relative mobility rates — comparing the chances of people from different origins of gaining advantageous destinations — rather than absolute rates. Arguably, as Saunders (1989, 1990) has pointed out, an analysis of relative mobility rates seriously understates the amount of social fluidity of the class structure (see also Payne, 1990).

The operationalization of relative mobility employed by Goldthorpe (and by Marshall *et al.*), in which people of different origins would have different chances of arriving at a given destination, were there to be statistical independence of origins and destinations, is not simple disparity or odds ratios, read directly from the mobility tables. Instead it is usually a calculation of relative chances under one crucial condition, namely that mobility can be subdivided into two kinds. The first kind is seen as relating to changes in the occupational structure: the expansion of non-manual occupations 'creates', through the distribution of destinations, new mobility 'opportunities'. If one is really interested in whether social policy modifies opportunity for upward mobility, then such structural mobility is noise in the system. The proliferation of indices of mobility over the years testifies to this dominant paradigm's attempt to sort out structural mobility from the second type, that which reflects outcomes of class competition over opportunity.

The latest version of this differentiation is log linear modelling, in which a series of terms are added or subtracted from a model; the object is to inspect the strength of factors by seeing how closely each model approximates to the observed mobility tables. In a model which uses birth cohorts to represent change over time,[3] and which contains origin and destination distributions (and therefore their changes over time), relative mobility does not change significantly. In other words, if we control for structural change, the residual patterns of mobility are virtually invariant in Goldthorpe's or Marshall's data.

If we return to the key introduction of log linear modelling in mobility analysis (Hauser *et al.*, 1975a, 1975b), the original argument can be read in two ways. One is the way in which Goldthorpe has taken it (and Marshall *et al.* have followed, since they wish to compare their results with his). The other is the exact opposite of

Goldthorpe's position: if relative mobility rates can be treated as a constant, then we should stop worrying about them and concentrate on the things that really do change historically — the structure of origins and destinations and the mobility associated with them. To imply, as Saunders says Goldthorpe and Marshall *et al.* imply, that some part of mobility — especially when it appears from this analysis to be the major part — is not relevant, not real mobility, not important for class formation, class consciousness, etc., has to be nonsensical. Try telling the people who have experienced it that, due to the evidence of a log linear model, they are mistaken in thinking they were born the sons or daughters of manual workers and now work as managers or professionals![4] While for the purpose of analysis and explanation we need to try to distinguish the causes of mobility, we cannot ignore one type once we have distinguished it from others (or, to be more accurate, minimize it in our discussions of how much mobility there has been).

Once we recognize that our need is to study absolute, not relative, mobility rates, then it becomes evident that we need to incorporate women into the analysis. The changes in the occupational structure of advanced capitalist societies in recent times has been in the expansion of white-collar occupations. Further, there has been an expansion in the proportion of jobs done by women and in the percentage of women engaged in waged work. Both men and women are potential candidates for the mobility opportunities generated by the changes in demand for labour. However, as we have shown above, women have exhibited a different pattern of mobility from men. Seventy-five per cent of service-class jobs are 'male jobs'; women are allocated to other classes, by structural processes which owe little to ability, natural right or the success of capitalism.

Further, women's participation in the labour force changes mobility opportunities for men. Abbott and Sapsford (1987) demonstrate that studies of intergenerational mobility give a false impression even of male mobility unless women are included in them. Women's participation in the labour market adds to the effect of structural changes, because certain classes of job become 'women's work' and men become excluded from them. In Table 2.6, for example, we can see that between 1921 and 1971 men's employment increased substantially, and substantially more than women's, as salaried or self-employed professional workers, lower-grade salaried professionals and technicians, and skilled manual workers. Conversely, women increased their employment (at the expense of men) as unskilled manual workers, as supervisors of manual workers, and above all as clerical workers and secretaries. Women come in at the bottom of the class — unskilled manual work, routine non-manual work — and thereby 'drive' men further up the occupational scale.

The real message is not only that women's mobility is different from that encountered by men, but rather that the mobility paradigm is itself inadequate. As soon as women are included, one comes face to face with the gendered segregation of the labour market and has to recognize that the differences in occupational distribution

Table 2.6 Changes in labour market structure, 1921–1971 *

Socio-economic group	Males 1921 %	Males 1971 %	Females 1921 %	Females 1971 %	Ratio 1971/1921 M	Ratio 1971/1921 F	Ratio of rates of increase: fem./male
S/e and higher-grade salaried professional workers	1.6	6.1	0.9	1.4	3.8	1.6	0.4
Employers and proprietors	7.7	5.2	4.7	2.9	0.7	0.6	0.9
Administrators and managers	4.3	9.9	2.1	3.3	2.1	1.6	0.7
Lower-grade salaried professionals and technicians	1.8	5.5	6.3	10.8	3.1	1.7	0.5
Inspectors, supervisors and foremen	1.9	4.5	0.3	1.2	2.4	4.0	1.7
Clerical workers and secretaries	5.1	6.1	9.8	28.0	1.2	2.9	2.4
Sales and shop personnel	4.1	3.9	7.5	9.4	1.0	1.3	1.3
Skilled manual workers	32.3	29.4	20.3	9.3	0.9	0.5	0.5
Semi-skilled manual workers	24.5	21.2	40.0	27.3	0.9	0.7	0.8
Unskilled manual workers	16.7	8.2	8.1	6.4	0.5	0.8	1.6

*Note: all figures are rounded to one decimal place. The 1971/1921 ratios indicate the degree of increase, separately for males and females: a ratio of 1.0 indicates no change, one smaller than that a decrease, and one larger an increase. The ratio in the final column compares the two rates of increase: a ratio of 1.0 indicates no difference between males and females, one smaller than that a larger increase for males than females, and one larger than that a larger increase for females than males.

Source: adapted from Abbott and Sapsford, 1987, Table 70, p. 180.

are 'real'. That is to say, the structures which mobility creates, and which create mobility, are not something that should be controlled for by statistical manipulation, but instead become an integral part of the problem. While it is true that Hauser's work in the mid-1970s discovered this from a different direction (see Hauser *et al.*, 1975), the full significance, that absolute mobility is the problem rather than relative mobility, has yet to be grasped by the comparative mobility researchers (e.g. Erikson and Goldthorpe, 1985). The failure to locate mobility in specific historical and physical locations, as part of wider sociological processes, flows directly from a narrow concentration on male mobility.

Notes

1 We should like to record our thanks to Roger Sapsford, who prepared and commented extensively on the manuscript.
2 The Essex Class Project's response rate was only 62.5 per cent of 'possible addresses'; however, comparison with Census data shows the resulting sample to be reasonably representative.
3 Change in mobility rates is calculated by comparing mobility in an older cohort with mobility in a younger one. It has long been recognized that this is a poor substitute for having two time-separated studies: men in the older cohort have had longer in which to achieve mobility, and they did so under historically unique conditions. Career progression, history and mobility rates are confounded together, so giving a poor measure, even before we get to log linear models (see Payne, 1987a, pp. 155–171).
4 Another way of thinking about this was suggested in a recent conversation with Robert Miller about the Irish Mobility Study. One of his log linear models, including occupational distributions, showed no residual differences in mobility between Catholics and Protestants in Northern Ireland. In other words, if Catholics had the same job distributions as Protestants, their mobility patterns would be the same. One might observe that if Catholics did have the same job distribution as Protestants then perhaps the political situation in Ulster today might be rather different. See also the critique of this approach put forward by Kelley (1990), particularly pp. 335–7.

Chapter 3

The Mobility of Women and Men

Tony Chapman

In recent years, a great deal of attention has been given to the study of women's employment in Britain (Dex, 1985). However, there has been relatively little work undertaken on the occupational mobility of women adopting the methodological and theoretical traditions of conventional social mobility research (Payne, 1976b; Chapman, 1984). Such an exercise is not without its problems, in particular with regard to the basic conceptualization of female class mobility (see Britten and Heath, 1983; Dale *et al.*, 1985). Even when, as in this chapter, we are concerned with inequalities of occupational opportunity rather than the broader issues of class structure, consciousness and action, several analytical problems arise.

The aim of this chapter is to explore some of these problems by attempting a 'conventional' social mobility analysis of women's and men's occupational mobility using data from the Scottish Mobility Study. The basic intergenerational mobility table will be analyzed initially to assess the extent of 'absolute' mobility. Following this, 'inflow' and 'outflow' tables will be analyzed to explore the relationship between origins and destinations. Finally, the notion of 'relative' occupational mobility will be applied to the mobility of women.

The Scottish Mobility Study Data

The Scottish Mobility Study (SMS) was carried out under the direction of Geoff Payne at the University of Aberdeen in 1974–75. The study was undertaken within the theoretical and empirical tradition of national sample mobility studies pioneered by Glass and his colleagues at the London School of Economics in 1949. The SMS research team, and the Nuffield Mobility Study researchers (Goldthorpe, 1980), attempted to replicate earlier research on Britain by Glass (1954) and on the United States by Blau and Duncan (1967).

The SMS data comprises nearly 5,000 interviews with men born between 1909 and 1955 and about 3,500 sub-interviews with their wives. The data on women to

Category	Occupational Type	% men	% women*
I	Professionals, large proprietors	11.8	1.5
II	Semi-professionals, higher technicians, small proprietors, farmers, farm managers	14.8	14.2
III	Lower technicians, manual supervisors, self employed artisans	13.9	1.7
IV	Routine non-manual workers	5.7	14.7
V	Skilled manual workers	20.2	10.6
VI	Semi-skilled manual workers	19.3	33.0
VII	Unskilled manual workers	14.2	24.3
	N =	4648	3650

*These percentages refer to the present or most recent full-time occupation of women and men respondents at time of interview.

Figure 3.1 Payne's Seven Category Occupational Status Scale

which this chapter refers are not therefore randomly sampled. Nor does it provide a proper cross-section of women in the labour market because all of the women in the study were married at the time of enquiry (Chapman, 1984; Payne, 1987a). This chapter uses the SMS seven category occupational status scale, based on occupational classification schema devised by Hope and Goldthorpe (1974). The occupational status hierarchy works on the principle of producing a scale which 'represented popular evaluations of the general "goodness" (in the sense of "desirability") of occupations' (Goldthorpe, 1972, p. 221). It should be stressed that these popular definitions referred to the occupational status of men. The seven category occupational scale, as defined by Payne (1987) is shown in Figure 3.1.

The occupational career points used in this paper refer to (1) the respondent's 'father's job' when the respondent was aged 14 years; (2) the respondent's first full-time job after leaving school, and (3) the respondent's *most* recent full-time job or present full-time job. Clearly, this latter data point is not ideal as it may refer to full-time employment which was abandoned some time ago, and may conceal the fact that a person may have been working part-time at the time of enquiry.

The Mobility of Women and Men in Scotland

In most conventional social mobility studies, the first stage of analysis involves a detailed discussion of a basic mobility table which embraces the whole sample. In this case, data are presented for *both* women and men over seven occupational status groups

Table 3.1 Occupational mobility of men and women, by their father's job when respondent aged fourteen: overall percentages

Father's Occupation	Men's and women's occupational position															
	I		II		III		IV		V		VI		VII		%	
	M	W	M	W	M	W	M	W	M	W	M	W	M	W	M	W
I	2.8	0.4	1.5	1.9	0.4	0.1	0.6	0.9	0.3	0.3	0.3	1.5	0.3	0.3	6.2	5.4
II	2.3	0.2	4.2	2.8	1.3	0.4	1.0	1.9	1.2	0.7	1.5	3.5	0.8	1.8	12.2	11.3
III	1.6	0.1	2.0	1.9	2.6	0.1	0.6	2.1	2.0	1.1	2.3	4.2	1.6	2.8	12.8	12.3
IV	0.9	0.1	0.8	0.9	0.3	0.1	0.3	0.8	0.5	0.2	0.3	1.1	0.2	0.5	3.3	3.8
V	2.0	0.2	2.8	3.0	3.7	0.5	1.4	3.6	8.6	3.4	5.7	10.2	4.7	7.2	28.7	28.2
VI	1.1	0.2	2.0	1.9	2.8	0.3	1.0	3.0	4.2	2.8	5.5	6.8	3.3	6.1	19.9	18.0
VII	1.2	0.2	1.6	1.7	2.7	0.2	0.9	2.4	3.6	2.1	3.6	5.8	3.4	5.6	16.9	18.0
%	11.8	1.5	14.8	14.2	13.9	1.7	5.7	14.7	20.2	10.6	19.3	33.0	14.2	24.3	100.0	100.0
															4648	3650

27

to compare patterns of intergenerational mobility. Women's and men's *present* occupational status (in 1975) is crosstabulated with their father's job status when the respondent was 14 years old.

Table 3.1 provides the basic table showing the absolute level of intergenerational mobility. Table 3.2 summarizes the extent of mobility calculated from Table 3.1. Over seven occupational categories, men were much more likely to be upwardly mobile than women (43 per cent of men against 32 per cent of women). More than 27 per cent of men and nearly 20 per cent of women were immobile, whilst nearly 50 per cent of women against only 30 per cent of men were downwardly mobile.

Table 3.2 Rates of occupational mobility over seven occupational categories and two occupational categories

	7×7		2×2	
	Men	Women	Men	Women
Upward	42.5	32.2	23.2	17.2
Stable	27.4	19.9	65.8	65.5
Downward	30.4	48.8	11.3	18.0

When a more narrow definition of mobility is adopted, by only counting movements across the manual/non-manual divide, the differences between women and men are less pronounced — although men were still more likely to be upwardly mobile.

On face value, it is surprising that so many women are upwardly mobile (although to a lesser extent than men) given our knowledge about women's less favourable position in the labour market (Martin and Roberts, 1984; Dex, 1985; Chapman, 1987). These findings can, however, easily be misread — and it is unlikely that greater equality in the labour market existed in 1975 than was expected. This anomaly can be explained quite easily.

By observing the marginal totals for men's and women's father's occupations shown in the basic mobility table (Table 3.1), it is clear that there is an overall similarity between the occupational distribution of men's and women's fathers. When men and women respondents' jobs are compared, striking differences occur. In the non-manual categories I-IV a relatively even distribution can be observed between higher professionals, lower professionals and technician/supervisory categories (cats. I, II and III). A substantially smaller proportion of men were employed in routine non-manual work (cat. IV). The majority of women non-manual workers were employed as lower professionals and routine non-manual workers (cats. II and IV). Only a little over 3 per cent of women were employed as higher professionals or technician/supervisory (cats. I and III). Amongst manual workers, Table 3.1 shows that women were more heavily concentrated in semi-skilled and unskilled jobs (cats. VI and VII) than men. Men outnumbered women by two to one in skilled manual occupations (cat. V).

In the case of men, it is clear that over a generation there had been a shift away from manual work and a concomitant growth in professional work. This reflects a general shift into non-manual work: the overall increase in non-manual work (excluding higher professionals) is 10 per cent. When women's occupations are compared with their fathers', it is clear that women are rather less likely to hold either a higher professional or skilled job.

Two preliminary conclusions can now be drawn. Firstly, that the high level of mobility recorded for women generally represents movements into semi-skilled, routine non-manual and lower professional jobs (cats. VI, IV and II). Within the terms of conventional mobility analysis it is not possible to dispute that upward mobility has taken place. Secondly, and more realistically, the apparent level of upward mobility observed may be misleading in the sense that a movement from a skilled manual background to a routine non-manual destination may provide women with few real advantages *vis-a-vis* status, pay, career prospects or employment security (West, 1982; Webster, 1986; McNally, 1979; Crompton and Jones, 1984).

Bearing in mind these problems, we can now move on to the analysis of 'outflow' and 'inflow' tables. The outflow matrix, Table 3.3, presents row percentages from which it is possible to assess the employment opportunities of men and women in comparison with their father's occupational status. It is clear from the first row of this table that amongst those respondents whose father was a professional, men had an excellent chance of achieving the same status. Some 70 per cent of men achieved lower professional status or better, while only 13 per cent had manual jobs. For women, the advantages of having a father of higher professional or lower professional status are less well marked. Only 45 per cent of women from such a background obtained either higher professional or lower professional status while 30 per cent had manual jobs.

To summarize the table as a whole, a fairly clear pattern emerges for men: the lower occupational status that fathers held, the less chance respondents had of gaining higher professional or lower professional status. The doors were by no means closed for men whose fathers had manual jobs: indeed, some 30 per cent of men from manual background attained status of technical/supervisory work or better. For women the pattern is far less clear. There is some evidence to suggest that fathers' occupations affect women's employment opportunities. This is particularly clear when the number of women from professional backgrounds who enter professional occupations is considered. The relationship between origin and destination for women from other backgrounds defies a statement of direct causality — indicating that the importance of social origins for women's own job status may be more limited. Before this assertion is taken too seriously, however, it is necessary to turn our attention to the 'inflow' table.

Table 3.3 Occupational distribution of men and women, by class of father when respondent was aged fourteen: percentage by row.

Respondent's father's occupation	Respondent's occupation															
	I		II		III		IV		V		VI		VII		%	
	M	W	M	W	M	W	M	W	M	W	M	W	M	W	M	W
I	44.8	7.6	24.8	35.9	6.3	2.0	10.1	17.2	4.9	5.1	4.1	26.8	4.2	5.6	6.2	5.4
II	19.0	2.2	33.9	24.7	10.9	3.1	7.9	16.9	9.5	6.3	12.7	30.5	6.2	16.2	12.2	11.3
III	12.8	0.9	16.0	15.6	20.5	1.1	4.4	16.7	15.3	8.9	18.4	34.2	12.6	22.5	12.8	12.3
IV	26.8	2.9	22.9	24.8	10.5	2.2	9.8	22.6	13.7	5.8	9.2	29.2	7.2	12.4	3.3	3.8
V	6.8	0.9	9.6	10.5	12.9	1.7	4.7	12.8	29.9	12.1	29.8	36.4	16.2	25.7	28.7	28.2
VI	5.5	1.0	10.0	9.2	14.2	1.6	5.1	14.0	21.0	13.1	27.7	32.1	16.5	28.9	19.9	21.1
VII	7.0	0.9	9.5	9.6	15.8	1.2	5.3	13.1	21.1	11.7	21.2	32.1	20.1	31.4	16.9	18.0
%	11.8	1.5	14.8	14.2	13.9	1.7	5.7	14.7	20.2	10.6	19.3	33.0	14.2	24.3	100.0	100.0
															4648	3650

Table 3.4 Occupational composition of men and women, by class of father when respondent was aged fourteen: percentage by column.

Respondent's father's occupation	Respondent's occupation														
	I		II		III		IV		V		VI		VII		%	
	M	W	M	W	M	W	M	W	M	W	M	W	M	W	M	W
I	23.3	27.3	10.3	13.7	2.8	6.5	10.9	6.3	1.5	2.6	1.6	4.4	1.8	1.2	6.2	5.4
II	19.6	16.4	28.0	19.7	9.6	21.0	16.9	13.1	5.7	6.7	8.0	10.5	5.3	7.5	12.2	11.5
III	13.8	7.3	13.8	13.5	18.9	8.1	9.7	14.0	9.7	10.4	12.2	12.7	11.4	11.4	12.8	12.3
IV	7.5	7.3	5.1	6.6	2.5	4.8	5.6	5.8	2.2	2.1	1.6	3.3	1.7	1.9	3.3	3.8
V	16.5	16.4	18.6	20.8	26.7	27.4	23.6	24.6	42.6	32.1	29.5	31.1	32.9	29.7	28.7	28.2
VI	9.3	14.5	13.4	13.7	20.3	19.4	17.6	20.1	20.6	26.2	28.5	20.5	23.0	25.0	19.9	21.1
VII	10.0	10.9	10.9	12.1	19.2	12.9	15.7	16.0	17.7	19.9	18.6	17.5	23.9	23.2	16.9	18.0
%	11.8	1.5	14.8	14.2	13.9	1.7	5.7	14.7	20.2	10.6	19.3	33.0	14.2	24.3	100.0	100.0
															4648	3650

Table 3.4 shows the social origins of men and women according to the status respondents have attained. The 'inflow' table shows that just over 40 per cent of men and women with higher professional jobs were from professional backgrounds. A similar proportion of higher professional men and women are from manual backgrounds. Although the number of women in higher professional jobs is very low, the indications are that a close link between origins and destinations is identifiable throughout the table. This does not contradict the evidence in Table 3.3 since no claim is being made that men and women were equally likely to get, say, professional work. Instead it is being stated that those who *do* gain professional work share similar origins.

From the analysis put forward thus far, three generalized findings can be reported. Firstly, that there is a good deal of upward mobility for both men and women, which does not give the impression of social closure. Secondly, that there appears to be a closer relationship between origins and destinations amongst men than is evident for women. Finally, despite the high levels of mobility recorded for women, opportunities were limited to a relatively narrow range of occupations. Women remained badly under-represented in higher professional, technician/supervisory and skilled manual occupations.

Creating Symmetrical Mobility

Before general conclusions are drawn about the applicability of conventional mobility analysis, it is necessary to take this analysis one stage further — in order to assess the extent of 'relative' social mobility. By creating a symmetrical mobility table, it has been argued, it is possible to demonstrate how much occupational mobility would have taken place had there not been substantial changes in the occupational structure (Heath, 1981; Goldthorpe, 1980). Symmetry is achieved by equalizing the marginal totals of the original mobility matrix (Table 3.1) and multiplying out the frequencies (see Heath 1981, Appendix 1). If a person's origin had no effect on his or her own achievements, then all the frequencies in the matrix would be the same. As Table 3.5 indicates, however, this is not the case; there is a link between origin and destination irrespective of changes in the occupational structure. When overall mobility rates are calculated (shown in Table 3.6) it appears that differences in rates of mobility amongst men and women are less pronounced.

How, though, could it be that women's mobility would have increased if no new jobs in the semi-professions and other non-manual work had been created? Two contradictory explanations emerge. First, it could be argued that developments in the occupational structure were not responsible for new opportunities for women, but that there had been a movement towards equal opportunities. Second, the data themselves could be misleading.

Table 3.5 Rates of intergenerational mobility for men and women assuming perfect symmetry[1]

Respondent's father's occupation	Occupation in 1975							%
	I	II	III	IV	V	VI	VII	
(a) Men N = 4648								
I	5.3	2.8	1.0	3.1	0.6	0.7	0.8	14.3
II	2.3	3.9	1.7	2.5	1.2	1.6	1.1	14.3
III	1.5	1.8	3.2	1.3	1.9	2.3	2.3	14.3
IV	3.1	2.6	1.6	2.9	1.7	1.1	1.2	14.3
V	0.7	1.1	2.0	1.4	3.7	2.5	2.7	14.3
VI	0.6	1.1	2.2	1.5	2.6	3.4	2.8	14.3
VII	0.7	1.0	2.4	1.6	2.5	2.7	3.4	14.3
	14.3	14.3	14.3	14.3	14.3	14.3	14.3	100.0
(b) Women N = 3647								
I	5.4	3.0	1.7	1.6	0.9	1.3	0.4	14.3
II	2.0	2.7	3.2	1.9	1.3	1.8	1.4	14.3
III	1.0	2.1	1.5	2.5	2.2	2.5	2.4	14.3
IV	2.7	2.7	2.3	2.7	1.2	1.7	1.1	14.3
V	1.0	1.3	2.1	1.8	2.8	2.6	2.6	14.3
VI	1.1	1.2	1.9	1.9	3.0	2.2	2.9	14.3
VII	1.1	1.3	1.5	1.9	2.8	2.3	3.4	14.3
	14.3	14.3	14.3	14.3	14.3	14.3	14.3	100.0

Note 1. The percentages in this table are derived from the data in Table 3.1.
The relative mobility frequencies are calculated according to Heath's Method (1981: Appendix).

33

Table 3.6 Rates of occupational mobility over seven occupational categories and two occupational categories for asymmetrical and symmetrical mobility tables

	Men		Women	
	Asymmetry	Symmetry	Asymmetry	Symmetry
7 × 7				
Upward	42.5	37.0	32.2	39.0
Stable	27.4	25.7	19.9	20.7
Downward	30.4	36.9	48.8	40.2
2 × 2				
Upward	23.2	16.3	17.2	18.1
Stable	65.8	66.9	65.5	63.6
Downward	11.3	16.5	18.0	18.2

Of course it is the method of analysis itself which creates a spurious finding, which warrants discussion at greater length than is possible here (Chapman, 1984). In brief it should be stated that in Table 3.1, distinct differences were shown to exist in the occupational distribution of men and women respondents. But amongst fathers, as would be expected, little variation occurred. If the occupational distribution of men is compared to that of their fathers', as illustrated in Table 3.7, it is clear that variations between the two generations give a fairly realistic representation of changes in the occupational structure as a whole (although see Payne, 1987b). This said, it is apparent that there are many new opportunities for the men in the sample compared with their fathers in all non-manual jobs. The obvious effect of *controlling* for changes in the structure of the labour market, therefore, is a reduction in the level of men's mobility — demonstrating that the relationship between origins and destinations is stronger than previously thought.

Comparing women with their fathers makes a nonsense of this technique. The operation of equalizing the marginal distributions has the effect of over-compensating for those occupational categories within which women were very much under-represented in comparison with their fathers. The impression is given that women's chances of mobility have been increased and that there is a stronger relationship between origin and destination than actually exists.

Conclusions

The analysis of 'relative' occupational mobility amongst women obviously raises serious questions about the value of utilizing comparatively sophisticated methods of data manipulation. Indeed, it is not even safe to assume that summary statistics drawn

Table 3.7 Occupational distribution of men and women compared with that of their fathers

	Occupational distribution						
	I	II	III	IV	V	VI	VII
Men							
Respondent's father	6.2	12.2	12.8	3.3	28.7	19.9	16.9
Respondent	11.8	14.8	13.9	5.7	20.2	19.3	14.2
Percentage difference	+5.6	+2.6	+1.1	+2.4	−8.5	−0.6	−2.7
Women							
Respondent's father	5.4	11.3	12.3	3.8	28.2	21.1	18.0
Respondent	1.5	14.2	1.7	14.7	10.6	33.0	24.3
Percentage difference	−3.9	+2.9	−10.6	+10.9	−17.6	+11.9	+6.3

from 'absolute' mobility tables for men and women are automatically comparable. Doubt must obviously be cast on the usefulness of calculating the *overall* extent of mobility, because the movements identified may not properly reflect the *same* upward movements. Certainly this applies to the validity of counting movement across the manual/non-manual divide, because such movements may not properly represent an improvement in status — especially amongst women. Additionally, researchers must be very cautious before assertions are made about the impact of changes in the occupational structure on new opportunities. For analysis to proceed on a more productive footing, it would seem to be necessary to enhance our understanding of changes in the structure of the labour market rather than to manipulate them away.

On the positive side, the above analysis provides some support for the cautious use of occupational mobility data adopting 'inflow' and 'outflow' tables. Patterns of intergenerational and intragenerational occupational mobility might best be examined through analysis of changes in labour market opportunities over time. Analysis will proceed in this direction in Chaper 7 of this volume.

Chapter 4

A Re-examination of 'Three Theses Re-examined'

Pamela Abbott

In their article 'Class Mobility in Britain: three theses examined', subsequently included as Chapter 2 of Goldthorpe *et al.*, (1980, 1987), John Goldthorpe and Catriona Llewellyn presented evidence about male mobility that impugned three conventional theses about class and mobility. These were:

> that of a marked degree of 'closure' existing at the higher levels of the class structure; that of a 'buffer zone' constricting the extent of mobility across the division between manual and non-manual occupations; and that of the offsetting or 'counterbalancing' of any rising trend in upward mobility *intergenerationally* by a declining trend in social mobility *intragenerationally*. (p. 40 of the 1987 Edition)

While these three theses were originally formulated with respect to male mobility and examined by Goldthorpe and Llewellyn using male data (from the 1972 Oxford Mobility Study), it is interesting to re-test them using female data (in this instance from the Open University *People in Society* Survey). The implied outcome of the examination by Goldthorpe and Llewellyn was that 'closure', 'buffer-zone' and 'counterbalance' are not useful models for *all* mobility, whether by men or women. It is for this reason that the present chapter is called 'Three Theses Re-examined'.

To spell out in more detail what we are examining, the three theses were:

> i The 'social closure' thesis (associated with e.g., Giddens, 1973; Bottomore, 1964; Miliband, 1969), which argued that those who occupy 'superior' positions in the class hierarchy may be presumed to be motivated to retain these positions for themselves and to pass them on to their children, and that they have command of the necessary resources to do so. Insofar as mobility does occur into the highest class it will be short-range; élite groups will contain few who have experienced long-range mobility.

The effect of social closure is that occupational groups at the peak of the hierarchy will be homogeneous with respect to origins.

ii The 'buffer-zone' thesis (associated with Parkin, 1971; Giddens, 1973; Bottomore, 1965; Westergaard and Resler, 1975), which argues that there is a high degree of social mobility around the manual/non-manual boundary but that this serves to block off longer-range mobility and, again, secure social closure. Thus in terms of origins, intermediate groups are heterogeneous while extreme ones are homogeneous.

iii The 'counterbalance' thesis (associated with Westergaard and Little, 1967; Westergaard, 1972; Westergaard and Resler, 1975; Parkin, 1971), which argues that education is now the main route to social mobility and that placement in the labour market is primarily determined by educational qualifications, given the increased professionalization, bureaucratization and technological complexity of the modern age. *Intra*generational work progress is no longer of much significance and it is no longer the case that men are able to achieve significant mobility via achievement at work. In other words, the intergenerational mobility which now occurs as a result of educational expansion, and reforms aimed at providing equality of educational opportunity, will be offset by a decline in working-life advancement.

On the basis of data from the all-male sample used in the Oxford Mobility Study Goldthorpe and Llewellyn rejected all three of these theses, arguing that there was a significant amount of occupational mobility both intergenerationally and intragenerationally, and being able to find no clear evidence for the existence of a 'buffer-zone'.

The question that arises is whether an examination of data on female social mobility would lead to similar conclusions. Goldthorpe and Payne (1986) argue that taking account of women in studies of social mobility does not fundamentally alter the conclusions drawn from studies based on male-only samples. They point out that the rates of mobility are similar for men and women in the British Election Study data, although they acknowledge that women are more likely than men to be downwardly mobile from their fathers' occupational class and men more likely to be upwardly mobile. This finding is confirmed not only in other British studies (e.g. Abbott and Sapsford, 1987; Chapman, 1984; Marshall *et al.*, 1988) but also in American studies (e.g. Tyree and Treas, 1974; Hauser *et al.*, 1974) and European ones (e.g. Erikson and Pontinen, 1985). However, by concentrating on rates of intergenerational mobility, Goldthorpe and Payne ignore the range of female mobility and its movement during the working life. In other words, they do not test the three theses outlined above using female mobility data. In this chapter each of the three theses is examined in turn, drawing mainly on data on female mobility from the Open University's *People in*

Society Survey, a national quota survey of class-related demographics and attitudes which has been carried out by undergraduate and masters-level Open University students since 1979. (The data analyzed are drawn from the samples collected in 1980–1984: for more details of the survey's design, see Abbott and Sapsford, 1987). We should note that the patterns of female occupational mobility found in that survey are essentially similar to those found by the Scottish Mobility Survey (Chapman, 1984) and the Essex Class Survey (Marshall *et al.*, 1988); see also Payne and Abbott in this volume.

In order to test the three theses, the full mobility tables for all women in the *People in Society Survey* will be included. The 'inflow' tables enable us to determine the class origins of women currently in each occupational class, while 'outflow' tables enable us to see the destination class for daughters, by each occupational class of father. The former kind of table lets us see the extent to which the class backgrounds of women in each occupational class are now homogeneous or heterogeneous, and the latter the extent to which occupational classes have been self-recruiting. For example, in terms of the buffer-zone thesis, Payne *et al.* (1976) and Goldthorpe and Llewellyn (1980, 1987) used inflow tables to demonstrate, by comparing origin and destination class, that there is considerable fluidity in male class mobility and that there is long-range as well as short-range mobility. They were therefore able to reject, for men, both the buffer-zone and social closure theses.

Social Closure

Goldthorpe and Llewellyn (Goldthorpe *et al.*, 1980) conclude from their analysis of intergenerational mobility in the Oxford Mobility Study data that there is no evidence of social closure; that is, those in the highest social classes seem able neither to prevent upward mobility into those classes nor to ensure that their sons achieved the same class position as themselves. While nearly half of the sons of Class I fathers achieved a Class I destination, so did about 12 per cent of the sons of men in Social Class VII. Furthermore, the class backgrounds (i.e. father's class) of men in Social Classes I and II are very heterogeneous. However, if we look at patterns of female mobility a very different picture emerges. Compared with men, very few women end up in Social Class I, irrespective of their fathers' social class. In the *People in Society Survey*, for example, if we look at the outflow rate we can see that only 8 per cent of the daughters of men in the highest social class were themselves in that class, and less than 1 per cent of women with fathers in semi- or unskilled manual jobs (Table 4.1). If we look at inflow rates, 50 per cent of women in professional or managerial occupations had a father in the same kind of occupation, while only 3 per cent had a father in the semi- or unskilled working class (Table 4.2). The class background of the very small proportion of women who end up in the highest social class is more homogeneous than that of corresponding men, but very few women of *any* background end up there — about 8 per cent of women were employers, managers or professional workers in 1981, compared with about 21 per cent of men (OPCS, 1984, Table 17). We can conclude from this that higher social classes may not be able to operate social class closure against lower social classes — although daughters of high-class fathers stand a higher chance than daughters of other fathers of achieving a high-class occupation — but men operate social closure successfully against women. Women are excluded from occupations in the highest social grades, irrespective of class background.

Table 4.1 The social mobility of women, by class of origin[1] ('Outflow' %)

Father's occupation[2]	Own occupation[2]					Total[3]
	A	B	C1	C2	D	
A	8	38	44	6	4	200
B	2	41	44	8	5	354
C1	2	24	46	10	19	310
C2	<1	14	32	19	35	693
D	<1	12	27	13	48	253
Totals	2	23	37	13	25	1810

Notes:
1. Open University *People in Society Survey* data
2. Classified by the Social Grading Scale
3. About 7 per cent of married working women were excluded — father's class unknown or coded as E (retired/unemployed for more than two years, permanently disabled, etc.)

Table 4.2 The social mobility of women, by destination class[1] ('Inflow' %)

Father's occupation[2]	Own occupation[2]					Total[3]
	A	B	C1	C2	D	
A	50	17	13	5	2	11
B	24	35	23	12	4	20
C1	15	17	21	13	13	17
C2	9	23	33	56	54	38
D	3	7	10	14	27	14

Notes:
1. Open University *People in Society Survey* data
2. Classified by the Social Grading Scale
3. About 7 per cent of married working women were excluded — father's class unknown or coded as E (retired/unemployed for more than two years, permanently disabled, etc.)

The Buffer Zone

They also argue from their analysis of the Oxford Mobility Survey data that there is no longer any sort of buffer zone preventing long-range mobility, if indeed there ever was one. That is, intergenerational mobility is not restricted to short-range movement around the manual/non-manual boundary. Sons who are upwardly mobile from the manual working class are as likely to move into professional or managerial jobs as they are to enter routine non-manual ones. Likewise, the sons of professional or managerial fathers who are downwardly mobile are as likely to end up in manual working-class occupations as in routine non-manual ones.

When we look at female mobility data, a very different picture emerges. In the *People in Society* data (Table 4.1) the daughters of professional or managerial workers who were downwardly mobile in terms of their own jobs ended up overwhelmingly in routine non-manual work. The daughters of manual fathers who were upwardly mobile into the middle-class also ended up in routine non-manual work. (39 per cent of working women in 1981 were classified as 'junior non-manual' in the Census, while the largest category of males, skilled manual workers, accounted for only 27 per cent of men OPCS, 1984, Table 17.) Clearly for women the presence of this very large category of routine non-manual work constitutes a real buffer zone. While the manual/non-manual divide appears to act as a barrier to downward mobility, upward mobility through the divide is frequent; however, the majority of these who are upwardly mobile climb no further than routine non-manual work.[1] (Abbott and Sapsford (1987) analyzed the data separately for full- and part-time female workers and found that the pattern was similar for both.)

Countermobility

The Oxford team also failed to find evidence that increased mobility via educational achievement is being counterbalanced by a decline in working-life mobility. While their analysis suggests that educational criteria are an important factor in initial occupational placement, they also found a considerable amount of intragenerational mobility. 50 per cent of men in Classes I and II who emerged as intergenerationally mobile in terms of the total measurement times had been downwardly mobile in the interim. That is, they had started work in an occupation lower down the hierarchy of classes and had then been intragenerationally upwardly mobile. Furthermore, of the men with a working-class background, 75 per cent had working-class jobs initially, but by 1972 only half of these were still in working-class jobs. The authors conclude that there is considerable intragenerational mobility but that once the higher classes have been reached individuals tend to stay there for the remainder of their working lives. Thus they reject the view that there is little upward mobility for men via occupational advancement.

Research on women has also found that educational qualifications are an important determinant of occupational class placement. Jones (1986), in her analysis of mobility among 16–29-year-olds (men, and women without children), demonstrated that class of origin and level of educational qualifications were important factors for both boys and girls, although she points out that for women the effect is more difficult to see, because of their heavy concentration in routine non-manual jobs. However, she found that 86 per cent of the daughters of manual workers who stayed on in education past the age of 18 had non-manual first jobs, compared with 63 per cent of those who left school earlier, while 76 per cent of the daughters of non-manual fathers who left school early were in non-manual employment.

The *People in Society* data also indicate strong relationships between education and occupational class. Table 4.3 shows the relationship between father's occupational class, own occupational class and whether the respondent stayed on at school beyond the statutory minimum age for leaving. Irrespective of class background, those in AB jobs had generally stayed on at school two years or more above the minimum, and only a small proportion had left at the first opportunity. Women in C1 and skilled manual jobs from AB backgrounds had generally stayed on for two or more years, but only half of those from C1 or manual backgrounds had done so. The vast majority of women in semi- or unskilled jobs were early leavers, except for those from an AB background. This analysis looks at all women in paid employment outside the home, and the present job may not always be a valid indicator of a married woman's potential occupational class, particularly if it is a part-time one. Numbers in each cell would be

Table 4.3 The education background and occupation of women[1]: percentage with 2 + years of post-compulsory schooling

Father's occupation[2]	Own occupation[2]					Total[3]
	A	B	C1	C2	D	
A	82	78	68	57	33	72
B	86	84	68	43	11	72
C1	100	78	49	50	3	52
C2	100	81	37	7	8	34
D	100	90	55	—	—	32
Total	86	82	53	18	5	

Notes:
1. Open University *People in Society Survey* data
2. Classified by the Social Grading Scale
3. About 10 per cent of married working women were excluded — father's class unknown or coded as E (retired/unemployed for more than two years, permanently disabled, etc.), or age or year in which left school not recorded.

too small for valid statistical analysis if the table were to be broken down further by marital status and full- or part-time employment. However, the overall analysis does suggest a strong relationship between education and present class; women in high-status jobs have generally spent longer in the educational system. (See Abbott and Sapsford, 1987, for a discussion of why years of post-compulsory schooling is a better indicator for the purposes of this kind of analysis than educational qualifications obtained.)

While educational qualifications are important in determining occupational placement for both men and women, women are much less likely than men to be upwardly mobile once they are in the labour market — to recover the occupational class of their father after initial downward mobility on entry to the labour market. The Scottish Mobility Study (see Chapman, 1984) found that on entry to the labour market 75 per cent of men and 77 per cent of women were downwardly mobile from their father's class. However, men tended to recover their position after a period of years. (Chapter 7 in this volume has a more detailed discussion of this point with reference to the Scottish data.)

Jones (1986), looking at National Child Development Study data, concluded that women experience more intragenerational stability in their careers up to the age of 23, although intragenerational mobility, whether upwards or downwards, is less common among women than men. Given that education is an important determinant of first occupation, she suggests that for many women their class destination is determined by their education. She then demonstrates that educational qualification is an important factor in female intragenerational mobility after entry to the labour market. Thirteen per cent of the daughters of middle-class fathers who had a manual job were countermobile. Of this 13 per cent, some two-thirds had, in fact, been educated beyond the age of 18. This compares with the 19 per cent of middle-class sons who experienced downward mobility on entry to the labour market, 8 per cent reaching middle-class occupations via education and work routes, and 11 per cent by work routes alone. (See also Greenhalgh and Stewart (1982) for a study which ranked occupations by hourly earnings rather than status but again came to similar conclusions.) These studies suggest that women's intragenerational mobility is very limited and that a woman is much less likely than a man to be upwardly mobile and correspondingly more likely to be immobile or downwardly mobile. The much more detailed analysis provided in a study carried out by the OPCS (Martin and Roberts, 1984) demonstrates clearly that while childless women are more likely than women with children to be upwardly mobile over their lifetimes, their level of upward career mobility is still not as high as that experienced by men.

Conclusions

Analysis of female social mobility shows considerable fluidity in the occupational class system, with women both upwardly and downwardly mobile. However, because of the distribution of female jobs between the occupational categories, women are more likely on average to be downwardly mobile from their father's class than are men and less likely to be upwardly mobile. High-status fathers are less able to secure high-status occupations for their daughters than for their sons. Furthermore, the large concentration of women in routine non-manual work has a significant impact on female social mobility. While the manual/non-manual divide acts as a barrier to downward mobility for them, the considerable upward mobility across the divide leads mostly to routine non-manual occupations and goes no higher.

Female patterns of intragenerational mobility are complex. Married women's domestic responsibilities, especially periods of withdrawal from the labour market and/or of part-time employment during the child-rearing years, have a marked effect on their class destination. If women returning to the labour market take part-time work, there is a strong likelihood that this will entail downward mobility: see Shirley Dex's chapter in this volume. However, even when single women are examined separately we find that they experience less intragenerational mobility than men and women are less likely to be counter-mobile. Both American and British studies suggest that educational factors are more important for women than for men in determining their occupational class, irrespective of how long they have been in the labour market. In the context of the counterbalance thesis, qualifications seem to be a major factor in female occupational placement: women are less likely to be promoted on the basis of work experience than are men.

These findings suggest that an analysis of male occupational class mobility by itself gives an inadequate picture of the nature of contemporary British society. It provides a distorted picture of what is going on, because the experiences of women are different from those of men — and these differences are not totally accounted for by women's domestic responsibilities.

In terms of the theoretical propositions that Goldthorpe *et al.* (1980) were explicitly concerned to test in the Oxford Mobility Study — 'social closure', 'buffer zone' and 'countermobility' — an analysis of data on women puts all of his conclusions in doubt. The findings for women challenge his conclusions that no evidence exists for the ability of those in higher social positions to provide these for their children, or for the restriction of mobility to short-range movement around the manual/non-manual divide, or for the notion that educational qualifications are the major stimulus for upward mobility. The *People in Society* findings demonstrate that in terms of social closure it is possible to support Goldthorpe to the extent that there *was* some long-range mobility, and high-status fathers were not necessarily able to secure high-status occupations for their daughters. The extent of long-range mobility was limited, however, and there is clear evidence that in the highest occupational categories men are able to operate social closure against women; there are few women in top jobs.

Finally, it is clear that a buffer-zone does exist for women at the manual/non-manual divide, with considerable mobility around this area — especially upward from manual work — but substantially less beyond it. While the occupational processes of post-industrial society are characterized by a large routine non-manual sector, there is no technical nor inevitable economic law that says that this sector must be occupied by women. However, given the predominance of women in routine non-manual work, and their experience of a buffer-zone process, what does this imply for class analysis? Two possible interpretations may be drawn (a point developed in the final chapter below). First, Parkin has suggested that the buffer-zone provides a phase of class adaptation in which new class values and behaviour are learned. If this is so, then female mobility may be less significant for class action or consciousness. On the other hand, as West asks,

> how can women workers be 'peripheral' if the 'underclass' they so neatly occupy is part of the 'buffer zone' which helps to prevent polarization of the two major classes? (West, 1978, p. 232).

Note

1. There is, of course, a debate as to whether routine non-manual work is in fact to be categorized as middle-class. In particular it has been argued that *female* routine non-manual work has been proletarianized. However, Martin and Roberts (1984) have demonstrated that most female non-routine manual workers have comparable conditions of employment to those of women in clearly middle-class occupations. (See also Abbott and Sapsford, 1987, for a more detailed discussion).

Chapter 5

The Changing Pattern of Early Career Mobility

Geoff Payne, Judy Payne and Tony Chapman

Although this analysis focuses on occupational, rather than class, processes, the question of classifying women in order to examine their mobility does not disappear. Women who are in unpaid roles as housewife and mother must either be treated as 'non-occupational', or possibly as in reserve positions in which a woman's former occupational identity is not entirely lost. In other words, to substitute her father's or husband's occupation (Acker, 1973, p. 937; Oppenheimer, 1977; Rutter and Hargen, 1975; Parkin, 1971) is not acceptable, as this would be to shift out of the occupational frame of reference and into that of class, while at the same time diverting attention away from the more general economic position of women as potential members of the labour force in their own right.

However, if a married woman as a housewife does not have an active occupational or class role of her own, she must (i) be excluded from an analysis of class mobility; or (ii) have her husband's class identity attached to her; or (iii) be identified by her former occupational identity when she last worked; or (iv) be identified by some combination of (ii) and (iii) (the Britten and Heath solution).

As observed above, option (i) has in practice been the one chosen in most mobility studies to date, and is the one on which we are seeking to improve. There are problems in using just the husband's class, as in option (ii): this ignores the social persona which the woman retains from her earlier life. Equally, option (iii) is not without its disadvantages: if a woman has not worked for thirty years, her identity is given by an occupation that was relevant a very long time ago, but which may even have ceased to exist under present-day technology.

These options have been expressed in terms of a woman's own adult identity, that is, in terms of her mobility 'destination'. A parallel set of choices exists for her mobility origins, where the problem becomes one of deciding how to include her mother as a factor in deciding the classification of her family of origin (a problem which applied equally to the mother of male respondents). The eventual choices will largely depend on the way the family is seen to operate as a unit of production or consumption, although none of the options is without some disadvantages.

Whether we adopt a life-style model or a narrower class-based view for an analysis of mobility, we also need to be clear about the ways in which a family bestows an 'identity' on one of its junior members. There are several mechanisms of inter-generational 'inheritance' which can in turn be related to occupational outcomes. Among the best-known half a dozen or so, the most commonly researched is education, by which we mean that the family background is a major determinant of the qualification level attained by the offspring. By the same token, direct inheritance of property, and job aspirations are two other recognized means of 'transferring' family background to the child. However, these are not so much an outcome of a lifestyle or status, as the products of the underlying class attributes of the parents, which have also created their life style. Three further but less well-researched mechanisms are self-presentation, informal job contacts, and household location.

While these six mechanisms are not an exhaustive list, they serve to demonstrate two points. First, these mechanisms on the whole depend on the parental class or occupational position. The extent to which each of the six mechanisms is equally dependent on both parents, and the extent to which each parent influences the offspring of his/her own gender are empirical questions which require more research. In short, we cannot easily amalgamate male and female roles on the basis of existing knowledge unless we restrict our notions of the linking mechanisms between origins and destinations.

However, as previously indicated, the present authors do not see the family of origin problem as being the main focus. The larger and arguably more significant gap in our knowledge is the mobility career of women as individuals in their own right, rather than as members of a family unit. Of course, we need to know something about origins in order to make sense of this, but it is better to solve part of the problem by side-stepping the origins issue than to be trapped so completely in the logical pitfalls of criticism that no empirical analysis is possible.

One way out of this dilemma — and it is no more than choosing the lesser of the evils — is to make an arbitrary distinction between origins and destinations, which will allow us to present some new evidence. If we retain the practice of identifying the family of origin by the father's occupation, two advantages do accrue. First, we by-pass the problem that in many cases (e.g. between the wars) the mothers were not in paid employment and so had no occupational identity. Second, we can make direct comparisons with earlier, male-only studies that used the father as the class identifier. Even though these are flawed, British sociology is not so generously endowed with empirical studies that we should rush to discard those we do have. Further, if we use the same origin measure (despite its flaws) we can concentrate on current careers as the source of any gender differences in occupational attainment (see below, p. 50). However, the chief disadvantage that has to be taken on board if we adopt this measure is that the modifying influence of the mother is unquantified, an influence which in terms of doing paid work has been growing steadily (see Chapter 6).

As for destinations, it is proposed that as far as possible, a woman should retain a separate identity. As both a single person and a married woman in paid employment, this is easy to operationalize. When a married woman ceases to work in this way, she can be classed either as retaining an occupational identity but temporarily not available for employment, or just possibly as adopting her husband's class until such time as she opts to resume paid work. This offers the main advantages that again we by-pass the problem of classifying the role of housewife, while setting up a position in which the woman's occupational identity is given the same logical priority as the man's. Against this it can be argued that we have not been consistent in the way that we have treated origins and destinations, and that the class position of the housewife has still to be clarified.

As noted earlier the typical paid work role for a woman is routine white collar (e.g. Hakim, 1979; Payne *et al.*, 1979a). In the SMS data on first job obtained on entering work, almost one in three of women (compared with one in thirty men) were shop assistants, or office workers (Hope-Goldthorpe category 2304) while another one in six were clerical specialists (category 2303).

In other words, just over half of all female employment on entering work was of a routine white-collar kind. Or was it? To label this work as 'white-collar' is already to locate it as on the non-manual side of the manual/non-manual distinction, a location which is open to debate (e.g. Goldthorpe, 1980; Westergaard and Resler, 1977; Wedderburn and Craig, 1974).

In previous analysis of the SMS data, two alternative conventions have been followed. For male respondents, clerical specialists (Hope-Goldthorpe category 2303) have been treated as non-manual, whereas sales personnel and general office workers (Hope-Goldthorpe category 2304) have been treated as manual (the latter comprise about 3 per cent of male first jobs and less that 0.5 per cent of current male employment). However, in an earlier paper which argued that female mobility opportunities at their current employment point were lower than males' (Payne, *et al.*, 1979a), sales work was re-classified as non-manual. This was because the ambiguity of its position was recognized, and treating it as non-manual 'loaded' the data *against* the authors' case in order to avoid any accusation of data manipulation. To be consistent, this second convention has been retained here, for both males and females.

In the following discussion, the data are drawn from the 1975 Scottish Mobility Study survey of males aged 20 to 64 and resident in Scotland (cf. Payne *et al.*, 1979a; Payne and Payne, 1981). When the household details indicated that the respondent was married or living with a woman, information was collected about her. Thus the term 'female social mobility' as used in an empirical sense in this paper refers to women presently married to or living with men aged 20 to 64, or more specifically to those women who in addition started work between 1930 and 1970, i.e. a group with some slight concentration towards the middle of that age-range.

Trends in Male and Female Mobility

Figure 5.1 shows the distribution of non-manual jobs among people starting work at different points between the years 1930 and 1970. The upper line is a plot of the percentage of jobs obtained by women which were non-manual, while below it is the percentage of female jobs which were filled by women upwardly mobile from manual working-class family backgrounds. The lower pair of lines show male first jobs in the same way. These graphs have three main features: (i) the female lines show higher percentages than the males; (ii) the two pairs broadly resemble each other; and (iii) the

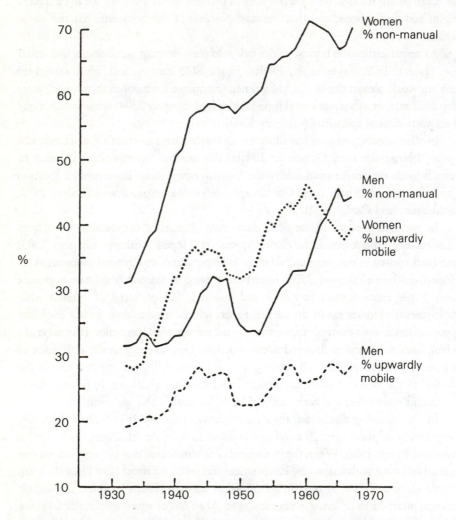

Figure 5.1 Five-year moving averages for non-manual employment and mobility on first entry to the labour market

pattern of upward mobility echoes that of the non-manual percentages in both cases, apart from the later part of the time series.

Taking the latter two findings first, it can be seen that, allowing for some small variations, non-manual occupations show a decade of expansion, a decade of stagnation or contraction, a further decade of expansion terminating in the 1960s with a sharp hiccup in growth affecting women more severely than men. In each pair, this pattern is repeated for the rate of upward mobility, except that in the last decade the symmetry disappears. For women, the mobility rate falls more steeply than the non-manual employment line, while for men the upward mobility rate flattens out while non-manual opportunity continues to rise. In other words, although upward mobility rates (calculated as movement across the manual/non-manual line at first job) are much higher than in the 1930s and 1940s, the share of non-manual occupations going to the children of *non-manual* fathers increases in the 1960s.

The pattern is not what one might intuitively expect. Given what we know about the Depression, we would not anticipate a growth of non-manual opportunity in the 1930s, nor would we expect to find the 1960s were a time of increasing social closure. The Scottish economy was already depressed in the 1920s, largely as a result of its dependence on the old staple industries of coal, iron and steel, shipbuilding and textiles. Male unemployment rose from 15 to 25 per cent in the 1930s, and in some of the old staples, it was to exceed 40 per cent and remain so until the war.

However, this period also saw both increases in productivity due to technological innovation (even in the old staples) and considerable economic concentration. Larger units of production required more extensive and complex administrative structures, and permitted greater division of labour with new technical specialism. In other words conditions were right for an expansion of non-manual opportunity even in industries which had a poor economic performance. It would seem that young workers benefited from such changes while older workers were more likely to remain unemployed, trapped in occupational specialisms which were not needed and, being adults, probably more expensive to employ. In as far as the occupational requirements of new technologies and scales of organization generated more non-manual jobs, it follows that increases

in non-manual employment and upward mobility do not seem to be incompatible with high unemployment, with rising productivity or with marked changes in the nature of capital (Payne and Payne, 1981, pp. 11-12).

These observations, made about male employment and mobility, would on the present evidence now seem to apply to *both* genders.

On the other hand, gender differences begin to emerge during the Second World War and its aftermath in the late 1940s. The first peaks in the non-manual employment in Figure 5.1 are reached during the war, with women reaching a plateau by the middle of the war, and young men by the end of it. The former workers remain at that level until 1950, whereas the men suffer a decline before their recovery starts perhaps two or three years later. The similarity between these profiles is a product of the war; the difference lies in gender responses in time of war. The removal of a significant proportion of the adult male labour force into the armed services, together with the setting up of a state-controlled wartime economy, created a demand for labour which women and very young men filled. The data in Figure 5.1 deals only with civilian jobs: school-leavers taking these jobs between 1939 and 1945 found themselves entering jobs that under normal circumstances would not have been open to them. This part of the time series reflects not so much a change in total opportunity due to an expansion of the non-manual sector, as a temporary change in recruitment practices.

Conversely, in the immediate post-war years, the opportunities for young men and women were depressed by demobilisation. The claims of demobilised armed forces personnel, together with the log-jam of those who had come onto the market during the war and were now firmly in post, made the next few years more difficult for those just starting work. In this respect, young men suffered more than young women, presumably because men were more directly affected by the demobilisation factor whereas more older women left work to become mothers (so creating vacancies) as a consequence of delayed family building patterns and an active media campaign to reassert 'domestic values'. As the 1950s progressed, the upward trends in both non-manual opportunity and upward mobility re-established themselves.

Leaving aside the last decade of the time series for the moment (see below), the broad similarities of the plot in Figure 5.1 suggest that some general process of economic change has similar effects on both males and females. Given that we have been dealing primarily with what Lee has recently called 'systematic' major changes in employment (1981, p. 61) this is perhaps not too surprising, but it is nonetheless of interest that gender does not at this level seem to play such a major part that the long-term external changes are obscured by the differences in male and female experiences.

However, to return to the first of our initial three observations, the female graphs show consistently higher percentages, a basic difference which requires investigation. In the early part of the period, the female upward mobility percentage is about 30 per cent: by the war years this has increased to 35 per cent and thereafter up to the 1960s it is nearer 40 per cent. In the final decade it declines to below 40 per cent again. From 1940 on, a majority of women entering work did so as non-manual workers, and from the mid-1950s this was running at two in every three. This pattern mirrors the census data for the same years. Nearly 70 per cent of women were currently in non-manual work in 1971 (i.e. their occupation at the time of census, not the occupations of women first entering work in 1971). In contrast, the majority of males started work as *manual* workers, and only in the last fifteen years did this drop *below* two in every three.

What we have here is a very simple but often overlooked fact, that employment opportunities determine mobility. If over half of all daughters are employed in non-manual work, and only about one-third of all daughters come from non-manual family backgrounds (as defined by their *male* parents), then there is a structural mismatch. Even if all daughters of non-manual families get non-manual jobs themselves, this still leaves about one in four of all jobs that are non-manual and have to be filled by recruiting from manual families. Although male respondents are also more likely than their fathers to be non-manual workers, due to the occupational transition effect (Payne, 1987a) this is nothing like so marked as in the case of women.

On the face of it, it would seem that rather than women being discriminated against, they have an occupational advantage over men which extends to social mobility (where the female percentage increases from a 10 per cent difference to 30 per cent at its peak in the early 1960s). However, the picture is not quite as simple as that. As we saw earlier, women are not employed in the same non-manual occupations as men. Men outnumber women in Classes 1 and 3 (professional and managerial, supervisory and self-employed), while women outnumber men in Classes 2 and 4 (semi-professional and routine clerical work). There is however very little difference in the overall totals in these four classes (27.4 per cent and 26.9 per cent). It is only when category 2304 is added to the non-manual count that the large difference between men and women emerges. This category adds a further 30 per cent to the female total. It follows that the previous apparent advantage of women must be qualified, in that the *female mobility experience involves a movement to the lowest and most marginal of the non-manual categories.*

There is therefore in a double sense a distinctive mobility experience for women. It will be recalled that the distributions of parental origins for the men and women are the same, because they are basically contemporaries. The distinctive mobility patterns are a product of the pattern of destinations, that is to say the distribution of occupational opportunities for men and women. Whereas an average of less than one in three men was upwardly mobile on starting work, the figure for women was closer to two in three. Even if that status were temporary (until marriage) or somewhat illusory (as it was only marginally non-manual) *it must still be regarded as an experience of upward mobility, given the logic underlying previous analyses of male mobility.*

By the same token, the period of the 1960s showed a marked change in mobility opportunities for both genders. Whereas non-manual opportunity continued to rise for men, but their upward mobility tailed off, for women there was a slight *fall* in the proportion of non-manual jobs obtained, and a drop of nearly 10 per cent in the rate of upward mobility. The fact that something affects both genders suggests a systematic change, but it is not clear what it is. The arguments used to explain earlier changes do not hold true. There is no war dislocation, and the authors know of no evidence that employers modified their patterns of recruitment which in some way discriminated against people from working-class backgrounds. On the contrary, we would have anticipated quite the reverse, as the 1960s have been perceived (not just by a generation of sociologists now entering middle-age) as a decade of greater openness when working-class etiquette, dialect and mannerisms became more acceptable. We also have evidence that later on, in the 1970s, overall mobility for men increased (Payne 1990). The 'swinging sixties' were the years in which British social mores underwent their biggest changes this century, but the present evidence suggests at least a temporary rigidification of the class structure at the macro level.

Components of Mobility

In a previous paper, we argued that the male mobility pattern in the 1960s could be explained by a change in the *type* of non-manual employment that was available in the various periods of time series. The essence of the argument is that manufacturing industries and the service sector have different profiles of non-manual jobs and recruitment policies, and in the 1960s the service sector dominates the picture. The manufacturing (or secondary) sector has fewer non-manual jobs, but fills proportionately more of them with men from manual backgrounds. The tertiary sector has far more non-manual openings, but has always tended to hire the sons of non-manual fathers. The reason for this is slightly complicated. The service sector involves more highly technical, knowledge-based occupations, while the state part of it at least is organized on a bureaucratic basis. That is to say, job applicants are expected to have formal educational qualifications. The sons of non-manual workers do better out of the schooling system, and therefore are able to fill more of the available places in service industries. Whereas the manufacturing sector makes a considerable contribution until 1960, but thereafter so many of the new non-manual opportunities are concentrated in the tertiary sector that mobility opportunities cease to increase (Payne and Payne, 1981, pp. 15-21).

The basic model can be applied to the female data, but from the outset it is clear that an identical pattern will not emerge. This is because we already know from Figure 5.1 that whereas for men, non-manual opportuntiy increased while mobility stabilised, for women non-manual opportunity decreased as did mobility. If the shift to tertiary sector dominance is the cause, it would seem to have hit young women harder.

The distributions of mobility within the three main industrial sectors — primary, secondary and tertiary — are given in Figure 5.2. The numbers of non manual occupations and upwardly mobile people in the primary sector are so small that there is little to discuss. Were we interested in 'non-mobility' it would be a different story. With such small numbers, no clear gender differences can be detected.

The 1960s saw over 10 per cent of all men being upwardly mobile in the tertiary sector, and less than 5 per cent upwardly mobile in secondary industries. Apart from the wartime peak, this pattern is not repeated elsewhere in the time series: the 1930s and late 1940s could be said to run closer to 7 per cent and 3 per cent. Among women the secondary sector contributed a steady 5 per cent or 6 per cent to the mobility rate from the 1930s while the tertiary sector's contribution climbed from 15 per cent to 40

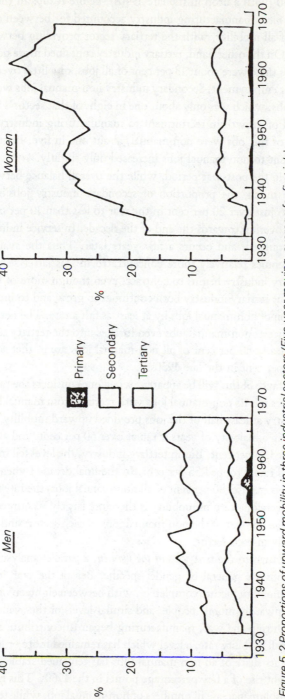

Figure 5.2 Proportions of upward mobility in three industrial sectors (Five-year moving average for first job)

per cent by 1960 (with a drop in the late 1940s), before it dips in the final decade.

Among the men, manufacturing industry accounted for between about one-sixth and one-third of all mobility, with the tertiary sector providing between two-thirds and five-sixths. On the other hand, tertiary industry contained more non-manual jobs: during the 1930s these were about 18 per cent of all jobs, or a little over one in three of all tertiary sector employment. Secondary industry non-manual jobs were only about 4 per cent of all jobs, which was only about one in eight of that sector's jobs. There was not a great deal of growth in recruitment to manufacturing industry because of the war, but more of the jobs were non-manual, about one in five. In contrast, tertiary sector recruitment to non-manual jobs increased only slightly.

However, in the post-war period, while the overall balance between the sectors did not change much, the proportion of secondary industry jobs which are non-manual fell from just over 20 per cent in the war to less than 10 per cent by the early 1950s before recovering towards the end of the decade. In service industries, the fall is much less pronounced, and occurs a few years later. Thus the availability of non-manual jobs becomes relatively more concentrated in this latter sector. In the final decade, secondary industry begins to contract, even though more of its jobs are non-manual ones. But tertiary industry both continues to grow and to increase its already larger proportion of non-manual jobs by at least as fast a rate. The net effect is to shift the overall balance of non-manual jobs even further into the tertiary sector, so that by the late 1960s nearly 80 per cent of all non-manual jobs are in that sector, compared with under 75 per cent in the late 1950s.

The importance of this will be apparent when one considers the rate at which each of the two sectors fills its non-manual jobs with recruits from manual backgrounds. In secondary industry at least half of the jobs provided upward mobility for almost all of the time series: in a majority of years it ran at over 60 per cent, and at its peak during the war it reached 75 per cent. But in tertiary industry, the level fell more often below 50 per cent, and rarely topped 55 per cent. In the final decade (when as we have just seen, this sector comprises 80 per cent of all non-manual jobs) the rate fell to around 40 per cent. The overall pattern of mobility is therefore largely accounted for by the size of the sectors, the number of the non-manual jobs in each sector, and the recruitment 'rules' that apply in each sector.

If we now turn to the first jobs *of the women*, a parallel analysis shows how far these explanations are general or gender-specific. Before the war, tertiary industry dominated the mobility picture completely, with between eighteen or nineteen out of every twenty upwardly mobile people, and similar levels of the available non-manual employment. During the war, manufacturing began to contribute about 4 to 6 per cent to the overall mobility rate, a level which has remained more or less constant ever since. Similarly its share of all non-manual jobs has remained stable at around 15 per cent, with a slight rise of a few percentage points in the 1960s. This has been achieved mainly by an absolute increase in numbers of non-manual jobs while total employment in manufacturing has contracted. It follows that non-manual jobs are a bigger proportion of that sector's employment: well over a third during the 1960s compared with a quarter just after the war and less than one-tenth in the 1930s.

The female upward mobility profile for the secondary sector resembles that for males: it seldom drops below 50 per cent, and is more typically around 55 per cent. However, the war saw less of a peak (about 65 per cent in the later stages) and the 1960s tend to run at closer to 50 per cent. In other words, the sector offers slightly poorer mobility chances, job for job, for women than for men, even if the broad profile is similar.

The tertiary sector is another matter altogether. Its total size, its share of all non-manual employment, and the proportion of its jobs that are non-manual all show an almost unbroken rise from 1930 to 1960. Only the years 1950 and 1951 break the succession. By the late 1950s, 85 per cent of service sector jobs were non-manual (compared with about 50 per cent in the early 1930s) which represents just over half of *all* employment for women (less than one-third in the early 1930s).

We already know that retailing and basic grades of office work are major sources of female employment, sources which are by definition predominantly tertiary sector activities. The characteristic profile of female employment in service industry should not, then, come as a surprise. It does, however, point to the fact that whereas men have experienced a small but marked shift towards tertiary sector employment, women have had this as a more typical feature of their occupational opportunities. If we were to ignore the reality of this concentration in routine white-collar work, and look just at the remaining female non-manual employment, it would show a profile which is not too different from that of males.

In the real world, however, the two elements of female employment cannot be separated, and the complete picture of mobility is dominated by the pattern of the tertiary sector. However, its own recruitment outcomes differ from those in manufacturing but not in the same way as for men. Here upward mobility is generally *higher* than in manufacturing with 55 per cent being the base line, rising to 65 per cent in the war and the 1950s. In the final decade of the time series, the rate descends to 55 per cent. This last coincides with a levelling-off of the sector's growth in employment, in its share of all non-manual employment and in the proportion of its jobs that are non-manual. Again, job for job, it offers better mobility chances for women.

Modifying the Sectoral Explanation

The most obvious result of comparing male and female workers in this way is that the explanations proposed for changes in male mobility cannot be directly applied to female mobility. There is not the same shift from secondary to tertiary sectors, nor do the recruitment practices within each sector operate in the same way for both genders.

Given that women do different jobs and are employed to a much greater extent in tertiary industry, this is to be expected. However, if the empirical patterns are dissimilar, this does not necessarily invalidate the basic model. Indeed, what is common to the two accounts is that tertiary industry holds the key to explaining mobility rates.

More theoretically, we find that it is informative to disaggregate total mobility into its constituent elements which are the product of the proportions of non-manual opportunities, and the way these are filled, within major industrial sectors which are themselves expanding and contracting. For men, the service sector does not become dominant until the 1960s, when its style of limited recruitment from the manual class stops any further rise in male mobility rates. For women, this sector is consistently more important throughout the time series, and when service industry ceases to expand its first job recruitment, mobility drops off too. This understanding of the basic structure of mobility draws, albeit a little tenuously, on ideas of sectoral shift during the development of modern capitalism, and the notion of occupational transition in advanced economies (Clarke, 1957; Payne, 1987b; Browning and Singleman, 1978).

In other words, mobility rates are accounted for by the demand for labour of various kinds under the particular economic conditions of any given period. The mobility experiences of the present adult population have been determined by the shift from primary sector employment to tertiary sector employment, and by the occupational transition from predominantly manual labour to non-manual labour, which characterizes late industrialism and the emergence of post-industrial society. Such an explanation of mobility rests primarily on these macro level economic processes, rather than on ideas about class closure — whether conscious or unconscious (e.g. Parkin, 1971; Johnson, 1972) — or on educational reform as a mechanism of enhancing working-class opportunities for career achievement (e.g. Glass, 1954, p. 24; Floud and Halsey, 1961, pp. 1-2; and discussion of males in Payne, Ford and Ulas, 1979b).

These latter explanations are not to be seen as incorrect or irrelevant, but rather as taking a secondary place. After all, it is one thing to identify the growth of the tertiary sector as lying at the heart of the matter, but another to discover the distinctive practices in the tertiary sector which determines its contribution to mobility rates (see page 85). In this chapter it is not possible to do more than speculate, but one aspect of tertiary industry seems a likely candidate. Much of the sector is public, that is, it takes the form of a government-controlled bureaucracy (health, education, welfare, administration, etc). Following the line of classical bureaucracy theory, one might therefore expect a more formal approach to recruitment, relying on paper qualifications. If this were true, we would expect non-manual employees to be better qualified than in other industries, and — because the children of middle-class families do better than those of the working class in the education system — the mobility rates to be lower. A preliminary analysis not presented here suggests that both male and female non-manual employees are indeed better qualified than in other industries, while mobility rates are lower for men and for the 'non-routine white collar' part of female employment (Payne, 1987a).

Conclusion

An account of female mobility must draw on two interconnected kinds of explanation, one dealing with occupations and mobility in general, and the other with gender-specific features of employment practice. The former, what might loosely be called the 'occupational needs' of modern capitalism (such as the growth of non-manual occupations and the shift to the tertiary sector) can in theory be supplied by recruiting men or women. In practice, women have been hired for some jobs such as shop assistant or routine office work to an extent that is less to do with 'occupational needs' than with gender attitudes. As women moved out of the private domain into the public, they were channelled into a subset of occupational roles. It can be argued that the development of capitalism was dependent on having those roles filled, but it is not evident that capitalism required them to be filled so overwhelmingly with female labour.

The distribution of employment destinations for women is different from that for men, so that what passes for upward mobility must also necessarily be different. This is one of the strengths of taking an *occupational* rather than a *class* mobility perspective, in that knowledge about gender employment patterns can be integrated into a discussion of mobility. For example, it seems likely that the higher rates of female intergenerational mobility in the tertiary sector reflect not just its greater number of non-manual jobs but that compared with manufacturing industry there are many more non-routine non-manual jobs for women in the service sector. In other words, in manufacturing industry, almost all jobs for women are routine office work: in the service sector, although low level jobs predominate, there are relatively more jobs of a higher level. We might also speculate that the trends of the late 1950s and 1960s owe a great deal to two uniquely female employment trends. On the one hand, the revolution in the distributive trades which spawned the supermarket cut opportunities for shop work, while on the other, older married women came back onto the labour market in increasing numbers, to compete with the school-leaver for available jobs.

Despite the methodological limitations of an imperfect sample, a 'male' occupational grading scale, and a rather crude solution to defining family origins, the analysis has nevertheless been useful as a test of several ideas both in mobility and in stratification theory more generally. On the debit side (if one can think in these terms), several features dear to recent sociology look decidedly less robust. The manual/non-manual distinction has been seen to have considerable limitations as a tool of research on female occupations. A doubt has been raised about the suggested tightening link between educational qualifications, occupational attainment and mobility. And indeed the basic idea of sectoral shift has been shown to require heavy qualification to allow for gender. On the credit side, the analysis of overall trends has shown that some changes had an effect on both men and women, even if the effects were not identical. The predominance of the tertiary sector as a non-manual employer stands out in this respect. The general approach of disaggregating mobility rates retains its utility.

Chapter 6

Gender and Intergenerational Mobility

Robert L. Miller and Bernadette C. Hayes

Until recent years mobility researchers in the British Isles have justified the absence of women in mobility and class studies on the grounds of their derivative status either from a father or husband (Heath, 1981). As more and more women participate in paid employment in the British Isles as well as in North America this justification has become increasingly untenable. As in the area of class analysis, the whole question of occupational mobility and attainment, especially in relation to female intergenerational occupational mobility, still begs to be answered for women. With some exceptions (e.g., Abbott and Sapsford, 1987; Dex, 1987; Hayes, 1987; Goldthorpe and Payne, 1986; Payne *et al.*, 1983), the empirical study of this issue has remained ignored by British and Irish sociologists.

In contrast to the British Isles, however, a growing body of research literature in North America has been devoted to female intergenerational occupational mobility patterns, particularly in contrast to those of men. To date, with the exception of some critics (Powell and Jacobs, 1984; Powers, 1982), published research on the occupational attainment of women suggests no differences in the mean level of occupational status attainment by the two genders, although there is less variance in the occupational status of women, given their under-representation at the lower and upper ends of status distributions (Spaeth, 1977; McClendon, 1976; Featherman and Hauser, 1976). Occupational prestige is considered to be invariant across the sexes (England, 1981). Furthermore, the processes by which women and men attain positions are more known for their similarities than differences, at least as far as the effects of family background and education on occupational status are concerned (McClendon, 1976; Featherman and Hauser, 1976). Father's occupation and farm origin, however, are found to have a slightly greater effect on the occupational attainment of males than females (it is sons that inherit farms) (Hauser *et al.*, 1974; Tyree and Treas, 1974) and the effect of education on occupational status has been found to be about equal for the two sexes or slightly greater for females than males (Marini, 1980; Treas and Tyree, 1979).

In a like manner, recently available British research which measures family origin exclusively in terms of father's occupation also documents this somewhat greater tendency for sons to 'inherit' their fathers' occupations than daughters (Abbott and Sapsford, 1987; Goldthorpe and Payne, 1986; Payne *et al.*, 1983; Heath, 1981). This remains especially true in relation to fathers of both the highest and lowest social class origins. For example, Heath (1981) and Abbott and Sapsford (1987) demonstrated that not only were daughters of professional status fathers more likely to be occupationally downwardly mobile than their brothers, but working-class women also showed a greater propensity to cross the manual/non-manual divide and end up on non-manual occupations than their male siblings.[1]

Despite the similarity of these results, however, the theoretical and methodological validity of this 'mainstream' of research has come under increasing criticism. While the basic nature of the problem is clear enough, that women need to be included more adequately in mobility analyses, the solution is not so simple. Just duplicating traditional procedures, only applying them to women, solves nothing. As all these studies have defined women's intergenerational occupational mobility in much the same way as a man's, a comparison of father's occupational status to the respondent's occupational attainment, these male-derived models may have been disregarding factors particularly relevant to women's intergenerational occupational mobility, specifically the influence of the *mother's* educational attainment and occupation (Pearson, 1983; Stevens and Boyd, 1980; Rosenfeld, 1978).

For example, United States researchers who have considered the contribution of both mother's as well as father's occupational origins to the destination of daughters suggest that maternal occupational status can be of primary importance in predicting female intergenerational occupational mobility patterns. In fact, not only was a mother's occupational status found to be significantly associated with her daughter's, but the effect of mother's occupation was of greater relative importance than that of the father in predicting a daughter's occupational inheritance (Rosenfeld, 1978). This result, moreover, held regardless of the racial composition of the American female sample. As Pearson's inter-racial research attests:

> For both races, mother's occupational status was associated with her daughter's destination. The influence of mothers on daughters generally exceeded the influence of fathers on daughters and fathers on daughters' spouses; and in the case of blacks, it clearly exceeded the influence of even fathers on sons (Pearson, 1983, p. 213).

This tendency for daughters to duplicate the occupational experiences of their mothers was found to be even more pronounced among Canadian women. Stevens and Boyd (1980), using data from the National Canadian Mobility Study of 1973, demonstrated that not only was a daughter's occupational activity significantly affected by her mother's occupation, but that this intergenerational relationship persisted even in the case of housework. This is in direct contrast to father's occupation which, although influential, failed to emerge as the primary predictor for their currently labour active female offspring. In fact, so great was this mother/daughter influence that even when the father/daughter association was controlled, a mother's occupational status continued to aid in the prediction of their daughter's occupation. As Stevens and Boyd explain, 'A mother's occupation does influence her daughter's occupation. In fact, we need only know the mother's occupation in order to be able to predict within reasonable limits her daughter's occupation; knowledge of the father's occupation is superfluous' (Stevens and Boyd, 1980, p. 192).

Similarly, the two available studies on female intergenerational occupational mobility in Northern Ireland and the Republic of Ireland also suggest the vital importance of maternal occupational status in predicting the occupational attainment of women (Hayes, 1987; Hayes, forthcoming). Using data from the 1973/74 Irish Mobility Study, Hayes (1987), in a comparison with females in the Republic of Ireland, not only demonstrated that women in both Northern Ireland and the Republic of Ireland inherited the occupational status of their mothers, but, as in the previously discussed Canadian study, this finding remained significant in relation to the category of housewife. More interestingly, however, when the contribution of both mothers' as well as fathers' occupational origins to the occupational destinations of Northern and Southern Irish women were investigated, a mother's occupational status was significantly associated with her daughter's occupational attainment and this effect of mother's occupation was of greater relative importance than either father's occupational or educational achievement and mother's education in predicting the occupational achievement of Northern Irish women (Hayes, forthcoming).

Finally, the only available research that simultaneously compares the effects of mother's and father's education and occupational attainment for North American men and women suggests that the educational and occupational attainments of mothers are likely to have greater effects on the occupational status of daughters than sons and that the educational and occupational attainment of fathers are likely to have greater effects on the occupational status of sons (Boyd, 1985; Boyd, 1982; Cooney et al., 1982; Marini, 1980). For example, Marini (1980) found that the status attainment of the same-gender parent had a greater effect than the status attainment of the opposite-gender parent. Furthermore, education tended to have a greater effect on the occupational prestige of females than males. Cooney et al. (1982) also reported significant gender interaction effects in relation to the educational and occupational attainment process of men and women. That is, whereas father's education and father's occupation had a greater positive effect on the occupational attainment of their sons than their daughters, mother's education and occupational status had a greater impact on the daughters. These results, in congruence with role modelling or socialization theory, suggest that both male and female offspring are more likely to model themselves after the same-sex parent than after the opposite-sex parent.

Data and Measures

The data used here are from a large-scale study of social mobility in the Republic of Ireland and Northern Ireland that was carried out in the early 1970s. Although women were not included in the main samples (the target population being limited to males aged 18 to 64 years in both parts of Ireland (Wiggins, 1977) this lack of direct data coverage is compensated for by the extensive amount of information gathered on female household and family members (Jackson, 1975). This information on the male respondents' female relatives (i.e., sisters, wives, mothers, mothers-in-law, grandmothers and daughters) includes material on the last job held, educational qualification, marital status and age.

In the manner of the 'status attainment' tradition (Blau and Duncan, 1967; Duncan *et al.*, 1972), a number of regression models are introduced to investigate the question of comparative male and female intergenerational occupational mobility in Northern Ireland and the Republic of Ireland. Similar to their predecessors, these statistical models seek to depict the relative strengths of association between individuals' socio-economic background (i.e., their parents' socio-economic statuses) and their own educational level and occupational status. Educational achievement is operationalized as an intervening factor in the relationship between parental socio-economic status and a man's or woman's own occupational status. This chapter compares male and female intergenerational occupational mobility using a modified version of the approach originated by Blau and Duncan, namely mothers' education and mothers' occupational status are included in addition to the educational attainment and occupational status of fathers as determinants of the educational attainment and occupational destinations of both their male and female offspring.

To explain briefly, path analysis is a method for studying patterns of causation among a set of theoretically specified variables. More specifically, it is a 'method applied to a causal model formulated by the researcher on the basis of knowledge and theoretical considerations' (Pedhazur, 1982; p. 580). Using standardized multiple regression equations, 'the objective is to compare a model of the direct and indirect relationships that are assumed to hold between several variables to observed data in a study, in order to examine the fit of the model to the data' (Loether and McTavish, 1980, p. 351). Thus, unlike ordinary regression analysis, the main advantage of this approach is that it enables one to measure both the direct and indirect effects that one variable exerts upon another.

Furthermore, 'path analysis' through regression allows the 'decomposition of the correlation between any two variables into a sum of simple and compound paths, with some of these compound paths being substantively meaningful indirect effects and perhaps others not' (Asher, 1976, p. 32). It is this specific 'data reduction' advantage which will be utilized in this chapter. By the technique of path analysis, the relative determining effects, both direct and indirect, of the background characteristics of both mother and father in determining occupational status of both daughters and sons may be investigated. While a given independent and dependent variable may be correlated, it is possible that all or much of this association is an 'artefactual' effect of stronger links between the dependent variable and other independent variables.[2]

The following six variables were included in the analysis for both men and women: mother's occupation; mother's eduction; father's occupation; father's education; offspring's education; and offspring's occupation. Education was measured in terms of a modification of the scaling of educational attainment developed by the CASMIN study for purposes of comparative analysis (Müller *et al.*, 1988). The CASMIN educational scaling gives a more valid measure of education in Northern Ireland than either using educational qualification or years of schooling alone since it can be thought of as combining the most significant aspects of both for subsequent job attainment. The Irish Occupational Index (see Boyle, 1976), a 'metric' or approximately 100-point scale of occupational prestige developed by the Irish Mobility Study, was employed as a summary indicator of occupational standing.

The group appearing in the analysis is restricted in a number of important aspects. Labour active male respondents aged 27 to 65 are matched with the sister nearest in age who was also aged 27 or above and who had been labour active at some point in her life. This method of matching only those 'pairs' of siblings who had both worked was chosen in order to minimize as far as possible the confounding effects of both a non-comparable sibling sample and variation in family background. Although this female group was not collected as a directly representative sample, given the large sample size overall and previous evidence as to the reliability of proxy responses (Duncan and Duncan, 1978; Hauser and Featherman, 1977), sample representation, particularly in terms of parental characteristics for directly matched sisters of the male respondents, is not considered a prohibitive problem. The exclusion of those under the age of 27 was to limit the effect of irregular and unstable job patterns known to be common to both males and females in younger age groups. The group subjected to analysis, therefore, consists only of 'matched pairs' of siblings in which both sister and brother have worked at some time in their lives with each member of a 'pair' having, of course, the same family background. By selecting 'pairs' by this rigorous criteria, a hypothetical 'twenty-first century' model of male and female employment is imposed upon the data in which *all* are equally likely to work, regardless of gender. One must note that this strategy does exclude a large proportion of the potential sample. A 'matched pair' of siblings only appears in the analysis if both of them have worked. While the loss of male respondents without female siblings should not overly bias the representativeness of the group, the exclusion of sisters who have never worked (whether housewives or not) may. (However, see Hayes (1987) for an analysis of female intergenerational mobility based upon data from the Irish mobility project that does deal with housewives.) While some male respondents will also never have worked, the proportion of women falling into this category will be much larger. One must recognize that this 'twenty-first century' model of equal labour force participation is, in reality, only partly realized. The data are drawn from a twentieth century sample. The jobs of many of the working women will in fact be jobs that they held at some time in the past. Among married sisters, the type and level of job will for many have been warped by the wife's 'career' being subservient to that of her husbands.[3]

Since the regression analyses are carried out in part to discover to what extent the mother's occupation exerts an effect upon both her male and female children, the group under consideration is further restricted by including only those 'pairs' who have a mother who is or was labour active. So, in this respect, the 'twenty-first century' model of equal labour activity regardless of gender is reinforced. The pairs of siblings have been matched by as strict a series of criteria that one can apply to the data — both the female and male siblings of each pair have worked and each pair comes from a family in which both mother and father were also labour active. While one must accept that the sample comes from a period in which the full labour market equality of activity for women was not the norm, the sample comes as close as any can to a model of equality of activity. Real gender equality of labour market activity does not exist yet and waiting until some undetermined future date when it is attained would preclude the possibility of an analysis following this approach for at least decades. So, while the group being analyzed is not typical in many respects, its 'atypicality' is necessary in order to approach an evaluation of the effect of the mother relative to the father upon the occupational attainment of their children. One should also note that the effect of the group's 'atypicality' will be to minimize any differences found between the sexes in the analysis; an analysis of occupational attainment that allowed for the labour market 'inactivity' of mothers who were housewives and the 'lack of occupational attainment' of women who are not labour market active themselves would be likely to find greater gender differences and stronger links between the status of the mothers and their daughters.

Results

Table 6.1 gives in the first column the results of a regression of the 'independent' variables of gender, mother's and father's occupational and educational levels, size of community of origin and religion (as a Protestant/Catholic dichotomy) upon the 'dependent' variable of educational attainment of those individuals making up 'matched pairs' of siblings for Northern Ireland. The second column reports a similar regression carried out upon the occupational levels of the sibling pairs (with educational level becoming an additional 'cause' of occupational level). In order to test whether the relationships between the independent variables and the dependent variable remained constant for both sexes, 'interaction' variables representing the unique effect in combination exerted between gender and each of the independent variables in turn, were also entered into the equations. In effect, the table gives models of hypothetical 'causes' of level of educational attainment and level of occupation. The values of the independent, causal variables' effects upon the dependent variables of siblings' education or occupation can range from +1.00, indicating a strong 'positive' effect, through 0.00, indicating no effect, to −1.00, indicating a strong 'negative' effect.

Table 6.1 Determinants of respondents' occupational and educational level, standardized regression coefficients

	Education	Occupation
Educational level		0.572***
Father's occupation	0.151***	0.078**
Mother's occupation	0.089*	—
Father's education	0.110**	—
Mother's education	—	—
Gender	—	−0.190***
Religion	−0.140***	0.076***
Interaction; gender and:		
Mother's education	0.203**	—
Religion	−0.140*	—
R²	0.145	0.367
N = 718		

Notes:
(a) Gender is coded as Female = 1, Male = 0 and Religion is coded as Protestant = 1 and Catholic = 0 for both the 'direct' effect and in the computation of interactions.
(b) Size of community and interactions with gender of educational level, mother's occupation and father's education and occupation are not significant for either education or occupation.
*** Coefficient significant at 0.001 level.
** Coefficient significant at 0.01 level.
* Coefficient significant at 0.05 level.

As discussed above, the 'typical' model of social mobility, limited to males only, excludes women as a matter of course; women being doubly excluded in that 'background' variables are also normally limited only to those that pertain to the father. Perhaps the most noteworthy general finding is that gender, both in the siblings' generation and in the generation of their parents, plays an important role. That is, the occupational level of the mother plays a significant, positive role in determining the educational level of *both* the female *and* the male siblings (a coefficient of +0.89 for Mother's occupation on Education; significant at the 0.05 level). In addition, there are significant effects of two 'interaction' variables upon siblings' educational level; the advantage of having a mother with higher educational attainment applies more strongly to daughters (+0.203) and the effect of gender upon educational attainment varies depending upon religion (−0.140). The presence of gender 'interaction' variables indicates that the mechanics of educational attainment are different for male and female siblings from the same family backgrounds. Furthermore, one should note that the effect of a mother's occupational attainment on the educational attainment of her offspring is significant and independent from that of the father. A male-based model of occupational mobility, therefore, would be too specific in that it would neglect both the effect of the mother upon educational attainment and the possibility that the intergenerational dynamics of educational attainment can differ between genders.

While gender plays a central role in the educational attainment of the siblings, the pattern for occupational attainment is simpler (the second column of Table 6.1). Common to virtually all 'path' or 'status attainment' models of social mobility in developed nations, the individuals' own educational level is the prime determinant of their occupational (+0.572, significant at 0.001 level); i.e., educational attainment associates strongly with occupational attainment. The status of father's occupation plays a significant, though secondary, role in occupational attainment (+0.078) and the other independent variables, with the notable exceptions of gender and religion (an 'advantage' to being of Protestant background of +0.076), do not appear. Neither father's educational attainment nor the educational or occupational level of the mother nor any of the 'gender interaction' variables appear in the regression equations for present occupational status.

The 'notable exception' of gender has a highly significant negative coefficient (−0.190, significant at 0.001 level). This can be interpreted as meaning that, while the effects of educational and occupational background variables upon occupational attainment of the two sexes are the same, the average level attained by the female of each pair of matched siblings is lower. This lower level of attainment is attributed solely to the effect of gender and cannot be assigned to the other factors covered by the analysis. Simply, put within the limits of the variables under investigation, the lower attainment of women is due to their being women and not due to a failure on their part to realize any advantages of family background or personal educational attainment. Table 6.2 displays the parameters of this lesser level of attainment.

Among non-manual occupations, men are clustered more in the manager and employer categories of both large and small enterprises while the bulk of women are in one of the routine non-manual categories of ancillary workers, junior non-manual workers or personal service workers. For the manual categories, women are more likely to be in the semi-skilled manual category while men dominate both the 'upper' manual categories of manual supervisors and skilled work and the 'lower' unskilled manual category. More men are own account workers, farmers and agricultural labourers.

The significance of religion for both educational attainment and occupational level in Northern Ireland deserves special mention. Being Protestant confers an advantage in educational attainment that is independent of family background and the

Table 6.2 Occupation by gender for matched sibling pairs

Occupation*	Male	Female
Managers & employers, 25 or more employees	2.9	0.5
Employers, less than 25 employees	6.5	2.1
Managers less than 25 employees	5.7	1.6
Professionals	3.0	1.6
Ancillary workers	3.7	15.1
Non-manual supervisors	0.4	0.8
Junior non-manual workers	8.0	26.5
Personal service workers	0.6	14.5
Manual supervisors	5.9	1.0
Skilled manual workers	26.5	8.1
Semi-skilled workers	12.6	20.1
Unskilled workers	6.6	2.9
Own account workers	5.2	2.4
Farmers	10.3	0.9
Agricultural workers	2.1	1.9
Total	100.0	100.0

*Occupational categories are based upon socio-economic groupings.

educational attainment of parents. Northern Ireland has an educational system divided along sectarian lines at the primary and secondary levels into a state (Protestant) sector and a Catholic sector. While there are clear indications that the Catholic schooling system is now 'catching up' with the levels of attainment reached by the state system (Osborne, 1986), this would not have been the case during the decades in which the sample being analyzed was educated. The interaction between gender and religion upon educational attainment, which, strictly interpreted, indicates a lower level of educational attainment particular to Protestant females compared with all others, can be better interpreted as an indication of the different significance of education for the two communities. The Catholic community in Northern Ireland, in reaction to restricted opportunities, has always adopted strategies of mobility that emphasize movement up through educational attainment for both sexes. In the Protestant community, however, alternative means of upward mobility and status maintenance have been more available and, particularly among Protestant males who attend the more select grammar schools, the significance of educational attainment can be seen more as a screening device rather than as a certificate of knowledge.

The importance of these 'alternative means' appears in the coefficients of occupational attainment, where Protestants are found to have an advantage. A large complex literature on the different opportunity structures available to the two communities in Northern Ireland already exists and a detailed examination of the topic is beyond the scope of this chapter. For these reasons, it will not be discussed further here except to note that the Protestant advantage in occupational attainment exists independently of family background and educational attainment factors and can be attributed to evolving differentials in occupational structure that are most apparent in *intra-* as opposed to intergenerational mobility. (See Miller (1979; 1983); and Hayes (1987) for discussions that explicitly consider the Protestant/Catholic differential within the Irish Mobility Project data.)

Considering differences between Northern Ireland and the results of a similar analysis carried out for the Irish Republic (Hayes and Miller, 1989), one notes that more variance in the occupational, and particularly the educational, levels of the siblings can be explained in the results for the Republic. This agrees with the general finding of the CASMIN study of comparative social mobility that, among industrialized nations, the Republic tends towards an extreme of less mobility and greater determination of occupational status by origin factors (e.g., Erikson and Goldthorpe, 1985). One also should note that a large proportion of the Northern Irish sample would have been affected by the educational reforms brough in by the 1947 Education Act for Northern Ireland while the equivalent provisions in the Republic would not have taken effect until after practically all of the Irish Republic sample would have completed their education. Lower social background effects upon educational attainment observed for Northern Ireland may in fact display to some degree the efficacy of the much-maligned attempt to open up educational access in the United Kingdom during the post-war period.

While the models of educational attainment for the two parts of Ireland differ to some degree (but not in a manner that would alter the conclusions below), the results for the determination of occupational status agree closely; the only difference of substance being that the 'cost' of being a woman is greater for female siblings in the Republic of Ireland. If the Republic is a more traditional society in its view of women, this is confirmatory evidence.

Conclusions

Returning to the debate on the place of women in occupational attainment at the beginning of this chapter, the results clearly do not confirm the male-centred view that women's occupational attainment mirrors that of men and that the role of the mother in the attainment of children, both male and female, is essentially irrelevant. The educational attainment and occupational standing of the mothers were found to exert effects upon the educational attainment of both their male and female offspring that were independent of the fathers'. This, with the strong direct link between educational attainment and occupational status, implies a significant indirect effect of mother's attainment and position upon the occupational standing of the siblings. The presence of significant interactions with gender in the model of educational attainment for matched siblings indicates that, even when the mothers are included, there are significant differences between the sexes in the 'attainment process'. Similarly, the significance of gender for the present occupational standing of siblings, along with the indirect effects of the background variables upon occupational standing working through the siblings' educational attainment, show that women's occupational attainment does not just mirror that of mens'.

At the same time, neither does the analysis indicate that the opposite extreme applies, a model of occupational attainment for one gender which is simply the 'negative image' of the other with children most significantly affected by the 'role model' provided by the parent of the same gender.[4] Rather, the reality, as one can apprehend it with this analysis, seems to fall in between the two extremes. A broadly similar pattern of effects upon attainment, that must take account of mothers, applies to both sexes. Within that broad similarity there are then significant variations between the sexes implying strongly that a model for one gender should not be imposed upon the other. One should not seek a resolution to a false debate, whether or not the occupational attainment of women is a process that differs fundamentally from that of men, but rather to develop a conception of social mobility that includes both women and men as special instances of a general case.

Notes

1 The apparent propensity for proportionately more women than men of working-class origin to cross a manual/non-manual divide in their own worklives may be more an indication of the different context of non-manual work for women in terms of remuneration, chances for promotion and the like rather than an indication that working-class women are more likely to 'overcome' their origins than working-class men.

2 Even the most cursory review of the sociological literature surrounding the use of regression models to depict inter- and intragenerational mobility will make the reader aware that these models are strongly associated with a view of social mobility — the 'status attainment process'. Much of the literature comparing male and female intergenerational mobility has been written in this perspective. This chapter, however, uses standardized regression models in response to this literature and as a valuable 'data reduction' tool; not as an expression of the 'status attainment model'.

3 Fewer than 10 per cent of the jobs reported for women were part-time work.

4 'Role models', and hence socialization theory, may still apply since, particularly in the case of educational attainment, the parent of the opposite gender may well be the one who is emulated. Also, multivariate procedures for categorical data that could include 'housewives' and the long-term unemployed could well find stronger, and gender-specific, linkages between parents and children.

Chapter 7

The Career Mobility of Women and Men

Tony Chapman

For many sociologists, the theoretical and empirical problems associated with the study of women's class mobility have been regarded as so fundamental that few attempts have been made to study women's occupational mobility. Social mobility research data can be used, however, to trace the occupational careers of women and men to some effect, providing that due caution is observed in the interpretation of data. It has already been noted in Chapter 3 that particular caution must be taken in the use of occupational scales because the distribution of women in the occupational structure is not the same as men's. Women tend to be concentrated more heavily in a relatively narrow range of occupations and industries in comparison with men. It is also clear, of course, that conventional notions of life-long occupational careers as operationalized by mobility researchers does not fit well with the occupational histories of women, and married women in particular (or indeed, for all men, at all times: see Martin and Roberts, 1984; Pahl, 1984).

This chapter provides an examination of patterns of occupational mobility of men and women in terms of their social origin, their first full-time occupation and their occupation at the time of interview in the Scottish Mobility Study (SMS). (Details of methodology can be found in Chapter 3 above). These patterns will be considered firstly with reference to those respondents who had been working for at least fifteen years so that there is a clear distinction between first job and present job; and secondly, using two cohorts of respondents who started work between 1910-1929 and from 1930-1949. In order to develop a more detailed analysis of patterns of recruitment on entry into the labour market between 1930 and 1970, a further trend analysis will be undertaken to conclude the chapter.

The following discussion focuses on a 'collapsed' version of the seven category occupational scale adopted in Chapter 3. Category 1 includes higher professionals and lower professionals, Category II comprises technician/supervisory and routine non-manual workers, and Category III is composed of all grades of manual workers (skilled, semi-skilled and unskilled). It is important to re-state that women tend to be concentrated in the lower status occupations in each grouping. For example, in

Category I, women were more likely to be employed as 'lower' professionals such as teachers and nurses, and not as 'higher' professionals such as chartered accountants or lawyers. It would be grossly misleading to assume that because a similar number of women and men are represented in Category I that equality of opportunity in the professional labour market had been achieved.

Intragenerational Mobility: the Second Step

Turning attention firstly to panel (a) of Figure 7.1 we see the *intra*generational mobility for women and men whose father had professional status. It is evident that for both men and women, there was a high degree of downward mobility on entry into the labour market. A very large proportion of men attained the same occupational status as their father later in their careers. Indeed, over half of men who were initially downwardly mobile (15 + 60) achieved professional status later in their careers (9 + 29), compared with only 13 per cent of women. More than half of the women in the sample remained in manual work compared with about one-fifth of men.

Amongst respondents whose fathers had jobs of intermediate status (Fig 7.1(b)) it is apparent that about 11 per cent of both women and men were upwardly mobile into professional work on entry into the labour market. Over time, however, men (11 + 16) from intermediate social backgrounds were more than four times as likely as women (0 + 6) to obtain professional work. Many more women (63 per cent) than men (43 per cent) were employed in manual work later in their careers.

A very large proportion of women and men whose fathers were manual workers (Fig. 7.1(c)) also had manual jobs. On entry into the labour market over 80 per cent of men and women were employed in manual work, but later in their careers 30 per cent of these men compared with less than 15 per cent of these women were upwardly mobile.

In summary, it can be stated that men were much more likely than women to be upwardly occupationally mobile both intergenerationally (Chapter 3) *and* intragenerationally. Amongst those respondents who were initially downwardly mobile, men were much more likely than women to achieve or surpass their father's occupational status later in their careers.

Changes in Career Mobility

One of the problems with the above analysis is that no account is taken of changes in the labour market which occurred over time. In Figure 7.2, a simple cohort analysis is presented. What becomes obvious from these data is that opportunities for upward mobility on entry into the labour market were enhanced for respondents born between

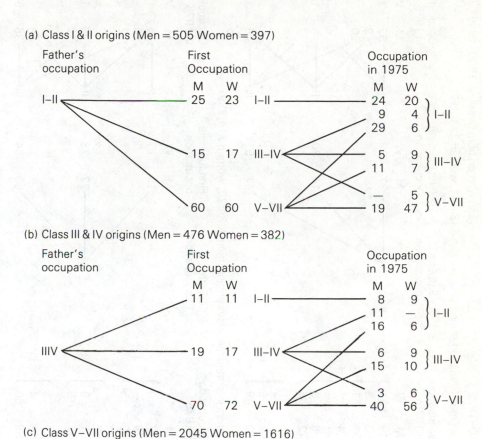

(a) Class I & II origins (Men = 505 Women = 397)

(b) Class III & IV origins (Men = 476 Women = 382)

(c) Class V–VII origins (Men = 2045 Women = 1616)

Figure 7.1 Three point occupational mobility patterns: flows representing 3 per cent or more of all in class of origin, men and women aged 35 and over

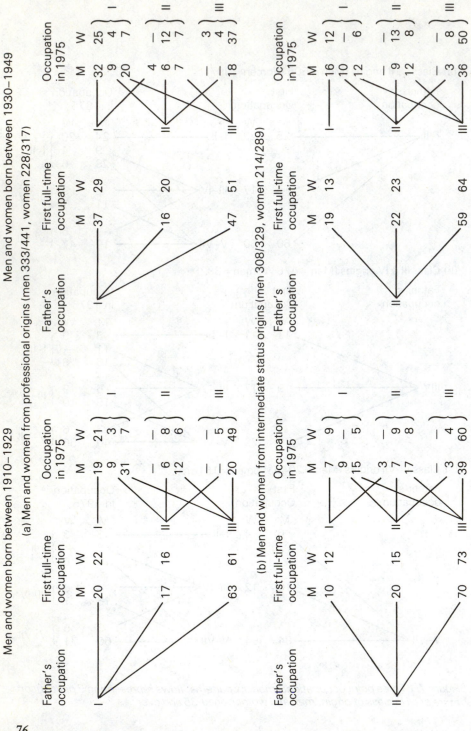

Men and women born between 1910–1929   Men and women born between 1930–1949

(a) Men and women from professional origins (men 333/441, women 228/317)

(b) Men and women from intermediate status origins (men 308/329, women 214/289)

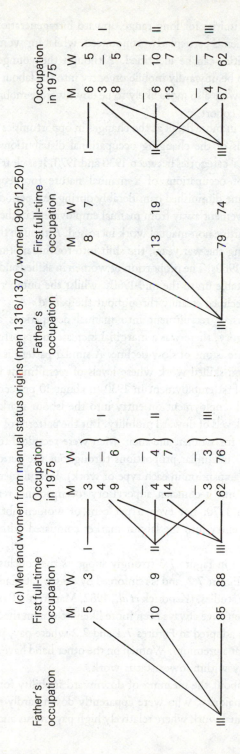

Figure 7.2 Three point occupational mobility patterns — flows representing 3 per cent or more of all in class of origin, men and women: 1910–1929 and 1930–1949

1930 and 1949. The opportunities for long-range upward intragenerational mobility for the younger cohort of men is particularly pronounced, whilst for women, no clear improvement in opportunities can be identified. Although the younger cohort of women were more likely to be upwardly mobile on entry into the labour market, the evidence suggests that they were also more likely to be downwardly mobile later on in their careers than the older cohort.

It is important to look in more detail at the changes in opportunities for men and women through an analysis of the changing occupational distribution of men and women in seven occupational categories between 1930 and 1970. It is clear from Figure 7.3 that the availability of occupations of a manual nature for people entering employment for the first time diminished considerably during this period. In the case of women, there was a movement away from manual employment in the mid- to late 1930s as opportunities in routine non-manual work increased. Although this trend was temporarily held back during the war years, the shift into routine non-manual work continued up until the mid-1960s. The proportion of women in skilled and semi-skilled work remained relatively stable up to the mid-1960s, whilst the number of unskilled manual women workers declined steadily throughout the period.

For men, the patterns of recruitment into manual occupations are less well defined. In the skilled category, there was a marginal increase in opportunities in the 1950s, but the overall picture is one of slow decline. A similar pattern is observed for unskilled work. It is in semi-skilled work where levels of recruitment fell the most from about 20 per cent of first employment in 1930 to about 10 per cent in 1970.

The decline in manual employment on entry into the labour market obviously helps account for increased levels of upward mobility. But the patterns of employment in non-manual work differ for women and men. Men were recruited to each of the four non-manual categories in similar proportions throughout the period (although the overall impression is of expansion in each type of work). Recruitment of women into higher professional and technician/supervisory occupations remained low throughout the period. In 1970, not even 5 per cent of women obtained higher professional status jobs on entry into the labour market compared with over 10 per cent of men.

The evidence presented in Figure 7.3 strongly supports the conclusions reached from the cohort analysis of Figure 7.2, and is reinforced by census data and more recent labour market participation studies. (Kendrick *et al.*, 1982, Martin and Roberts, 1984). In terms of recruitment, men have always been more likely to obtain the higher status jobs in the three categories adopted in Figures 7.1 and 7.2 where pay, prospects and employment security were at a premium. Women on the other hand have continued to be employed predominantly within lower status work.

This raises questions about the meaning of downward mobility for many men. For many men, indeed a majority, who were apparently downwardly mobile, their destination was skilled manual work where relatively high pay, status and job security

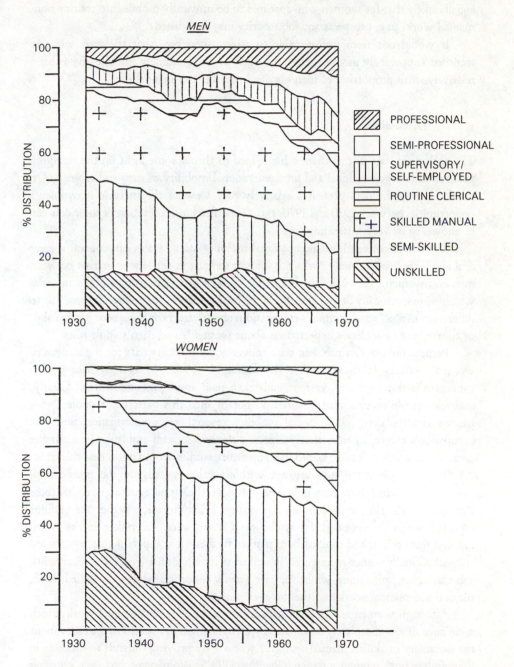

Figure 7.3 Occupational distribution of men and women over seven occupational categories by year of entry into the labour market: five year moving averages.

could be achieved. This is important for the purposes of interpretation, because it is equally likely that for women who appeared to be upwardly mobile into routine non-manual work, pay, prospects and job security may be limited.[1]

It would not seem unreasonable to assert, therefore, that the men who are recorded as upwardly mobile were more likely to be 'genuinely' mobile given that a relatively small proportion of men obtained routine non-manual jobs.

Discussion

The analysis of data in this chapter has helped to throw some light on the changing patterns of intergenerational and intragenerational mobility of men and women. On the face of it, the data present a relatively rosy view of the increase in women's opportunities between 1930 and 1970. But a superficial interpretation of these data can be shown to be very misleading.

The use of conventional occupational mobility status scales can conceal a great deal about the true inequality which is known to exist in the labour market between men and women. This is partly due to the uneven distribution of women in scales which were specifically designed to study the labour market experience of men, due to differences in men's and women's expectations about careers in the labour market and, of course, due to society's expectations about women's and men's adult roles.

Perhaps the greatest problem with conventional mobility data for the analysis of women's careers is the fact that the sociologists who instigated these studies conceptualized careers as long-term unbroken paid employment histories. Clearly, many women's occupational histories do not fit into this pattern. (Yeandle, 1984; Martin and Roberts, 1984). Social mobility researchers' preoccupation with the occupational careers of men clearly reflects a general societal ambivalence about the careers of women. It is to be hoped that any future studies would not repeat this error.

The data presented here are not without value — despite the problems of interpretation which have been indicated. It is nevertheless necessary, given that these data refer to the middle decades of this century, briefly to ask whether the findings reported would be replicated if a similar sized study were undertaken in the 1990s. Judging from census and recent labour market studies,[2] it is apparent that women are still substantially under-represented in skilled-manual, higher grade technical work and the higher professions, whilst they are heavily concentrated in semi-skilled work, routine non-manual work and the lower professions.

Although women are making inroads into areas of skilled manual work which were once almost completely dominated by men, changes in traditional attitudes about the suitability of skilled manual work for women are proving difficult to dislodge in the minds of both women and men (Chapman, 1987). Women are, however, entering the higher professions in larger numbers than was the case up to 1970. There are now many more women who become graduates and enter the professions in large numbers.

Nevertheless, recent evidence suggests that even amongst graduates, the prospects of women are still relatively limited in comparison with similarly qualified men in terms of employment status, pay and career prospects (Chapman 1989).

For the 1990s and beyond it is likely that the number of women who are recruited into professional, technical and skilled jobs will continue to increase, especially given recent forecasts about the shortage of young people (Pearson *et al.*, 1989). Many employers are attempting to ease women's entry into careers and to retain them with new equal opportunities packages and policies to reduce the impact of childcare on career opportunities (Hibbert, 1988a, 1988b, 1989; Holland, 1989).

It is questionable, however, as to the long-term commitment of employers to the recruitment of women when the impact of the so-called 'demographic time-bomb' (Beavis, 1989) fizzles out. Similarly, governments, employers and trade unions may weaken their resolve to promote the education and training of women in the face of a future contraction of labour demand.

Historical analysis of the labour market inevitably throws up many examples of women being invited for a 'temporary stay' in those jobs where men have traditionally dominated.[3] The analysis presented here of patterns of occupational mobility of women and men between 1930 and 1970 in Scotland provides little room for optimism. For despite major changes in the structure of the labour market, women continued to be badly under represented in those jobs which offered the highest status, pay, security and prospects; whether they were manual, professional or white-collar workers. The new patterns of the 1990s will show whether this pessimistic interpretation of the historical evidence is justified.

Notes

1   There is no space here to develop these arguments with reference to recent literature or for a more detailed analysis of the SMS data (see Chapman, 1984). Crompton and Sanderson (in the next chapter) help to develop discussion on the career potential of women and men in similar types of work.

2   See Martin and Roberts (1984) for the largest study on women's employment of the 1980s. For a review of recent Census data, see Chapman (1987).

3   There is much good historical analysis on women's labour market participation; see John (1986), and Bradley (1989). For useful analyses of women working in jobs which are traditionally reserved for men, see Riley (1980) and Cockburn (1983).

Chapter 8

Credentials and Careers

Rosemary Crompton and Kay Sanderson

In 1979 Hakim's study for the Department of Employment described the emergence, since the 1960s, of the 'two-phase' or 'bimodal' profile of female employment. Before the war, most women had left the labour force permanently on marriage or at the birth of their first child. Increasingly however, this pattern had been replaced by one in which women returned to work from their thirties onwards, and indeed, in 1971, labour force participation rates for women in their forties were equal to those of women in their early twenties.

The Women and Employment Survey (Martin and Roberts, 1984) which reports on interviews carried out in 1980 with a national sample of 5,588 women of working age, suggests that important changes have occurred even since 1971. The results show that 'Progressively more women have been returning to work soon after childbirth and between childbirths and it is now a minority of women who have a bimodal employment pattern . . . a growing proportion of women are becoming continuous workers' (Dex, 1984, p. 1). For each successive birth cohort, the survey reveals longer periods spent in employment and increasing attachment to the labour force. However, as is well known, the increasing participation of women in the formal economy has not been evenly distributed throughout the occupational structure. That is, women's employment tends to be concentrated into particular *occupations* (e.g. secretarial work), and/or, at lower levels in the job hierarchy if women are employed in the same occupations as men (e.g. teaching). Part of the explanation for this distribution of female employment must lie in the fact that women's increased labour force participation has overwhelmingly been achieved through part-time work (Martin and Roberts, 1984: 119). Part-time work enables women to fit family/domestic work together with participation in the formal economy. However, for many, the shift to part-time work is associated with a drop in occupational status, and indeed, semi-skilled domestic and shop-assistant work appears to have emerged as a 'secondary' labour market relying almost entirely on part-timers. Part-time jobs are less secure and have fewer benefits than full-time jobs. These conditions also apply to part-time jobs in the female professions of nursing and teaching. Here, although no drop in occupational status is associated with the switch to part-time work, a feature of such employment — indeed, of part-time employment as a whole — is that promotion opportunities are virtually non-existent.

The 'part-time factor' is but one of a number of characteristics of female labour in general which would contribute to an explanation of the structure of women's employment which rested largely on 'supply side' factors (often generally described as 'human capital' theories: Chiplin and Sloane, 1982). In addition, women's working lives, as the Women and Employment survey demonstrates, will usually be interrupted to a greater or lesser extent due to childrearing. In anticipation of this, so the argument runs, women themselves do not gain work-related qualifications necessary to the pursuit of a linear career, that is, do not augment their 'human capital'. In any case, employers are reluctant to invest in the training of this potentially unstable workforce.

'Supply-side' explanations stand in contrast to those which would stress not so much women's *preferences* in structuring their job choice, but rather, the nature of the *demand* for female labour which effectively constrains what women can achieve in employment terms. (Bruegel 1978). In broad terms, demand side explanations of the structuring of female employment may be grouped into two categories: firstly, those feminist arguments which stress the role of *men* in organizing, more or less systematically, formally and informally, to keep women out of better-paid 'men's jobs' (e.g. Hartmann, 1976), and secondly, those such as 'reserve army' or 'radical labour market' theorists who argue that it is of significant advantage to 'capital' (male or female) to have permanently available an unskilled, lowly paid element in the workforce. (Braverman, 1974; Edwards, 1979).

The significance of women's work patterns — or otherwise — is of considerable importance to a number of other social science debates, particularly in the area of social stratification. In his defence of the 'conventional view' (i.e. that the 'class situation' of the wife is properly 'derived' from that of the male 'head of household'), Goldthorpe (1983) argues that the labour force participation of married women is highly determined by the class position of the husband. Heath and Britten's (1984) rebuttal of Goldthorpe's argument cites evidence from the Women and Employment Survey which suggests that women do have an independent commitment to *particular* kinds of work, and that 'Women are far from being a homogeneous group of marginal workers' (Dex, 1984). They also use data from the longitudinal National Survey of Health and Development to argue their case that 'women's own qualifications are *more* important than their husbands' class as an explanation of their career paths' (Heath and Britten, 1984, p. 486).

Improving the quality of the female labour supply through qualifications, moreover, might have far-reaching effects for male, as well as female, careers (Crompton and Jones, 1984; Crompton, 1984). The high rates of male social mobility in the years following the Second World War were substantially sustained by two factors: (i) the rapid expansion of so-called 'service class' occupations (professionals, managers, administrators etc.) in a situation of rapid economic growth combined with the extension of state provision of health, education, etc., and (ii) the recruitment of women — often part-time — to fill the lower levels of the burgeoning sector of 'service' occupations (Goldthorpe, 1980). As earlier work has shown (Crompton and Jones, 1984) — and as educational statistics demonstrate — these first female re-entrants had little in the way of formal qualifications of either a school leaving or 'vocational' variety. This fact, combined with their broken employment records, provided a more than adequate justification/explanation for their permanent occupation of the lower levels of job hierarchies — however extended their eventual labour force participation might prove to be. However, if women were to make systematic inroads into higher-level occupations and careers, then clearly, unless there was a proportional increase in these occupations, male career prospects would be reduced.

There are a number of very good reasons, therefore, to be interested in any increase in the level and range of qualifications gained by women. In this chapter, we will be constructing in one section a theoretical framework which we hope will enable us to develop a number of informed suggestions about the possible consequences of an increase in women gaining work-related qualifications (empirical findings are reported later). In looking only at women gaining work-related qualifications we are, of course, fully aware that we are dealing with a minority of women. The National Training Survey, for example, reveals that only 24 per cent of women interviewed had gained post-school qualifications of any kind. Our focus is in fact even narrower as, of the women who did have such qualifications, 47 per cent of those held were clerical or commercial, whereas we have researched mainly in the area of professional or semi-professional qualifications (figures calculated from Table 3.7, Elias and Main, 1982). One advantage of this relatively narrow focus is that all of the qualifications we have investigated are of a standing which would normally substantially enhance the 'human capital' of individuals who gained them — other things being equal, they should significantly improve the job prospects of their possessor and thus improve the 'quality' of female labour in general.

We might appear to be prejudging the debates surrounding 'supply side' versus 'demand side' explanations of the structure of female employment in the attention we pay to women's qualifications — which are clearly a 'supply' characteristic. We would stress, however, that this is not our intention. In the first place, we would consider it mistaken to attempt a final resolution as the relative merits of 'supply' and 'demand' explanations. To explain the complex structure of occupational segregation as a whole will obviously require explanations derived from both traditions, depending on the particular occupation or industry which is under investigation. Secondly, we are acutely aware of two closely related phenomena: (i) that qualifications alone do not provide an automatic 'ticket' to a successful career, and there is evidence that some women may be employed in jobs for which they are massively over-qualified, (Elias and Main, 1982) and (ii) that many of the qualifications acquired by women are 'gendered' in that they anticipate the gender segregation of subsequent employment. For example, in 1982, 17,000 young women — over 5 per cent of all female school leavers — embarked on secretarial training, in constrast to only 300 boys. Similarly, 6,800 girls went into nursing courses, against only just over 100 young men.[1] Although the gap between male and female school leaving achievements is narrowing — more girls than boys achieve at least one 'A' level, and the proportion of boys (10.7 per cent) and girls (9.2 per cent) with three 'A' levels is practically identical — important variations by *subject* still persist. For example, in 1982, girls accounted for 66 per cent of 'A' level passes in arts subjects, as compared to 32 per cent in science and technology.

Despite the general increase in the proportion of women gaining qualifications of all kinds, therefore, important elements of continuity still remain. In this paper, however, we will mainly concern ourselves with occupations where women have not, historically, been represented to any great extent. Our empirical evidence will demonstrate that there has been a recent, and substantial, increase in the proportion of young women gaining such qualifications. Firstly, however, we will examine the relationship between qualifications and careers, and what these might mean to women — and men.

Qualifications and Careers

'Career' is a term that we would use in a fairly loose fashion to describe the construction and/or determination of adult life experiences. It need not necessarily involve only market or waged work — the most obvious example here would be the wholly domestic career of the full-time housewife. It could also include other strategies such as 'dropping out' or other alternative lifestyles. In this paper, we shall be focusing mainly on employment careers, which incorporate waged work. Many women, of course, will combine both 'employment' and 'domestic' careers, and thus their employment careers will be *discontinuous*. However, in everyday language — and much of industrial sociology — the notion of 'career' refers to a continuous period in the labour force, with the same or different employer or seeking work, during which the individual does his or her best to make rational decisions which advance their employment 'career'. This is the 'pure' or 'linear' career (Hearn, 1977; Atkinson, 1984) and the evidence of the Women and Employment Survey suggests that it will be experienced by very few women. (Dex, 1984a; 104). The 'pure' or 'linear' career experience is congruent with the developmental theory of occupational choice, which assumes that the 'pre-career' individual engages in a process of rational selection amongst the alternatives available. Roberts has argued that the developmental theory is, quite simply, wrong, and that it is structural, particularly local market factors which largely determine occupational 'choice'. 'Despite the existence of a nominally free labour market, individuals do not typically choose their jobs in any meaningful sense; they simply take what is available' (Roberts, 1975 p. 138). However, as Becker had stated: 'Career contingencies include *both* the objective facts of social structure and changes in the perspectives, motivations and desires of the individual' (quoted in Speakman, 1980 p. 109) (my emphasis). Indeed, it is apparent that, whereas the 'individual-ambition' model may reasonably describe a large element of middle-class social experience, the structure-opportunity model is of greater relevance to working-class 'careers'.

A similar parallel may be drawn between men and women. Women's employment experience is more likely than men's to be 'reactive' rather than 'active' — even when women have been relatively successful in the 'public' sphere. (Fogarty, Allen and Walters, 1971). However, often it is the case that *some* room for manoeuvre is available — and is usually taken — accepting the 'rules of the game' without seriously attempting to compete; the 'uncareer' — a search for work which may provide *meaning* but not a pure 'career' in respect of upward mobility, and finally, the 'non-career' — where work is viewed as a 'game' rather than work. (Hearn, 1977). All of these categories refer to 'career' related to market work. Dex (1984) initially describes a series of ideal-typical 'careers' encompassing market and non-market work using the Women and Employment data, viz: (i) the 'domestic career' — no return to work after childbirth; (ii) the 'phased career' — women who return to work after all births, usually part-time (such 'phased careers' have, Dex argues, elements of both 'uncareers' and 'non-careers'); (iii) restricted family careers — an early return to work after the 'family break', usually for financial reasons; (iv) 'unexpected' or 'unplanned' careers — a discontinuous working pattern resulting from 'unplanned' factors such as divorce or a late birth, and (v) the 'continuous career' — including both the childless career and returning to work after all births.

As Dex's categories are derived from life history data — i.e. a sequence of events that has already occurred — this typology is, not surprisingly, structured around characteristic life-cycle 'events' of particular significance to women. The data are simply not sufficient for us to ascertain whether such careers were *planned* or not — for example, a 'continuous career' might be a consequence of infertility or divorce, rather than any conscious plan. Nevertheless, whilst accepting that domestic events will have a very significant impact on women's 'careers', (and it should be remembered that divorce or an unexpected baby is not without significance for men either) it would not be legitimate to assume that all, or even most, women have no career plans at all — whether for a 'domestic career' of home and marriage, for work and domesticity in various combinations, or continuous work. Indeed, it is reasonable to suggest that the increase in the extent of 'women's working lives' discussed in the first section of this paper will have enhanced the salience of career planning for many young women, and that the increase in their gaining qualifications of all kinds may be a manifestation of this.

It should not be forgotten, however, that a fairly substantial proportion of women have always undertaken further training. For example, in 1972, 24 per cent of female school leavers, in contrast to 19 per cent of male, went into higher education or further education (combined figures), and in 1982, the gap had widened still further — 32 per cent of girls, 22 per cent of boys. However, more detailed breakdowns reveal that, even on the rather limited classifications available, substantial proportions of girls *train* for 'gendered' occupations. In 1984, 30 per cent of female school leavers entering further and higher education (373,300) commenced training for either initial teacher training, catering, nursing or secretarial work — areas where, *overall*, only 9 per cent of school leaver entrants were male.[2]

All four of these 'women's occupations', not surprisingly, manifest the characteristically 'female' patterns revealed by the Women and Employment Survey. Nursing and catering *require* flexible hours of working, teaching may obviously be combined with the care of school-age children, routine secretarial work is dependent only on access to an easily portable machine. The demand for these services is universal and the qualification is transportable. They are not dependent on a particular geographical location — a nurse, for example, would probably not have much difficulty finding a part-time job after she had moved with her bank manager husband. In short, such qualifications positively facilitate discontinuous careers and part-time working. In contrast, other qualifications, more usually undertaken by men, are clearly acquired as an integral element in a *continuous* career. A good example of this would be the Institute of Bankers examinations. As previous research has demonstrated (Crompton and Jones, 1984) these are becoming increasingly essential in order to achieve promotion within the major clearing banks. However, as the banks operate an informal 'no-poaching' agreement as far as career staff are concerned, the Institute of Banking qualification would not be particularly relevant to a discontinuous part-time career.

This link between particular types of qualification and characteristic employment career paths may be usefully extended and developed. Brown (1982) has suggested three ideal typical strategies underlying individual choices and actions in relation to work and employment. These are (i) the Entrepreneurial — where resources are such that self-employment is possible; (ii) the Organizational — where advancement is sought within an employing organization (bureaucrats or 'locals'), and (iii) the Occupational — where skills and qualifications are used to move from employer to employer (professionals or 'cosmopolitans'). A fourth category, the 'careerless' (see also Hearn, Roberts, op. cit.) relates to those expecting only or mainly immediate rewards from work. However, as it is characterized by lack of conscious planning it would be misleading to identify this as a 'stragety'.

Qualifications, it may be suggested, may usefully be thought of lying along an (approximate) continuum relating to these strategies. At one pole are the 'pure occupational' qualifications. In some cases their possession constitutes a 'licence to practice'. Any person wishing to set up as an independent practictioner cannot do so without those qualifications, and they are a prerequisite for employment in the occupations concerned. They include the classic service professions which deal directly with clients — medicine, law, chartered accountancy, dentistry, etc. Such qualifications have a universal validity which is unconditionally accepted by employers and clients. (We would also note that in the case of the client professionals, the amount of work undertaken may be controlled by varying the caseload. This may be an important feature if part-time work is contemplated). We would also include in the 'occupational' category recognised craft qualifications, and the RSA typing and secretarial examinations, etc. A further feature of occupational qualifications, which we have already noted, is that they are transportable — both from employer to employer and as geographically. At the other pole are located 'pure organizational' qualifications — that is, qualifications which are specific to an organizational career. Because most qualifications are externally validated, there will be relatively few that are of *no* relevance outside the employing institution. (Possible examples might be employer-sponsored courses such as NEBSS (National Examinations Board for Supervisory Studies) supervisor courses.) However, the essence of organizational qualifications is their identification of the individual as promotion material. This occurs whether such qualifications are *formally* required or not. They include, for example, the Institute of Banking already discussed, the Institute of Purchasing (local government), the Chartered Insurance Institute, the Chartered Building Societies Institute, etc. The business of insurance companies, banks and building socieites is closely regulated by the state, but the possession of the relevant qualifications by the individuals concerned is not a prerequisite for their operation. Setting up in independent practice — even by those with relevant qualifications — is not usually possible. (An exception might be made in the case of insurance brokers, finance companies (moneylending), etc., but again specific qualifications are not required in order to set up in business.) Employers do not require all of their employees to possess these qualifications. The most important functions of these organizational qualifications, therefore, is not as a 'licence to practice' but rather, as an increasingly necessary element in the successful pursuit of a linear, bureaucratic, organizational career.

It is often difficult to draw a firm distinction between 'organizational' and 'occupational' qualifications because in practice, the category into which a qualification should be classified will depend crucially on the *context*. For example, accountancy qualifications have both 'organizational' and 'occupational' aspects. Only chartered accountants may take responsibility for public audits, so in this sense, chartered accountancy may be said to constitute an occupational 'licence to practice'. The Chartered Institute of Public Finance and Accountancy (CIPFA) also gives an auditing qualification, but it is organizationally (public service) based. The Institute of Cost and Management Accountants (ICMA) and Certified Accountants may not take responsibility for audits. Thus these latter qualifications tend more towards the organizational category, although they are not, like banking and insurance examinations, organizationally *specific*. Accountancy qualifications — particularly chartered accountancy — may be the basis for independent practice and thus an entrepreneurial career. The high status and widespread recognition of accountancy qualifications will clearly facilitate an occupational career. Finally, and particularly in the case of a more management oriented qualification such as ICMA, whole or part qualifications may obviously be part of an organizational career strategy. Accountancy qualifications, therefore, could represent an element of either an 'organizational' or an 'occupational' strategy — and exactly *which* would depend on contextual information. Thus there will be a considerable overlap in the middle ranges of the continuum.

Part of the difficulty in classification stems from the multiple competences that qualifications may be taken to represent. As has often been noted, qualifications may be employed as a screening device which are used by the employer to infer information about an employee's personal characteristics, application, capacity for hard work, etc., as much as for the information they convey about *particular* skills. This is classically so with school leaving GCE 'O' and 'A' levels — the information acquired in 'A' level history or geography, for example, is likely to have little practical application to a young person's first job. This use of qualifications as a *general* indicator may be contrasted with a situation where *specific* competences are indicated by *particular* qualifications — a plumber, for example, is unlikely to be hired on the strength of 'O' levels alone. However, although this distinction is easy to grasp in the abstract, it is not maintained in practice. Qualifications which might appear to be quite specific — for example, building society examinations — may be used as indicators of *general* competences as well as the specific competence supposedly encompassed by the qualification itself.

Brown's ideal types, as he freely acknowledges, were formulated with reference to male employment career patterns. Nevertheless, they may be usefully adapted to 'female' employment career paths. There are Entrepreneurial, Organizational and Occupational *practitioners*, as well as careerists, and particular combinations of occupations, qualifications and career paths may be identified, on the basis of our existing knowledge as mainly 'male', mainly 'female', or both.

Occupational qualifications may be used to pursue either an entrepreneurial or an occupational career. Entrepreneurial careers include both small business operations — which may, of course become larger if the careerist is successful, as well as self-employment, which can include both full-time professional practice as well as part-time, and freelance 'temping' as either a secretary, nurse, supply teacher or computer programmer. The *full-time* business persons or professional practitioners are the entrepreneurial 'careerists'; part-time, temporary, intermittent work is carried out by entrepreneurial 'practitioners'. Entrepreneurial careerists are mainly men, entrepreneurial practitioners, women. Attwood and Hatton's (1983) research on hairdressing affords a good example. Most female apprentices were quite consciously planning to retire on marriage/children, but to return either via a 'shampoo and set' salon or as low paid (and often black economy) home hairdressers. Male apprentices in contrast, are working towards a career as stylist/manager/owner in/of a glamorous, city centre salon.

'Occupational' qualifications may also be used to pursue an occupational career. The *male* occupational model assumes that the careerist will use spells with different employers as stepping-stones on a linear, upward career. The qualifications in medicine, law, accountancy, etc. which the occupational careerist possesses are universally-accepted guarantees of competence which facilitate this upward movement. However, as we have suggested, such guarantees of competence are also relevent to a discontinuous career requiring mobility (both temporal and geographical) as well as to the continuous, linear, ideal-type.

In contrast to both Entrepreneurial and Occupational careers, only those individuals anticipating a continuous, linear career have usually undertaken the associated 'organizational' qualifications on the assumption that a 'bureaucratic career' will follow from loyal and continuous organizational service. Thus women, although often employed by large organizations in jobs hypothetically linked to a continuous career ladder (e.g. routine clerical work) have not, on the whole, acquired the relevant qualifications which would signal an upward mobility intention. Indeed, in many cases, they have actively been discouraged from doing so, as the organizations' manpower planning (sic) assumes the continuing presence of a female 'secondary' labour force with high turnover rates. (Llewellyn, 1981; Crompton and Jones, 1984). They are, in short, the unqualified organizational 'practitioners' and women leaving such work (without qualifications) may effectively become 'careerless' — hence the often-observed downward occupational mobility amongst women re-entering the labour force. The association between careers and qualifications, and the gender bias of related employment career patterns, is drawn together in Figure 8.1.

We should be cautious, therefore, about assuming that the increase in the proportion of women gaining formal academic, professional, and semi-professional qualifications will inexorably lead to a substantial increase in the proportion of women with continuous careers. An increase in occupational qualifications may result in *discontinuous* entrepreneurial and occupational careers, that is, in 'practitioners' rather than 'careerists', and 'practitioners' are likely to be female, rather than male. At the very least, however, such outcomes would reduce the proportion of totally unqualified female labour to be used for 'reserve army' purposes, and the tendency for women's occupational status to fall on re-entering the labour force might become less widespread. 'Organizational' qualifications, however, are rather different. The bureaucratic career is in essence both full-time and continuous — part-time *bureaucratic* careers are a contradiction in terms — although the organization might hire part-time occupational/entrepreneurial 'practitioners'. Women undertaking organizational qualifications are, therefore, at least in the short run, giving a clear signal as to their promotion intentions to pursue a continuous bureaucratic career. If they are successful, long-term careers might well ensue.

Career (i) (Brown's [1983] ideal-types)	Type of Qualification		Career (ii)	Gender Association
I Entrepreneurial	Occupational (e.g. pharmacy chartered accountancy, etc. — see also III below)	(i)	'Careerists' small businesses self-employed, full-time professionals, etc.	Mainly male.
		(ii)	'Practitioners' Part-time workers, freelance, 'temping'.	Mainly female older/retired men.
II Organizational	Organizational (e.g. banking, local government qualifications)	(i)	'Careerists' Bureaucratic careers.	Mainly male
	None	(ii)	'Practitioners'	Mainly female
III Occupational	Occupational (e.g. teaching, nursing, accountancy — see also I above).	(i)	'Careerists' Full-time Occupational mobility characteristically upward.	Mainly male.
		(ii)	'Practitioners' Part-time sometimes full- time Occupational mobility characteristically sideways.	Mainly female.
IV Careerless	None*			Male and Female

* Note that a lack of formal qualifications will render invididuals apparently in I, II and III in constant danger of slipping into this category.

Figure 8.1 Employment careers, qualifications, and gender

As we have already discussed, girls' school leaving qualifications have been steadily improving relative to boys' and indeed parity has (almost) been achieved. This improvement has been reflected in university admissions; in 1984, women comprised 43 per cent of candidates accepted through UCCA, as compared to only 31 per cent in 1970. It could be argued however, that this increase in academic qualifications amongst women is but one manifestation of a more general 'diploma disease', as young people facing increasing difficulty in obtaining employment seek to improve their acceptability to employers. Thus an increase in the level of purely academic qualifications may not necessarily result in any changes in the gender composition of the occupational structure.[3] The same point, however, does not apply to more specific, work related qualifications. The numbers of 'home' students in training for subjects like medicine, dentistry, optics and pharmacy, for example, are controlled by both the state and the professional bodies themselves. This control will be likely to increase the chances of employment for the qualified graduate. Other qualifications are dependent, to a greater or lesser extent, on a sponsoring employer if they are to be obtained at all; for example the Chartered Institute of Public Finance and Accountancy, the Chartered Insurance Institute (CII), etc. Thus the numbers qualifying, within broad limits, are being controlled by the employers, and people obtaining such qualifications are likely to be already in employment. An increase in the proportions of women gaining these kinds of qualifications, therefore, is a much stronger indicator that a gender shift may be occurring within the occupation concerned. Table 8.1 summarizes some of our empirical findings. It demonstrates that the proportion of women gaining a range of qualifications has shown a recent, and substantial increase. For example, in 1970, women were 20 per cent of first year medical students, but 45 per by 1983. In 1974, women were only 9 per cent of those passing CIPFA's final qualifying examinations, but they were 36 per cent by 1984. Finally, in 1970, women were 3 per cent of the CII's final pass lists but were 26 per cent by 1983.

As careers take time to develop, and as these young women are at the very beginning of their careers, it is not surprising that these recent trends have had little impact, as yet, on the aggregate statistics. They are not evident, for example, in the economic activity tables of the 1981 census — although the situation is complicated here by the OPCS' changing definition of a 'professional'.

In assessing likely future tends, it is also necessary, as we have indicated, to take into account whether a qualification tends more towards the 'occupational' or 'organizational' ideal type, and thus whether they facilitate *both* 'careerists' and 'practitioner' strategies, or are of practical relevance to the 'careerist' strategy only. Medicine, dentistry, optics and pharmacy provide straightforward examples of *occupational* qualifications. An increase in the proportion of women qualifying for these occupations, therefore, will not necessarily be reflected in an increase in the proportion of women undertaking a linear career in these professions, but merely an increase in the

Table 8.1 Trends in women studying and qualifying: various professions (total numbers)

	1970	1975	1980	1983	1984
First year enrolments at British Universities:					
Medicine	2870	3420	3806	3770	
% Women	30%	34%	41%	45%	
Dentistry	772	934	935	885	
% Women	27%	31%	35%	42%	
Pharmacy	592	789	803	597	
% Women	57%	55%	64%	62%	
Optics	—	—	217	225	
Women			51%	52%	
New Members:					
Institute of Chartered Accountants	—	3342	3316	—	2732
% Women		7%	16%		23%
Chartered Association of Certified Accountants	—	1204	1837	—	1378
% Women		6%	11%		21%
Successful candidates in Final Exams:					
Chartered Institute of Public Finance and Accountancy	—	159	215	—	301
% Women		6%	19%		36%
Institute of Cost and Management Accountants	—	1391	1305	1246	—
% Women		3%	10%	16%	
Institute of Bankers	1469	1416	1554	843	—
% Women	2%	4%	12%	21%	
Chartered Insurance Institute	1253	829	818	1144	—
% Women	3%	8%	20%	26%	
Building Societies Institute	39	106	174	344	—
% Women	0%	1%	8%	14%	
Law Society (Solicitors) (Summer Examinations	—	2662	—	—	2002
% Women		19%			47%
Council for Legal Education — Bar (All Examinations — 1975: Michaelmas only 1984)	—	619	—	—	394
% Women		16%			29%

Sources: UCCA Statistics and published pass lists: data supplied by Institutes. Every effort has been made to relate these figures to home students only. However, because of variations in record-keeping by the professional bodies concerned, these figures may not always be absolutely accurate. This problem, however, has no effect on the overall trends revealed in the table.

number and availability of part-time and/or discontinuous 'practitioners'. Elias and Main (1982), for example, have reported that professional qualifications appear to increase the probability of working part-time: 'The singular characteristic of these qualifications is that, institutionally, they offer the possibility of part-time employment with none of the usual low wage penalties that accompany the non full-time job' (1982, p. 105).

In contrast, insurance, building society and banking qualifications are closer to the 'organizational' type. The individual taking these qualifications is actively signalling his or her intention to embark on a linear career. Thus it is more reasonable to assume that an increase in women gaining these qualifications will be reflected in an increase of linear careerists in the future. Finally, as we have already suggested, accountancy qualifications may be used to facilitate a wide range of career options at both the 'careerist' and 'practioner' level. (Although this is a rather different point, it is interesting that the increase in those qualifying has been highest in the 'public service' CIPFA, and relatively lower in the 'industrial' ICMA). Nevertheless, our evidence demonstrates that the quality of the female labour force is steadily improving and whether 40 year olds in 2005 have had continuous or discontinuous, full-time or part-time, careers, we may expect that fewer, proportionately, will have been crowded into low-level jobs and low-status occupations. There may nevertheless be considerable variations depending on both the types of qualifications women acquire and, where relevant, the organizational or occupational response.

Historically, low-status, truncated career 'niches' for women have emerged in occupations where professional qualifications have supposedly bestowed a notional *equality* of occupational status. Teaching is the best-known example — although not, perhaps a particularly good one. Until comparatively recently there was not parity of esteem between different teaching qualifications. In particular, there was an acknowledged difference — reflected in pay — between graduate and certificate only teachers. A less well known, but better example that we have examined in some detail is pharmacy. The professional qualification (MPS — Member of the Pharmaceutical Society) bestows equality of professional status on men and women alike. However, the pattern of employment/careers subsequent to qualifying has displayed distinct and gendered patterns.

Woman pharmacists have predominated in hospital pharmacy, men in 'community' or retail pharmacy. Hospital pharmacy offered both security of employment and the opportunity for part-time work — both useful for women pharmacists fitting professional employment together with the demands of home and family. Retail pharmacy, particularly if the pharmacist sets up as an independent retailer (i.e. embarks on an entrepreneurial career) has historically involved the working of very long hours (six-day week, six o'clock closing, weekend working, and regular performance of 'rota' which involves Sunday opening and seven o'clock closing) — which would clearly be very difficult to accommodate to domestic needs.

Table 8.2 Pharmacists: membership by sex and principal occupation[+]

	1972	1977	1981	1984
Community Pharmacists:				
Men	14570	12772	12706	—
Women	3170	3767	5114	—
Total	17750	16539	17820	18795
% Women	18%	23%	29%	—
Hospital Pharmacists:				
Men	990	1441	1422	1468[*]
Women	1690	1821	2178	2336
Total	2680	3262	3600	3804
% Women	63%	56%	61%	61%
Industry:				
Men	1300	1147	1097	—
Women	70	143	198	—
Total	1370	1290	1295	1289
% Women	5%	11%	15%	—
In any other pharmaceutical or non-pharmaceutical occupation				
Men	1540	1138	1090	—
Women	450	240	319	—
Total	1990	1378	1409	1317
% Women	23%	17%	23%	—

Sources: Pharmaceutical Journal Vols. 209, 219, 221, 228, Pharmaceutical Society Surveys
* Calculated — incomplete data.
+ These tables relate to *registered* pharmacists only. Unregistered pharmacists may not practice. However, for the qualified, registration is a simple matter and may be renewed, for example, after a period out of employment.

Thus men have predominated in retail pharmacy, and in the private industrial sector. There have, however, been interesting and recent developments. Table 8.2 shows that the number of women pharmacists practising in all areas is increasing, whereas the number of men practising has been remarkably static — although there has been a slight decline in men in community practice and a slight increase in men in hospital practice. Table 8.3 shows an increase in part-time working by *both* sexes, combined with a decrease in male, but an increase in female, full-time working.

Community pharmacy has seen an increase in both full-time and part-time women. There is relatively little part-time work being done by younger female pharmacists, but between the ages of 30–45 a sizeable *majority* are working part-time. Given the rather anti-social hours associated with community pharmacy, there has been a growing demand for 'relief' or 'locum' pharmacists to work on a regular basis during busy periods or on the pharmacists' day off, or to cover for pharmacists on holiday or off sick. The current pro-rata rate for relief pharmacists is £45 or more per

Table 8.3 Pharmacists: membership by sex and normal extent of occupation

	1972	1977	1978	1981	1983	1984
Full time:						
Men	16250	14342	14379	13874	13651	13377
Women	2700	3396	3922	4573	5037	5273
Total	18950	17738	18301	18447	18688	18650
% Women	14%	19%	21%	25%	27%	28%
Part-time:						
Men	1880	2156	2212	2441	2546	2515
Women	2570	2575	2801	3236	3474	3681
Total	4450	4731	5013	5677	6020	6176
% Women	58%	54%	56%	57%	58%	60%
All Members: (includes those not working)						
Men	20010	19604	19399	19130	19200	18901
Women	6800	7504	8353	9373	10144	10485
Total	26810	27108	27752	28503	29344	29387
% Women	25%	28%	30%	33%	35%	36%

Sources: Pharmaceutical Journal Vols. 209, 219, 221, 228 Pharmaceutical Society Surveys.

day, and increasingly, both women and older, retired male pharmacists have been recruited to fill this role. The range of part-time opportunities — and thus the possibility of pursuing 'practitioner'-type entreprenueurial and occupational careers, has therefore been increasing.

Women in the hospital service put their career at risk by opting to work part-time; and until recently promotion was very unlikely for part-timers. Promotion prospects with the hospital service are, in any case, currently problematic. Reorganization in 1974 has caused a 'log-jam' of relatively young pharmacists at the principal level thus blocking promotion at the lower levels. This is a feature of the service which has apparently been more discouraging to men than women. Women have long been a majority of hospital pharmacists, and although the expansion (and salary improvement) in the mid 1970s increased male participation (see Table 8.2), the decline of opportunities since then has seen a subsequent reduction in the number of men practising.

Developments in pharmacy, therefore, reflect a fascinating combination of continuity and change. Overall, male and female career paths in pharmacy would appear to be converging — more women are working full-time, more men are working part-time; more women are working in community pharmacy, more men in hospital pharmacy. However, the pattern of part-time working over the life cycle is crucially different for men and women, and reflects characteristically 'male' and 'female' employment patterns. The increase of men in hospital pharmacy has abruptly slowed down since linear career prospects have deteriorated. Thus the initial impression of apparent convergence — (which may, eventually, occur) — must be tempered by an appreciation of the persistence of gender-related career differences, even though these are changing. The increase in the number and proportions of women gaining qualifications in pharmacy, therefore, appears to have resulted in an increase in entrepreneurial and occupational 'practitioners' as well as a possible increase in linear 'careerists', although in exactly what proportions, it is as yet impossible to say.

Although we have not, as yet, investigated their role in any depth, employers will obviously play a major role in the structuring of career paths. In the case of pharmacy, for example, the role of a major employer such as Boots the Chemists is likely to become even more important in the future as the number of small retail pharmacies declines. Additionally, as we have previously noted, the role of employers is absolutely central to future developments in respect of 'organizational' qualifications. Most employers will actually sponsor employees undertaking qualifications such as banking and building society examinations through day release, paying examination fees, etc. The giving or withholding of such sponsorship is clearly a way in which the numbers qualifying may be controlled. Women have been widely considered as 'not worth' sponsoring — thus the relatively well-documented example of banking, where women have been actively discouraged from taking the examinations (Crompton and Jones, 1984; Llewellyn, 1981; Heritage, 1983). However, the increase in the number of women acquiring organizational qualifications in banking, insurance and building societies, suggests that the number of women sponsored is currently increasing. (Although this proposition is difficult to prove, we are convinced that this is one area in which Equal Opportunities legislation has had a marked effect.)

Although accountancy qualifications are less obviously 'in house', here, too, the employer sponsorship plays a crucial role. Student members will actually be in employment themselves — student accountants are not the same as undergraduates. Thus numbers qualifying will (certainly in the case of chartered accountancy) be controlled by the numbers of accountancy trainees taken on by the employers.

In the case of banking, insurance, building society and accountancy qualifications, therefore, the numbers qualifying may, within reasonably flexible boundaries, be controlled by the employers. Despite this important similarity between these qualifications, however, there are nevertheless differences in the likely work experience of those who qualify which may prove to have important, and different, consequences for women. Accountancy, as we have suggested, may provide a foundation for *either* 'careerist' or 'practitioner' work strategies. Doing the books is a task that may be undertaken part-time, by a qualified or unqualified woman. Indeed, the existing opportunities for part-time work in accountancy have been positively cited as a reason why more women should enter the profession (Silverstone, 1980). It seems reasonable to suggest, therefore, that employers will not have to engage in organizational restructuring, or devise new or very different career paths, in order to employ trained female accountants part-time or re-employ them if they wish to return to work. As in pharmacy, therefore, the increase in women training for accountancy may result in an increase in both female 'practitioners' *and* 'careerists' — although futher empirical research is needed in this area. 'Practitioners' may be expected to maintain their occupational *status*, but may find it difficult to switch into linear careers, particularly in large organizations.

In contrast, in banks, insurance companies and building societies, occupational status is crucially dependent on an individual's position within the bureaucratic hierarchy. (The same is broadly true, of course, for accountancy, but whereas it is possible to hire oneself out as 'an accountant', one cannot do so as, for example, 'a bank manager'). In these organizations, qualifications and linear careers have historically gone hand in hand. There is no obvious place within the organization for the *qualified* 'practitioner' — all 'practitioners', male and female, are invariably unqualified (Fig. 8.1). Thus the occupational status of unqualified 'practitioners', in contrast to that of qualified 'practitioners' such as part-time pharmacists, is explicitly low. The increased numbers of women gaining banking, etc. qualifications, therefore, if all other things remain equal, will result in *either* an increase in female organizational 'careerists' or an increasing proportion of *qualified*, low status 'practitioners' which could create tensions within the organization. A further possibility, which will be explored in future research, is that organizations may respond by developing avenues within the organization for qualified 'practitioners' as well as qualified 'careerists'.[4]

Summary and Conclusions

In this paper, we have raised a number of questions relating to the likely impact of the increasing proportion of women gaining qualifications on women's — and men's — careers in the future. 'Career' is a term that we have used rather broadly to refer to ideal-typical categories which describe characteristic patterns of employment amongst men and women. Some qualifications — those that we have described as occupational — are largely associated with either 'entrepreneurial' or 'occupational' careers. We have suggested that such qualifications are, in practice, a useful adjunct to the predominant career paths as revealed by the work history data gathered by the Woman and Employment Survey. That is, they facilitate entrepreneurial and occupational 'practitioner' careers, which incorporate the flexibility and mobility associated with discontinuous employment without a drop in occupational status, but also without the linear progression associated with continuous 'careerists'.

'Organizational' qualifications, however, may not be so readily adapted to discontinuous careers as they are historically associated with career patterns which are crucially dependent on continuous employment within a large organization (or a series of similar large organizations) resulting in a linear, upward career path. In such organizations, therefore, qualified women, if they are to gain any of the advantages usually associated with the possession of such qualifications, will have increasingly to undertake continuous careers. Unless, of course, employers consciously develop new strategies to accommodate a discontinuous, qualified, workforce.

Our final comments, therefore, relate to the nature of demand rather than labour supply. The 'flexibility' and 'adaptability' of women in relation to employment has been cited as a positive characteristic which should be encouraged in respect of 'labour' more generally, in order that Britain may move into and keep pace with increasingly rapid rates of social and technological change. (Atkinson, 1984). If organizations do create suitable niches for qualified 'practitioners', therefore, it is possible that women might become the basis of a *qualified* and flexible 'reserve' — thus relieving organizations of some of the need to retain a full-time, skilled, 'core' labour force. Any reduction in the 'core', however, might reduce opportunities for those who wish to pursue full-time careers — i.e. men. If more men are forced into 'discontinuous' careers despite having undergone a formal occupational training, it is possible that they will be unwilling to accept, as women *have* done, the loss of prospects associated with discontinuity. Although, therefore, we have recognized in our discussion that an improvement in the level of women's qualifications cannot simply 'read off' as implying a proportionate increase in the number of women in continuous careers, there are other factors at work which may nevertheless lead to the increasing convergence, over the next few decades, of male and female career paths.

Notes

1 Calculated from DES *Statistics of Education*.
2 Even here, however, there have nevertheless been substantial changes. Using the training for these four occupations as a crude 'index of segregation in training', in 1972 no less than 50 per cent of all girl school-leavers going into further and higher education went into training for these occupations.
3 The improvement in female academic qualifications raises interesting possibilities. Faced with an excess of labour, employers may respond with a variety of strategies, but one of the most common — as the 'diploma disease' implies — is to *increase* the level of qualifications required for the job — even though they may not necessarily be job related. In the climate of recent legislation and opinion, however, it will have been difficult to reject a female applicant if her qualifications are *better* than those of a roughly equivalent male.
4 Women have continued to increase their representation in all of the professions discussed in this chapter during the years since this article was written. The implications of this continuing trend are further discussed in R. Crompton and K. Sanderson (1990) *Gendered Jobs and Social Change*, Unwin Hyman, London. This book also incorporates more recent data on women's qualification and employment trends in pharmacy, accountancy and building societies.

Chapter 9

Marriage Partners and their Class Trajectories

Gill Jones

The 'conventional view' is that the social class of women is determined by the occupational class of their fathers before marriage and their husbands after it: 'the way in which women have been located in the class structure has reflected their general position of dependence' (Goldthorpe, 1980, p. 282; 1983). This view is part of the separation in much of the sociological literature of the public and private spheres of work and home. It has led to a blinkered vision through which women were seen in terms of their domestic roles, while men were seen as breadwinners primarily located in the work place (the home was not by this definition a place of work). Although recent research on female employment, household endeavours, and intra-household inequalities in terms of class of partners, and differential access to goods and income has challenged this view (Pahl, R., 1984; Crompton and Sanderson in the previous chapter; Paul, J., 1983; Brannen and Wilson, 1987), there is still little acknowledgment that a man's domestic circumstances are relevant to his labour market behaviour and class location.

Research on marital mobility tends to reflect this persisting tunnel vision, focusing on the wife's class mobility through marriage but not that of the husband (cf. McRae, 1986). The possibility that a wife's social class might be affected by the class position of her choice of spouse is acknowledged in a sociological world in which a woman's class is often ascribed to her from the occupational class of her husband or father. The idea that a man's social class might (or might not) be enhanced through marriage cannot easily co-exist with the theory that his social class is determined by his occupational attainment. In order to understand the social mobility of men as well as women, it is nevertheless important to consider their home circumstances, including their domestic responsibilities and their choice of spouse.

The study described here[1] forms part of a wide-ranging analysis of social class and gender variation in the transitions of adulthood, and takes a new approach to the study of marital mobility. Firstly, it is based on symmetry, examining the class positions of young men and women at or near the time of their marriage. The extent and nature of mobility through marriage for men and women will be examined. Secondly, it argues for a longitudinal approach to class. A typology of class trajectories from class of origin to class at marriage is used in order to consider the convergence of the two partners' class histories at marriage. This allows marital mobility to be studied in the context of other class mobility. The study examines the extent to which marital mobility provides a route to upward social class mobility. Can social mobility through marriage make up for lack of mobility routes in the labour market? Are these routes alternative or complementary? To what extent are they gendered? The following analysis of the class trajectories of marriage partners before marriage will indicate the extent to which a father's class position is reflected in that of his unmarried adult children, or a husband's class position reflects that of his wife (and vice versa), before the differential occupational class mobility which is likely to occur after the couple have children.

Marital Mobility

The expression 'marital mobility' originally meant marriage between persons of different social standing, of either gender. This notion of marriage as a means of social mobility was introduced by Sorokin:

> Such a marriage usually leads one of the parties either to social promotion or degradation. In this way, some people have made their careers; some others have ruined them. (Sorokin, 1927: 179).

More recently, however, the term 'marital mobility' has come to be applied mainly to women and, as Heath has pointed out, to be based upon fundamentally sexist assumptions. In particular, it 'assumes that a woman's status or class position is determined by her husband's occupation, and it implies that the woman's own achievements have little to do with her husband's fate' (Heath, 1981 p. 111). Thus, Rossi states (1971 p. 110):

> What a man 'does' defines his status, but whom she marries defines a woman's. In meeting strangers one can 'place' a man socially by asking what he does, a woman by asking what her husband does.

Indeed, from this perspective, one can add 'and a young woman from what her father does'. Until research began to examine patterns of occupational class mobility among women (Martin and Roberts, 1984; Dex, 1985), marital mobility was the main focus of the study of women's class histories: little research on the marital mobility of men was undertaken.

It is not surprising, then, that the study has fallen into disrepute. Research in the United States tended to juxtapose women's marital mobility with the occupational mobility of men, as gendered routes to the higher social classes. Chase (1975), for example, remarked that women had greater mobility through marriage than did men through occupations, and concluded that women were less tied than men to their class origins. Though Glenn *et al.* (1974) disagreed, the bulk of this research was based on a fundamental belief that women could only derive status from others. Marital mobility of women was measured in tables of their husband's class by their father's class. By this definition, most people married within their class ('class endogamy') while marrying up was generally balanced by marrying down. Heath notes that:

> There is both more downward and more upward mobility through marriage for women than there is through the labour market for men. In this sense a woman's 'class fate' is more loosely linked to her social origins than is a man's. (Heath, 1981: 114).

Goldthorpe and Payne (1986: 539) take a more reserved position, that 'class origins need not always influence to exactly the same degree the class fate of the men and women who share them'. Comparisons of this type are problematic, particularly when it is not always clear how marital or occupational mobility should be measured, or indeed what they represent.

McRae's (1986) study of 'cross-class families' is innovative in identifying marital mobility among men; she defines as 'cross-class', marriages between manual worker husbands, and wives in intermediate or higher non-manual work, treating women in routine non-manual work as in equivalent, rather than higher, class positions to those of male manual workers, on the grounds that:

> if they in fact do not better the conditions confronting men in manual employment, there is little reason to assume that marriage between women in routine non-manual work and men in manual work are 'cross-class' at all: husbands and wives in these families will share the same class position. (McRae, 1986: 6).

She found though that among the cross-class families thus defined, the social backgrounds (i.e. class of origin) of partners tended to be very similar. 'Pure' cross-class families in which both social backgrounds and current occupational classes were disparate, were relatively uncommon. Studies suggest that most people marry within their class. This begs questions about how their class should be measured, particularly in the case of the socially mobile. The study described here examines the relationship between marital mobility and other inter-generational and intra-generational social mobility in young adulthood. Does marital mobility offer the socially mobile the opportunity to crystallise newly gained class positions, or can downward marital mobility confirm loss of status? Can women who fail to achieve upward mobility through education or the labour market become upwardly mobile through marriage 'instead'?

The study of marital mobility should not be rejected as sexist. It could broaden our understanding of the position of married men and women as individuals and as family members in the class structure.

As Allen (1983 p. 142) points out:

> it may be that a woman's class fate *is* more loosely linked to her social origins than a man's . . . Some check on the woman's (wife's) occupational position and educational level at the time of marriage would begin to give more indication of the processes involved.

This chapter represents an attempt to re-examine marital mobility from this standpoint.

The Data

The research involves secondary analysis of the General Household Survey (GHS). The GHS is a national survey of households from which a subset was extracted of 12,036 people aged 16 to 29 years, by combining data from the 1979 and 1980 surveys. It is a cross-sectional data set, providing a picture of people's situations at a particular time (OPCS, 1979, 1980a).

The following analysis includes as marriage partners all those who describe themselves as 'living as man and wife', whether or not they are legally married. Because the GHS is based on a sample of households, married men and married women, though treated individually, will often belong to the same household (though some marriage partners, mainly husbands, will be excluded from the subset if they are over 29 years of age); analysis of couples based on wives will therefore show the obverse picture to an analysis of couples based on husbands. Only couples without children have been included in the analysis. The effect of this is to concentrate the analysis on couples in early marriage, but some bias towards those who delay childbirth is thus inevitably introduced. The intention is to get as close as possible to examining the class of marriage partners *at marriage* and thus avoid over-estimating the degree of marital mobility among women. This would result if the analysis included women who have been downwardly mobile in occupational class terms after having children (Dex, 1985; Martin and Roberts, 1984).

The occupational class schema which has been used throughout this chapter is derived from the OPCS socioe-conomic groups used in the Census (OPCS, 1980b), with some modifications (see Table 9.1). The data relate to a period of relatively low unemployment; few married respondents had never had a job and their class positions could therefore be partly based on their current or last occupational class.

This occupational class schema has been used in the research as the best available

Table 9.1 Derivation of occupational class schema

Occupational class, occupations included and socio-economic groups in the GHS

Class	*Occupations* include	GHS SEG
1	*Higher Professionals*:	5, 6
	Accountants, medical practitioners, lawyers	1, 2
		3, 4
2	*Intermediate Non-manual and Lower Professionals*:	7, 16
	Managers, self-employed business men, teachers, nurses	
3	*Junior Non-manual*:	8, 9
	Office Supervisors, typists, clerks, telephonists, shop assistants	
4	*Skilled Manual*:	11, 12
	Foremen, drivers, craftsmen, skilled production workers	15, 17
5	*Semi-skilled Manual*:	10, 13
	Personal service workers, bar and restaurant staff, lower-skilled	18
	production workers, packers	
6	*Unskilled Manual*:	14
	Labourers, cleaners	

measure, although it is acknowledged that the nature of the occupational class structure as represented here, while largely adequate for men, only partially reflects the social class position of many women in terms of their educational level, career prospects or class of origin. If the schema were used without any modification to compare the class of marriage partners, upward mobility of women would be over-estimated, since not only are the largest group of women in junior non-manual work, but also many of these women are the daughters and wives of men in manual work. In order to allow gender comparisons using the occupational class schema, the following analysis uses two modifications: in the first part of the analysis, the original six classes have been regrouped into three (higher non-manual, intermediate and lower manual). In the second part, in which a longitudinal class schema is introduced, a different approach has been taken: the classes have been dichotomized into non-manual and manual, but in the case of women in junior non-manual work, their class has been partly determined on the basis of their educational level. Those in junior non-manual work with education beyond the age of 18 are included with non-manual classes, while those who left education before the age of 18 are classed as manual workers, in 'proletarian' jobs (following Heath and Britten, 1984). In default of an occupational class schema which can overcome the problems of comparison at a more fundamental level, these methods do at least allow a more meaningful comparison of the class of husbands and wives.

Endogamy and Marital Mobility

Do people marry others of the same occupational class as themselves? This is not an easy question to answer for a number of reasons. Firstly, on what basis is their class most appropriately measured? Marriage partners are in temporary positions on life-time class trajectories at marriage. The occupational classes which are measured cross-sectionally in an analysis of marital mobility are therefore likely to be occupied by both the respondent and the spouse on a temporary basis. Secondly, as explained above there

Table 9.2 Class endogamy

Spouse's current or last occupational class by own current or last occupational class, among married respondents aged 16–29 with no children.

Column % and standardized residuals

Occupational class of spouse	Occupational class of respondent			
	1 + 2 %	3 + 4 %	5 + 6 %	All %
Class of wife				
1 + 2 Higher non-manual	47	16	12	24
	6.9	− 3.5	− 2.7	
3 + 4 Intermediate	42	63	54	56
	− 2.6	1.9	− 0.2	
5 + 6 Lower manual	11	22	34	21
	− 3.3	0.6	3.2	
All (= 100%)	(210)	(419)	(120)	(749)
Row %	28	56	16	100
Sign: p < 0.001 Cramer's V = 0.26				
Class of husband				
1 + 2 Higher non-manual	58	25	13	31
	7.2	− 2.4	− 4.2	
3 + 4 Intermediate	35	60	60	54
	− 3.8	2.0	1.0	
5 + 6 Lower manual	7	15	27	15
	− 3.1	− 0.4	4.1	
All (= 100%)	(225)	(512)	(173)	(910)
Row %	25	56	19	100
Sign: p < 0.001 Cramer's V = 0.26				

Source: GHS (1979; 1980)

is the difficulty of comparing the occupational classes of husbands and wives with a class schema which is best suited to describe male positions.

In the following analysis, mobility is measured first according to the current or last occupational class of the partners themselves, then the analysis is repeated, controlling for each partner's class of origin, as measured by their father's occupational class.

Table 9.2 is a crosstabulation of spouse's class by the respondent's own occupational class, first for husbands and then for wives, using a three-class schema which takes some account of the gendered structure of occupations. The use of this schema means that where a husband in manual work is married to a wife in junior non-manual work this would be regarded as class endogamy, rather than upward marital mobility of the husband or downwards marital mobility of the wife. The approach is similar to that of McRae (1986) but categorizes nurses in Class 2.

The table shows the degree of class endogamy, measured by the occupational class of both spouses. The analysis calculates standardized residuals (by subtracting the expected cell frequency from the observed cell frequency, and dividing by the square root of the expected cell frequency) from fitting a model which hypothesizes no association between the spouses' occupational classes. Use of standardized residuals controls for marginal distributions, in this case differences in the gender composition of different classes. As a rule of thumb residuals of more than two or less than minus two can be regarded as significant. The table shows that the model of no association does not fit the data: there is a high degree of class endogamy. This is especially the case among those in the higher occupational classes (1 and 2) who show a strong tendency to marry each other rather than outside their own occupational class (the standardized residuals are 6.9 for men and 7.2 for women). Also showing a strong tendency to marry each other (though not as strong as among the Classes 1 and 2) are those in the lower manual classes (standardized residuals of 3.2 for men and 4.1 for women). Those in the intermediate classes (3 and 4) show less endogamy when the size of these occupational classes is controlled for. The data therefore show that while endogamy exists, its degree varies between classes. It seems that, as in the analysis of intergenerational mobility (Jones, 1987a), occupational class congruence in early marriage occurs mainly among those in the two extremes of the class structure, the higher non-manual and the lower manual classes.

While these findings suggest that people seek out marriage partners of their own occupational class, most studies of marital mobility have been based on class of origin rather than current occupational class, particularly in the case of the wife. Respondents' own class could thus be coincidental: it may be that young people marry others of the same class of origin, particularly when they themselves have been mobile inter-generationally and intragenerationally. Class endogamy may therefore relate more to their class of origin rather than their current occupational class. Tables 9.3 and 9.4 test this hypothesis. They extend Table 9.2 by controlling for the father's occupational

Table 9.3 Class endogamy — Men 16–29 years

Wife's current or last occupational class by own current or last occupational class, controlling for father's occupational class, among men with no children.

Column % and standardized residuals

Father's class and occupational class of wife	Occupational class of respondent			
	1 + 2 %	3 + 4 %	5 + 6 %	All %
Father in class 1 + 2				
1 + 2 Higher non-manual	50	24	26	37
	2.0	− 1.8	− 0.8	
3 + 4 Intermediate	44	70	37	54
	− 1.3	1.9	− 1.0	
5 + 6 Lower manual	7	5	37	9
	− 2.2	0.9	2.7	
All (= 100%)	(93)	(74)	(19)	(186)
Row %	50	40	10	100
Sign: p < 0.001 Cramer's V = 0.29				
Father in class 3 + 4				
1 + 2 Higher non-manual	45	12	9	19
	5.5	− 2.4	− 1.7	
3 + 4 Intermediate	43	63	60	58
	− 1.8	1.0	0.2	
5 + 6 Lower manual	12	25	31	23
	− 2.0	0.6	1.2	
All (= 100%)	(82)	(251)	(55)	(388)
Row %	25	65	14	100
Sign: p < 0.001 Cramer's V = 0.25				
Father in class 5 + 6				
1 + 2 Higher non-manual	50	19	10	22
	2.9	− 0.5	− 1.6	
3 + 4 Intermediate	42	54	54	52
	− 0.7	0.3	0.2	
5 + 6 Lower manual	8	27	36	26
	− 1.7	0.1	1.2	
All (= 100%)	(24)	(74)	(39)	(137)
Row %	18	54	29	100
Sign: p < 0.005 Cramer's V = 0.24				

Source: GHS (1979; 1980)

class, first for husbands and then for wives. Standardized residuals from a model of no association are again given, as well as column percentages.

Table 9.3 shows the data for men. Analysis of the standardized residuals shows that the model of no association fits best among people whose fathers are in semi-skilled or unskilled manual work, suggesting that for these couples endogamy can be partly explained by class of origin. The main exception is among those who have been upwardly mobile intergenerationally. Those who have been upwardly mobile into Classes 1 and 2, and whose fathers are in lower occupational classes, tend to marry wives who are in Classes 1 and 2. In the case of these intergenerationally upwardly mobile, the class of origin has not therefore affected the choice of wife, in class terms. Marriage between those who are in the higher non-manual classes cannot therefore be explained by their class of origin alone.

The table shows that men who have been mobile intergenerationally marry according to their own occupational class rather than their class of origin. This is not surprising where upwardly mobile men are concerned, since marriage to wives who are in the same occupational class as themselves, but a higher class than their fathers, would appear to be a means of confirming their achieved class position. Thus the upwardly mobile of working-class origin, might confirm their new middle-class position through marriage to a middle-class wife. Results are more surprising in the case of the downwardly mobile middle class. Table 9.3 shows that men in this group whose fathers are in higher non-manual work and who are themselves in lower manual work, tend to marry wives who are also in lower manual work. Just as the upwardly mobile appear to confirm their 'achieved' class positions through marriage, so do the downwardly mobile.

The data for women are shown in Table 9.4. The basic pattern appears to be similar to that for men. Percentage comparisons suggest that a woman's class of origin is an important factor in her choice of spouse. However, comparison of the strength of association (Cramer's V) statistics on Tables 9.3 and 9.4 show that the occupational class of the father has little more effect on a woman's choice of marriage partner than it does in the case of men. A woman's class of origin is therefore no better a predictor of her husband's occupational class than a man's class of origin of his wife's occupational class.

Table 9.4 shows that among women, as among men, where fathers are in the lower manual classes there is less association between the occupational classes of the marriage partners. For this group, class of origin of the wife (rather than her own occupational class) appears to have a stronger effect on the choice of husband (measured by his occupational class). In contrast, women who have been upwardly mobile intergenerationally show the same pattern as equivalent men, in marrying a husband in the same occupational class as themselves. There is also, as with men, a relative tendency for those in Classes 1 and 2 to marry into the same classes regardless of the occupational class of their fathers.

Table 9.4 Class endogamy — Women 16–29 years

Husband's occupational class by own occupational class, controlling for father's occupational class, among women with no children.

Column % and standardized residuals

Occupational class of husband	Occupational class of respondent			
	1 + 2 %	3 + 4 %	5 + 6 %	All %
Father in class 1 + 2				
1 + 2 Higher non-manual	68	32	22	44
	3.4	− 2.1	− 1.7	
3 + 4 Intermediate	25	59	63	47
	− 3.0	2.0	1.2	
5 + 6 Lower manual	7	10	15	9
	− 0.8	0.2	1.0	
All (= 100%)	(91)	(124)	(27)	(242)
Row %	38	51	11	100
Sign: p<0.001 Cramer's V = 0.27				
Father in class 3 + 4				
1 + 2 Higher non-manual	54	24	15	29
	4.6	− 1.5	− 2.3	
3 + 4 Intermediate	39	59	55	54
	− 2.0	1.1	0.2	
5 + 6 Lower manual	7	17	29	18
	− 2.4	0.0	2.6	
All (= 100%)	(97)	(271)	(85)	(453)
Row %	21	60	19	100
Sign: p<0.001 Cramer's V = 0.23				
Father in class 5 + 6				
1 + 2 Higher non-manual	33	20	8	18
	1.8	0.4	− 1.8	
3 + 4 Intermediate	59	66	64	64
	− 0.3	0.2	− 0.1	
5 + 6 Lower manual	7	14	29	18
	− 1.3	− 0.8	1.9	
All (= 100%)	(27)	(85)	(52)	(164)
Row %	17	52	32	100
Sign: p<0.05 Cramer's V = 0.20				

Source: GHS (1979; 1980)

It appears from this study that endogamy occurs in relation to the marriage partners' patterns of social mobility. Men and women who are equivalent in their social mobility marry one another. The findings have shown the relative importance of a partner's own occupational class *vis-a-vis* that of his or her father's class.

The findings from Tables 9.3 and 9.4 are borne out by subsequent loglinear analysis, shown in a footnote.[2] It is clear from the analysis that the strongest predictor of a spouse's occupational class is the respondent's own occupational class, not their class of origin, and this is almost equally true for men and women. Father's occupational class on its own is a weaker predictor and indeed equally weak for men and women. Although there is a weak association between father's class and spouse's class within the occupational class categories of both sexes, this is largely confined to women in Classes 1 and 2, who have a relatively high propensity to marry men in Classes 1 and 2, if the women's fathers were in Classes 1 and 2. Sixty eight per cent of such women married spouses in Classes 1 and 2, compared with 50 per cent of equivalent men.

Within this general framework, there appears to be another pattern emerging, though the evidence is slight. Upward mobility of women in terms of occupational class is restricted, and is often determined by their educational level prior to their entry into the labour market rather than their attainments at work (Jones, 1986). Women who lack educational qualifications and enter the labour force in an occupational class which is lower than their class of origin, i.e. who are downwardly mobile intergenerationally, may seek 'counter-mobility' through marriage rather than in the workplace. Marriage might thus be seen as an 'alternative route' (Raffe, 1979) to counter-mobility, used by women because of their relative lack of work routes such as career structures and training programmes which are available to men (Crompton and Sanderson, Chapter 8). Downwardly mobile women of middle-class origin have been found to marry earlier than others from middle-class backgrounds (Jones, 1986). Do they marry back into their class of origin?

Downwardly mobile women show (Table 9.4) a pattern slightly different from that of downwardly mobile men. Men in this group were seen to marry women of the same occupational class as themselves, thus confirming their downward mobility through marriage. Among women there is less of such a tendency. Women who have been downwardly mobile intergenerationally into classes 5 and 6 and have fathers in Classes 1 and 2 tend not to marry men of the same class as themselves. There may be some indication here that some women achieve counter-mobility through marriage, regaining their class of origin through marriage rather than through work.

As Allen (1983) suggested, in order to understand more clearly the extent to which a woman's class fate is linked to her social origins, it is necessary to look at her occupational position and educational level at marriage. Table 9.5 shows the statistics resulting from crosstabulation of the partners' characteristics on each of three variables. The Phi statistics show that the greatest association is between the

Table 9.5 Elements of endogamy

Comparison of education, class of origin and own current occupational class associations between marriage partners under 30 years without children.

Statistics resulting from a crosstabulation of husband's characteristics by wife's characteristics for each of the following variables:

Variable	Sign. p =	Phi	N =
Age at leaving school	0.0001	0.47	735
Father's class	0.0001	0.17	664
Own occupational class	0.0001	0.32	710

Source: GHS (1979; 1980)

educational levels of marriage partners (0.47), then their own occupational class (0.32) and, lastly their class of origin (0.17). Class of origin is therefore less significant in the choice of marriage partner than the characteristics of the partners themselves, male or female. It should be seen as the starting point of the partners' personal class histories, rather than as a crucial element in itself.

A Typology of Class Trajectories

The analysis so far has been based on cross-sectional measures of class, whether class of origin or current occupational class, using three classes. A different approach will now be taken, based around two classes. A longitudinal class schema was developed for the research on which this chapter is based because of the inadequacies of conventional cross-sectional indicators of social class for measuring inequalities and differences in youth. The study identified a high degree of class mobility in early work careers, both in relation to class of origin and in terms of occupational class careers (Jones, 1987a). Current occupational class might therefore be seen as a temporary position on a 'class trajectory' (Wright, 1978), and an inaccurate reflection of life chances. While this is true of all people, it is particularly the case among young adults.

The modified typology of 'youth classes' used here though longitudinal in its conception is still in fact based on cross-sectional data in the GHS. It describes the trajectory taken from class of origin, through age of leaving education (used as a proxy variable for the occupational class of the respondent's first job), to class of current job. The full typology was developed with longitudinal data from the National Child Development study (Shepherd, 1985) and has been described elsewhere (Jones, 1987a). Occupational class has broadly been dichotomized into manual and non-manual work for male respondents and fathers. Since this is not a meaningful division of female occupational class, the modified approach described earlier has been taken for women in junior non-manual work who have been divided according to their educational level.

The typology distinguishes six ideal type class trajectories, referred to as 'Youth Classes', according to which most, though not all, married or cohabiting respondents could be identified in the data set.

1 *Stable Middle Class*
    comprising those of middle-class backgrounds who follow non-manual careers;
2 *Education-Mobile Working Class*
    those of working-class backgrounds who achieve upward mobility into non-manual work through full-time education;
3 *Counter-Mobile Middle Class*
    those of middle-class backgrounds who enter manual work or, in the case of women, low-grade non-manual work, and later retrieve their non-manual class positions through work or a combination of work and education routes;
4 *Work-Mobile Working Class*
    those from working-class families who achieve upward mobility into non-manual work through work routes;
5 *Downwardly-Mobile Middle Class*
    middle-class early education-leavers who enter manual work, some of whom will become counter-mobile in time, while some will remain downwardly mobile;
6 *Stable Working Class*
    those from working-class backgrounds who are early school leavers and in manual work.

Intergenerationally mobile and apparently intragenerationally mobile groups are thus identified. The upwardly mobile working class are further divided according to the route (via education, or via work careers) through which they appear to have achieved upward mobility. Distributions of these Youth Classes for men and women in the GHS are shown in Table 9.6.

The Youth Class typology has been applied to the study of transitions to adulthood (Jones, 1986), including the analysis of early housing careers (Jones, 1987b). It will now be brought into play for the study of the class histories of marriage partners. It is hypothesized that it is the configuration of the elements which make up a class trajectory which is relevant in the study of marital mobility.

McRae (1986) developed a typology of cross-class families which can be linked with the Youth Class typology, though it describes only the ways in which a husband may 'marry up'. Her 'Occupationally Upwardly Mobile Wife' can be seen as the result of marriage between a stable working-class husband and an educationally or

Table 9.6 Youth class in the GHS

Among all men and women, aged 16 to 29 years		
Youth class	Male %	Female %
Stable middle class	10	12
Education-mobile W–C	5	7
Counter-mobile M–C	8	2
Work-mobile W–C	9	3
Downwardly-mobile M–C	16	19
Stable working class	52	56
All (= 100%)	4760	4684

Source: GHS (1979; 1980)

work-route mobile working-class wife; her 'Occupationally Downwardly Mobile Husband' is the result of marriage between a stable middle-class wife and a downwardly mobile (possibly later to become counter-mobile) middle-class husband. Her 'Pure Cross-Class Family' in terms of the typology presented here would appear to consist of a stable working-class husband and a stable middle-class wife, where both class of background and current occupational class differ, and where there has been no visible inter or intragenerational mobility. Though the focus of the present analysis is somewhat different from that of McRae's study, these types can be identified in the following tables.

The Class Trajectories of Marriage Partners

Tables 9.7 and 9.8 result from a crosstabulation of wife's and husband's class trajectories in the GHS. Table 9.7 shows column and row percentages (showing absolute mobility) while Table 9.8 shows the standardized residuals from a model of no association (and thus shows relative mobility, controlling for the size of the marginal distributions). It should perhaps be pointed out that these tables have been derived using a modified data set which contained only couples *without children* where both were aged under 30 years; frequencies are therefore lower than in the previous tables which were based on individuals aged 16 to 30.

It is clear from Table 9.7 that there is a strong association between the class trajectories of marriage partners in terms of absolute rates. Over half of stable middle-class men and women marry partners with similarly stable class histories, and the pattern is even stronger among the stable working class. Class stability is therefore increased by such marriages. The picture is far less clear among the mobile groups, however; in particular, gender differences begin to appear. In order to understand the

Table 9.7 Class trajectories of marriage partners (%)

Among married couples both under 30 years with no children
Row percentages
Column percentages

Husband's class trajectory	Wife's class trajectory						
	STABLE M-C %	ED-MOB W-C %	C-MOB M-C %	WK-MOB W-C %	DOWNWD M-C %	STABLE W-C %	ALL %
Stable M-C	55 51	25 30	1 8	2 11	10 9	8 3	16 (93)
Education-mobile W-C	41 22	24 17	0 0	2 6	11 6	22 4	9 (54)
Counter-mobile M-C	13 7	13 9	2 8	4 11	24 14	46 9	10 (55)
Work-mobile W-C	12 7	10 8	7 31	2 6	15 9	56 13	11 (61)
Downward M-C	8 5	10 8	5 23	2 6	21 14	56 13	11 (63)
Stable W-C	4 9	9 29	2 31	4 61	18 48	63 59	44 (251)
All	18 (101)	13 (77)	2 (13)	3 (18)	17 (96)	47 (272)	100 (577)

Cramer's V = 0.27 Significance $p < 0.0001$

Source: GHS SIR Files (1979; 1980)

Table 9.8 Class trajectories of marriage partners

Among married couples both under 30 years with no children
Standardized residuals from a model of no association

Husband's class trajectory	STABLE M–C	ED–MOB W–C		Wife's class trajectory			
			C–MOB M–C	WK–MOB W–C	DOWNWD M–C	STABLE W–C
Stable M–C	8.6	3.0	–0.8	–0.5	–1.6	–5.6
Education-mobile W–C	4.1	2.2	–1.1	–0.5	–1.0	–2.7
Counter-mobile M–C	–0.8	–0.1	–0.2	0.2	1.3	–0.2
Work-mobile W–C	–1.1	–0.8	2.2	–0.7	–0.4	1.0
Downward M–C	–1.8	–0.8	1.3	–0.7	0.8	1.0
Stable W–C	–5.3	–2.0	–0.7	1.1	0.7	3.7

Source: Derived from Table 9.7, above.

relative rates of marital mobility, and control as far as possible for gender differences in the distributions of 'Youth Classes', we need to examine the standardized residuals.

Table 9.8 shows that even when the size of marginal distributions is controlled for, within the stable groups there is a strong relative tendency for endogamy. This occurs particularly within the stable middle class (the standardized residual is 8.6, compared with 3.7 among the stable working class). Similarly, it is shown to be relatively very unlikely for anyone, male or female, with a stable working-class trajectory to marry a partner in the stable middle class. Otherwise, the only group with a clear picture is the education-mobile of working-class origin: men and women in this group appear either to seek out others in the same group, or, relatively more frequently and more interestingly, to marry partners in the stable middle class. This is particularly the case among education-mobile men (standardized residual of 4.1, compared with 3.0 for women). The finding suggests that educationally-mobile men in particular may crystallize their new-found class position through marriage into the stable middle class.

Among the other mobile groups the picture is far more confusing. This is partly because very few married counter-mobile or work-mobile women have been identified in the data (they have been included in the table largely for the sake of symmetry). There appears to be a strong likelihood that counter-mobile women will marry men in the work-mobile group, but numbers are too small to be sure. Otherwise, there seems to be no significant association (with a standardized residual of plus or minus 2) between the class trajectories of partners in any of the mobile groups other than the education-mobile. There does seem to be some indication, though, that the downwardly-mobile middle class and the counter-mobile might be more likely to marry one another than members of other groups (the standardized residuals are both 1.3). It has been found earlier that some downwardly mobile men will regain middle-class status through counter-mobility (Jones 1987a). Counter-mobility is less available for women than for men and downwardly-mobile women tend, perhaps instead of seeking mobility through work-related routes, to marry earlier than other women of middle-class origin (Jones 1986). They may achieve counter-mobility through marriage instead. It is therefore interesting that they show a relative tendency to marry men who have been upwardly mobile or counter-mobile through work routes.

The table shows the degree of heterogeneity within current occupational class groupings. Although the stable middle class, the education-mobile, the counter-mobile and the work-mobile can all be described as currently middle class, their patterns of endogamy vary considerably. There is similar heterogeneity within the currently working class. The table shows the importance of a longitudinal approach to class if marital mobility is to be understood. The findings suggest that where class histories are complex, so too are patterns of mobility in marriage. In other words, people whose class trajectories have taken them across class boundaries, either in comparison with their father's class or within their own class careers, are just as likely to marry across class boundaries as well.

Conclusions

The empirical findings in this chapter began with an analysis of marital mobility on conventional lines, but focusing on men as well as women. The analysis then moved on to apply a measure of class trajectory to the analysis of partners' classes at marriage. The overall aim has been to question the assumptions underlying earlier studies of marital mobility and to consider whether there may be an alternative approach to the subject which may make a contribution to the debate on the class positions of men and women.

The study has shown that the class characteristics of the wife are as important as those of her husband or her father in a study of class endogamy. A wife's education and own occupational class at marriage affect her choice of spouse more than her class of origin. The longitudinal approach has revealed that marriage partners may often have similar class trajectories. People with stable class careers tend to marry one another, while those who are socially mobile continue their pattern of upward or downward mobility in their marriages. There is some evidence here that marital mobility could be a means of counter-mobility for women, though analysis is restricted by the data. It seems clear, however, that for men and women who are upwardly mobile through educational routes, marriage might be seen as a factor which consolidates achieved class. The education-mobile men and women from working-class origins tend to marry into the stable middle class. Similarly, but more surprisingly, many downwardly mobile middle-class men, far from retrieving their class position through marriage, appear to consolidate their loss of class status by marrying women in the lower manual classes. Further research is needed to examine the class identification of these men and women with complex class careers.

Marriage generally seems to occur between two partners of similar occupational class and education, who may be on similar class trajectories. Marital mobility reflecting different class trajectories appears to be most associated with downwardly mobile middle-class women. The earlier part of the analysis suggested that for some women marriage compensates for the relative absence of mobility routes for women through work and that, for those who are unable to achieve upward mobility through education or the work place, mobility through marriage may represent an alternative means of improving their class position.

The study of the social class of marriage partners at marriage is relevant to the debates concerning stratification by class and gender. It has been found that while a women's own occupational class is a better indicator of her life chances than that of her husband if she is in full-time work, this is not the case among part-time workers, or of course housewives. Arber (1987), for example, found that a husband's occupational class is a better predictor of a wife's health status than her own occupational class unless she is in full-time paid work. The notion of ascribing a wife's social class according to the occupational class of her husband is problematic because it overlooks inequalities within the home (Brannen and Wilson, 1987). It could, however, be argued, following the findings in this chapter, that a husband's occupational class may be an appropriate proxy variable for that of the wife where she is not in paid work, or where her occupational class has become lower as a result of disruptions to her working career, *in some circumstances*. These circumstances are likely to be where the wife had a stable class career before childbirth. Where the wife's class trajectory crossed class boundaries before childbirth and marriage, her husband's current occupational class is less likely, whatever her own employment status, to reflect her class position.

Notes

1 The work which forms the basis of this chapter was largely completed under an ESRC linked PhD studentship in the Department of Sociology at the University of Surrey, where Sara Arber and Nigel Gilbert embarked me on a research career. I am grateful to OPCS and the ESRC Data Archive for the use of the GHS. My thanks to all who have commented on earlier drafts, to Charlie Owen who helped me extend the analysis later, by providing me with a hierarchial data set, and to Lindsay Paterson at CES who provided statistical advice.
2 I am grateful to John Goldthorpe for comments on an earlier draft drawing my attention to the need for loglinear modelling here. The following analysis is based on data in Tables 9.3 and 9.4.

Model	d.f.	Residual deviances	
		Males	Females
Independence model	20	190.7	174.8
Respondent-Spouse class only	16	99.4	69.0
Father-Spouse class only	16	154.8	137.9
Respondent-Spouse, Father-Spouse	12	63.5	32.1
All 2-way associations	8	13.1	5.2

The above table shows that the Respondent-Spouse association is the single most important association for men and woman alike. Father-Spouse association is weak (equally weak for both sexes). Adding Father-Spouse after Respondent-Spouse leads to a bigger percentage reduction for women than for men, mainly because of women in Classes 1 and 2 as explained in the text. The most parsimonious acceptable model fits all three 2-way associations. In all, the loglinear analysis thus confirms the earlier findings from the cross-tabulations shown.

Chapter 10

Occupational Mobility over Women's Lifetime

Shirley Dex

Women's lifetime occupational mobility is significant for a number of reasons. Two main areas of importance are considered in this paper, labour market theories and class analysis based on social mobility studies. Both of these sets of theories have been obliged to evaluate women's place, partly in the light of their increased labour market participation, but also in response to feminist criticisms. As far as labour market theories are concerned, women and gender divisions have been incorporated only into segmented labour market theories, and then in ways which are not entirely satisfactory. Also, a better conceptualization of women's place within segmented labour market theories has been lacking lifetime occupational mobility data for women (and for men), which is a necessary basis on which appropriate sectors and their interrelationships could be mapped out. To the extent that social mobility analyses provide a foundation for class analysis, mobility over a lifetime is also an important aspect of the discussion. Women's employment and occupational mobility have been used by some to justify ignoring their class position (if they are married) (e.g. Goldthorpe, 1983). However, it is this author's view that an understanding of women's lifetime and life-cycle mobility is a necessary foundation for the conceptual developments which are required to understand women's place in class analysis, a view elaborated elsewhere (Dex, 1990). As Payne (1987a, b) has argued convincingly, labour market and social class analyses are two aspects of the same sociological interest. Thus, the way individuals are allocated to certain occupations and move within and between them is the subject matter of labour market theories, but clearly, these same mechanisms must to a large extent underlie social mobility and class analyses.

This chapter seeks to examine women's lifetime occupational mobility as a way of providing a better understanding of women's place in labour markets, and hence in the class structure. The main features of women's lifetime occupational patterns are documented with a view to showing in what sense women have careers, how their occupational mobility varies over the life-cycle, in what sense labour market sectors exist, and how labour market mechanisms which affect women underlie their social mobility and class positions. The chapter does not engage in extensive reviews of the relevant literature because it is covered elsewhere in this volume. However, a few points about existing segmented labour market theories are worth making. When these theories were imported into Britain from North America, a brief examination of some of the characteristics of women workers in the aggregate led to the claim that British women fitted the description of secondary workers; women had lower pay than men, they were concentrated in unskilled and insecure jobs, they were said to be more likely to be made redundant than men and less likely to be upwardly mobile (Barron and Norris, 1976; Bosanquet and Doeringer, 1973). Some studies took up this framework and made empirical investigations, in the first instance of men's work, (Blackburn and Mann, 1979), or carried out tests of bimodality in the distribution of earnings, (Psacharopoulos, 1978). For a more extensive review of the segmented labour market literature, see Piore (1975) and Loveridge and Mok (1979).

Feminists and others have not been slow to criticize the role attributed to women in this framework. One criticism is that women are treated as a homogeneous mass of workers located in a single segment which is rather a crude conceptualization (Beechey, 1978). Other criticisms are that the theories are not sufficiently specific about women's positions in the industrial and occupational structures; nor do they explain the post-war expansion in Britain of large numbers of women's jobs in the state sector, because the theories tend to concentrate on manufacturing industires (Beechey, 1978). Segmented labour market theories have also been criticized for underestimating the role of trade unions and not recognizing the extent to which unions can constrain the capacity of capital to pursue rational labour market strategies. Rubery (1978) extended this latter point by arguing that too much attention has been paid, in the initial American version of the theory, to the actions and motivations of capitalists. The facts about women's employment experiences do not always fit with the descriptions of the models; in particular, women do not appear to be more vulnerable than men in general. Their location in the services sector and in part-time work turns out to have given them a measure of security and protection *vis-a-vis* full-time male workers (Dex and Perry, 1984). Over time, and sometimes even coincident with the criticisms, research work has emerged which has countered some of these criticisms (Edwards, 1979; Bonacich, 1976), although some of this work can still be criticized for the way it treats women. Some other small-scale pieces of empirical work on particular industries have been helping to uncover more of the processes underlying women's occupational segregation in Britain. These studies all confirm the need to have empirical grounding to replace speculative theorizing about women's work including part-time work, if a useful and accurate theory is to emerge (e.g. Coyle, 1982; Armstrong, 1982; Craig *et al*. 1982; Rubery and Wilkinson, 1980; Craig *et al*., 1985; Craig and Wilkinson 1985; Brown, 1982; Dale *et al*., 1984).

This paper seeks to contribute to filling in some of the gaps by examining women's work histories in an attempt to plot out some of the labour market structures where women participate. An investigation of women's occupational mobility over the life-cycle also has the additional advantage that it provides an empirical base for life-cycle theories which in the past have been lacking. There is still a need for a framework which integrates both women's and men's labour market experiences, but unfortunately, that cannot be the focus of this chapter.

The Women and Employment Survey

Information about women's employment histories became available through the Women and Employment Survey (WES) carried out by the Department of Employment and Office of Population Censuses and Surveys in 1980. The WES data were the first systematic large-scale recording in Britain of women's employment and occupational histories over their whole life up to the interview. It contained the employment histories of 5,320 women between the ages of 16 and 59 in 1980. In addition, women were asked a series of questions about their current status at the interview. (Further details about the sample and response rates etc. can be found in Martin and Roberts (1984, Technical Appendix)). The availability of these data has meant that a nationally representative sample of British women's employment experiences could then be documented. The fact that women were of a range of ages meant that different amounts of information are available, and some problems of analysis arise from this fact.

A restricted range of occupations (12) were used to classify women's jobs.[1] Some of the problems attached to these groupings are described in Dex (1987). It was possible to merge this occupational record with the life and family events of the women. The fact that this information relies on memory recall raises certain questions about its accuracy. As far as it is possible to tell, the data seem to be of a high quality. Martin and Roberts (1984) add, however, that 'some caution should be attached to the interpretation of retrospective information'.

The twelve occupational categories set a limit to the occupational movements which we can see in these data. If we had a larger number of categories, we might be able to see more movements between them. Since we are hoping to identify patterns of occupational movements, it could be argued that the patterns are therefore dependent on the set of occupational categories used. One way of testing whether any identified patterns are artefacts of the categories or whether they reflect women's experiences is to see if examples can be found of each pattern in other sources; for example, in case studies. Checking of this sort confirmed that the patterns found were realistic (Dex 1987).

Women's Occupations and Life-cycle Occupational Mobility

Women have tended to be located in a narrow range of occupations, notably clerical work, semi-skilled factory work and semi-skilled domestic work. The WES data illustrates this. Table 10.1 shows the distribution of women through the WES occupational categories for women in Britain in 1980. In 1980, 30 per cent of all employed women were in clerical jobs, 10 per cent were in semi-skilled factory work and 11 per cent were in semi-skilled domestic jobs. The proportion of women in semi-skilled factory jobs has been declining as the size of manufacturing employment has been declining. Of the women employed in part-time jobs, however, 20 per cent were in semi-skilled domestic work and only 20 per cent were in clerical jobs. Other sources also show that women constitute a high proportion of certain occupational categories. For example, women constitute as much as 75 per cent of the workforce of typists, secretaries, canteen workers, office cleaners, hairdressers and some other occupations (Joseph, 1983). More precise measures of the extent of occupational segregation have been developed to capture and measure precisely the extent of this concentration (Hakim, 1979).

The Women and Employment Survey also asked women whether women or men did the same sort of work as they did at their workplace. The replies are another measure of the extent of occupational segregation. Table 10.2 is taken from Martin and Roberts (1984), the official report of the WES data, and the figures show the large extent to which women are employed in jobs where only women are employed. However, the results vary by occupation, and by the hours worked. Teachers had the lowest proportion who worked only with women, 25 per cent. The highest

Table 10. 1 Occupations of employed women in WES in 1980

	Full-time %	Part-time %	Total %
Professional	1	1	1
Teaching	8	3	6
Nursing, medical and social	7	6	7
Other intermediate non-manual	9	3	6
Clerical	39	20	30
Sales	6	12	9
Skilled manual	8	6	7
Semi-skilled factory	13	7	10
Semi-skilled domestic	4	20	11
Other semi-skilled	3	5	4
Unskilled	2	17	9
Total	100	100	100
N thousands	1.877	1.477	3.354

Source: Martin and Roberts (1984, p. 23)

Table 10.2 Proportions of full and part-time employed women in different occupation groups according to whether only women do same work. (Sample in parentheses)

Occupations	% of women in 'women only' jobs					
	Full-time		Part-time		Total	
Teaching	24	(148)	32	(38)	25	(186)
Nursing, medical & social	42	(120)	46	(90)	44	(210)
Other intermediate non-manual	42	(131)	*		42	(153)
Clerical	64	(691)	80	(241)	68	(932)
Sales	54	(111)	67	(168)	62	(279)
Skilled manual	66	(136)	77	(78)	70	(214)
Semi-skilled factory	76	(245)	78	(93)	73	(338)
Semi-skilled domestic	70	(64)	79	(261)	78	(325)
Other semi-skilled	50	(58)	40	(52)	45	(110)
Unskilled	59	(44)	77	(232)	74	(276)

*Too small to show percentages
Source: WES Martin and Roberts (1984, Table 3.10.)

proportion who worked only with women were the semi-skilled domestic employees, 78 per cent. There is clearly a tendency for lower level occupations to be more highly segregated and for part timers within occupations to be more highly segregated than full timers. We can now consider the valuable work history data contained in WES in order to complement the picture of women's place in the occupational structure which can be gained from cross-sectional descriptions. If there is no change over women's life-cycles in their occupations, then the cross-sectional snapshot picture will be fairly complete. However, if as is the case, women experience occupational mobility over their life cycle, then a different picture will emerge from looking at the work-history ciné-picture.

An analysis of women's lifetime occupations from these data enabled a set of occupational profiles to be identified and described. The precise methods used to identify such profiles are described elsewhere Dex (1984b), and a full description of the set of the profiles and their frequencies can be found in Dex (1987). These descriptions are not repeated here since they are not central to the main point of this paper. Some of the results which emerged during the identification of women's occupational profiles are important for the task in hand, however, and these are described below.

The examination of women's lifetime occupational histories revealed that women have preferences for certain sorts of work and that an occupational ranking can take place based on these preferences. The ranking turns out to overlap with a ranking based on the earnings gained in these occupations, although it does not always coincide with what would be thought to be conventional rankings. Women were also seen to have attachments to certain occupations, although not to others. Occupations which displayed a large measure of attachment were clerical, skilled, semi-skilled factory, teaching and nursing. The attachments were displayed by women moving between jobs in these occupations voluntarily. Most job-changing is voluntary. When women lost their desired occupation involuntarily and ended up in a different occupation for their next job, these jobs were often short-lived, and women returned as soon as possible, it seemed, to their original occupation. Thus women's preferences persisted through disruptions and over childbirth.

The ranking of occupations which emerged from this exercise, and which overlaps with an earnings hierarchy provided by Joshi (1984) for these data is as follows:

1 Professional/Teacher
2 Nursing
3 Intermediate non-manual
4 Clerical
5 Skilled
6 Semi-skilled factory
7 All other occupations (i.e. sales, child care, semi-skilled domestic, other semi-skilled and unskilled).

Downward occupational mobility consists of any move down this scale, or any move from a supervisor to non-supervisor status. Upward mobility is, of course, the reverse. In practice, many of the upward moves were solely a move to supervisor status within the same occupation. However, almost all downward moves consisted of changes in occupational category. The professional occupations are grouped together with teachers in this list because there were so few women professionals in this sample. Similarly, at the other end of the scale, some unskilled jobs may be of a lower rank than other semi-skilled jobs, but it was difficult to distinguish between unskilled and many semi-skilled jobs in this survey. Perhaps the most surprising feature of this list is that sales work comes at the bottom of the list alongside other semi-skilled jobs and below other manual occupations. Sales has conventionally been classified as non-manual employment and has had a status above manual work. It is clear from these women's data that sales is at the bottom of women's preference ranking but also near the bottom of the earnings ranking. We should perhaps consider a reclassification of most women's sales work to be alongside low-level manual work in consequence. On the basis of this ranking, women's lifetime occupational mobility could be quantified and the results of this exercise are described below under two headings. We can examine the two types of vertical occupational mobility; downward and upward.

Vertical Occupational Mobility

The amounts of downward occupational mobility are listed in Table 10.3 for women of different ages. The figures display the proportions of women in each age group who

Table 10.3 Downward occupational mobility

Number of downward occupational transitions	Age group, Percentage				
	16–19	20–29	30–39	40–49	50–59
At least *ONE*	12	37	52	57	61
At least *TWO*	—	10	15	20	22
At least *THREE*	—	2	3	5	7
N = number in age group who have worked	303	1232	1410	1135	1157

had at some stage in their employment history experienced either one or more downward moves. Not surprisingly the percentage of women who have ever experienced downward occupational mobility increased as their age increased; obviously, the longer is one's employment record, the more chance there is of experiencing occupational mobility of any kind. In the over 50s group, 61 per cent of the women had had at least one experience of downward mobility whereas only 37 per cent of women aged 20 to 29 had had this experience. Experiencing two or more moves down the occupational scale over a lifetime was rare and only 7 per cent of the 50 to 59 age group had at least three experiences of downward mobility.

An examination of the sub-groups of women with children and childless women (figures not shown) revealed that the former have had more experiences of downward mobility than the latter; 59 per cent of women aged 40–49 with children, but only 45 per cent of childless women had had at least one downward move; the gap is maintained irrespective of age. We would have expected this finding on the basis of other studies. What is perhaps more surprising is that the gap is not wider. We might have expected childless women to have far less experience of downward mobility. The fact that half of them have had this experience by the end of their working life suggests that there are some important causes, other than childbirth. In the case of the 50–59 year age group, being demobbed after the war could have produced this experience. The fact that 45 per cent of childless women aged 40–49 also had at least one experience of downward occupational mobility suggests that the large frequencies cannot be attributable to special circumstances like the war. Childless women appear to have their experience of downward mobility mainly between the ages of 20 and 40 since, after that age, the figures hardly increase. The question of what causes this mobility, if it is not childbirth, will be examined below.

The amounts of upward occupational mobility are displayed in Table 10.4. There is an increase in the frequence with age, and experiencing two or more upwardly mobile moves is far less likely than experiencing one such move. By the end of their

Table 10.4 Upward occupational mobility

Number of upward occupational transitions	Age group, Percentage				
	16–19	20–29	30–39	40–49	50–59
At least *ONE*	17	40	51	57	63
At least *TWO*	1	12	18	22	28
At least *THREE*	—	3	5	8	9
N = number in age group who have worked	303	1232	1410	1135	1157

working lives, however, 63 per cent of these women had had at least one upwardly mobile move. Childless women had more occurences of upward moves than women with children, especially between the ages of 30 and 39 (figures not shown).

One of the most interesting features of the quantities of upward occupational mobility listed in Table 10.4 is their similarity in size to the frequencies of downward occupational mobility. For each age group there appears to be similar amounts of downward and upward occupational mobility. However, approximately one-fifth of upward mobility consists of movements into supervisor status whereas very few of the downward occupational movements are solely movements out of supervisor status. The marked increase with age of an upward mobility experience again disappears when the 54 women are excluded whose experience resulted from their working during the war. These figures do not reveal whether the women who experienced downward occupational mobility were the same ones to experience upward occupational mobility.

An examination of both types of vertical mobility illustrated that the upward (or downward) occupational mobility figures on their own would not represent women's experience on the occupational hierarchy. What seemed most likely was that downward movements are followed by upward moves which are a retrieval of an earlier status which is lost during their work cycle. This pattern was part of the description of profiles and their disruptions referred to earlier. The figures illustrate that having children decreases a woman's chance of upward occupational mobility and increases the chance of downward occupational mobility. However, there are sufficiently large proportions of women with children experiencing upward occupational mobility and childless women experiencing downward occupational mobility to indicate, again, that differences in women's experiences of childbirth are by no means the whole explanation of different experiences of vertical occupational mobility.

Timing of Vertical Occupational Mobility

We have already seen something of the way experiences of vertical occupational mobility occur at different ages. Both downward and upward mobility showed marked increases in frequency when women were between the ages of 20 and 40. The fact that women with children had more experiences of downward mobility than childless women gave the impression that childbirth and childrearing are causes of downward occupational mobility but this may not be the case. We can be more precise about the timing of women's experiences of vertical mobility since the complete work history records of these women were available. An examination of the timing of downward mobility will help to locate the origin of the experience more precisely.

The timing of vertical mobility experiences over the life cycle of women with children is displayed in Table 10.5. Here, women's life-cycle experiences are split into four stages; up to their first birth; their last job before their first birth to the first job after childbirth; any returns to work between childbirths after the first; and job changes since the return after their last child. These figures are the percentages of all experiences of vertical occupational mobility, including supervisor changes, which occurred during the various work-cycle phases. The base on which these percentages are calculated, therefore, is *not* the number of women with such an experience, but the number of vertical occupational movements for this group of women, and some women, as we have seen, have more than one move.

The age groups over 30 have a fairly stable pattern of downward occupational mobility experiences. Approximately one third of the moves took place during the initial work phase before childbirth and another quarter over the first break for childbirth. In the case of women who are old enough to have finished their childrearing phase (40–59 years), both have approximately one quarter of their downward occupational mobility experiences in their final work phase — the rest being between births. In the younger age groups, under 30, downward occupational mobility was relatively more frequent before childbirth, presumably because these women have not progressed very far through their work cycle.

The amount of downward occupational mobility occurring over the childrearing phase is by far the greatest; 40–45 per cent of all downward moves occurred at this time for most age groups. The percentage of downward moves which occurred over the transition from the last job before childbirth to the first job after childbirth, is very high at 25 per cent. This is a very high proportion when we remember that this is a single occupational transition. The other phases can cover a large number of job changes and therefore, at least in theory, a higher absolute number of experiences of vertical occupational mobility. Thus the findings provide some support for Chaney's (1981) findings from her small-scale study, that much of the downward occupational mobility took place over the first childbirth break. It must be noted however, that childbirth is far from being the only significant time when women experience

Table 10.5 Timing of occupational mobility for women aged 20–59, with children

| | Age groups at interview — per cent | | | | | | | |
| Timing of occupational mobility | Downward mobility | | | | Upward mobility | | | |
	20-29	30-39	40-49	50-59	20-29	30-39	40-49	50-59
Up to first birth	52	36	33	35	74	53	41	43
First birth to first return	17	25	24	22	4	6	7	10
Second or later births to return after last child	23	20	17	15	9	14	11	9
Since last child	8	19	26	28	13	27	41	38
Total	100	100	100	100	100	100	100	100
N* =	371	868	860	903	334	869	871	1006

* Sample consists of total number of vertical occupational changes.

downward occupational mobility and that over half of these experiences take place outside the childrearing phase.

The pattern which emerges from the upward occupational mobility figures in Table 10.5 is quite different from the timing of the downward movements. There is again some variation with age which is a result of the different stage of completion of the work cycle. Upward occupational mobility most frequently occurs during the initial work phase or during the final work phase for women who have children. Approximately 80 per cent of upward occupational mobility movements take place during these two phases, with slightly higher proportions during the initial work phase. It is still the case that upward mobility during the initial work phase can be a retrieval of status lost by a disruption, for example, by moving at marriage, rather than being an indicator of occupational advancement — although some of the latter does occur. Some of the upward moves prior to childbirth are promotions to supervisor status. Upward occupational mobility occurs least frequently over the first break for childbirth; only 6–10 per cent of all cases. It is perhaps worth noting, however, that there is some upward occupational mobility over family formation.

These two sets of figures provide a consistent picture; a large amount of downward occupational mobility occurs over the childbirth phase and only a small amount of upward occupational mobility. Much of the downward and upward occupational mobility cancels out for these women rather than showing a net decline or improvement in status. Very few of the jobs held before childbirth were part-time jobs so that downward occupational mobility during this phase, which is approximately one third of all downward movements, cannot be linked to women's part-time working status. On the other hand, the higher proportion of upward mobility which occurs during the initial work phase may be linked to the predominance of full-time jobs at this time.

Much of women's downward occupational mobility occurs, as we have seen, across their first break from work for childbirth. The occupational transitions between the last job before childbirth and the first job after childbirth are displayed in Table 10.6 for all women who had ever returned to work after having at least one child. The diagonal elements reveal the proportions of those who set out in a certain occupation who retained their occupational status at their first return to work. The sizes of the diagonal elements show that teachers are most likely to retain their status (as are professionals but they are a very small group); at this time 85 per cent of women who were teachers before childbirth were still in teaching at their first return to work after childbirth. Over one half of nurses and semi-skilled factory workers also retained their status. Intermediate non-manual, sales, childcare, and other semi-skilled workers have the least chance of being in the same occupation after childbirth; these occupations experienced large outflows. At most, 39 per cent of women who were in these semi-skilled occupations before childbirth were still in them afterwards.

Most of the movement out of occupations at the top of the list is downward

Table 10.6 *Occupational transitions between last job before childbirth and first job after* *

| | First job after childbirth | | | | | | | | | | | | | |
	Professional	Teacher	Nurse	Inter-mediate non-manual	Clerical	Sales	Skilled	Child Care	Semi-Skilled factory	Semi-Skilled Domestic	Other Semi-Skilled	Unskilled	Total	N =
Professional	91	–	–	–	9	–	–	–	–	–	–	–	100	71
Teacher	–	85	2	2	1	4	4	1	1	1	–	–	100	115
Nurse	3	3	61	1	6	7	4	3	1	10	3	2	100	160
Intermediate non manual	3	3	3	39	19	19	–	2	2	5	3	5	100	62
Clerical	1	1	2	2	49	14	3	4	6	11	3	6	100	964
Sales	–	–	4	2	8	37	3	4	11	14	6	10	100	376
Skilled	–	–	4	3	6	10	43	3	12	7	2	11	100	240
Childcare	–	–	–	–	–	19	6	13	25	19	6	13	100	16
Semi-skilled factory	–	–	1	–	3	10	3	2	52	12	4	14	100	754
Semi-skilled domestic	–	–	2	–	3	8	6	–	17	43	5	16	100	126
Other semi-skilled	–	–	–	–	1	3	3	3	12	14	39	19	100	142
Unskilled	–	–	–	2	5	–	–	–	12	24	7	50	100	42
Proportion of each first return occupation which is part-time job	82	56	71	54	63	72	60	86	53	83	64	94		N = 3008

* Sample All women with children who have ever returned to work after childbirth, excluding any occupations inadequately described.

vertical mobility. There is a small amount of upward mobility. Much of the movement at the bottom of the list of occupations is horizontal mobility between the various types of semi-skilled work. The vast majority of the jobs in the first three of these occupations are part time, as the bottom row of the table illustrates. These results suggest that there is a relationship between the experience of downward occupational mobility and the move to part-time work, but this needs to be tested in the context of a multivariate model. Such a model is described in Dex (1987). The results showed that moving to a part-time job after childbirth increased women's chance of downward mobility by approximately 30 per cent.

The figures in Table 10.7 show, for women with the longest work history records (aged 40–59), the proportions who experienced downward occupational mobility on their first return to work after childbirth. The figures in Table 10.7 are something of a summary of those in Table 10.6, although they differ in that the origin refers to particular occupations in Table 10.6. In Table 10.7 the origin refers to women who stayed in the occupation specified throughout their work history prior to childbirth; that is they had the specified occupational profile.

Table 10.7 Downward occupational mobility over childbirth and status recovery for women aged 40–59

Profile before childbirth	Per cent experiencing downward mobility at first return after childbirth	Per cent recovering status after losing it over childbirth
Teacher	19	0
Nurse	43	19
Clerical	37	32
Skilled	42	32
Semi-skilled factory	15	95
All other semi-skilled	11*	28
Total N	1780	1780

*Based on unskilled work being downward occupational mobility from the rest of the semi-skilled occupations.

The results in Table 10.7 confirm that teachers have a very low likelihood of experiencing downward occupational mobility across childbirth. Also, semi-skilled factory work appears to be subject to relatively little occupational downgrading over the childbirth break. The figures showing the percentage recovery are also displayed in Table 10.7. There we see that semi-skilled factory workers can most easily recover their status if they lost it; 95 per cent did recover their status. Teachers who lose their status have little chance of recovering status and the rest lie somewhere between.

Conclusions

Several patterns of women's occupational mobility emerge from this analysis of the WES data, each different from the mobility experiences of men. These patterns result from the combination of women's supply-side preferences and constraints which vary over their life-cycle, with the structure of labour market opportunities; the structure has in parts moulded itself around women's acceptance of child-care responsibilities over the family formation period through the growth of part-time work. In this sense, labour market opportunities are not just a given of the situation, but they can, and do, evolve to capitalize on the sexual division of labour. Women's priorities also appear to vary over their life-cycle. Much downward occupational mobility resulted from women taking part-time jobs after childbirth. At the same time women were also found to exhibit occupational attachment and preferences in the way they returned to their chosen occupations, even after temporary disruptions and downward mobility. Thus, recovery of lost occupational status was common. In this sense they have lifetime occupational attachments which might reasonably be called careers. Certain parts of the labour market exhibit less mobility than others. Both the likelihood of downward mobility and any subsequent recovery were related to the origin occupations, and teachers were the most likely to retain their status over the whole of the life cycle. Thus there are certain occupations which offer women careers, despite any break for childbirth, and where a type of internal labour market is more highly developed.

These results point to a model of labour market structures and segmentation,

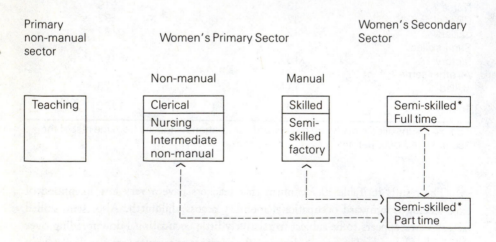

*Semi-skilled includes selling, child care, semi-skilled domestic, other semi-skilled, unskilled and a very few semi-skilled factory or low grade clerical.

Figure 10.1 Labour market segmentation and women's employment.

although one which applies mostly to the women's labour markets. In part, this structure has been seen to form around the acceptance of an interruption in women's labour market participation for childbirth. Rather than women being in a single undifferentiated sector as the crude versions of segmented labour market theories suggested, women's occupational histories suggest that a more complex structure of market segments exists for women. The basic structure of such a model is displayed in Figure 10.1, although the model may be limited to some extent by the range of WES occupational categories. In outline it captures the broad dimensions of women's position in labour market structures in Britain over the past few decades and it is consistent with women's occupational segregation.

Women can be found, firstly, in the *Primary Non-Manual Sector*, when they have teaching jobs. Women and men share these jobs which have many of the characteristics of primary jobs in the original dual labour market formulation; notably, they have internal labour markets, lower turnover, higher pay and promotion prospects. Some types of trained nursing jobs may also be part of this sector, although there is a higher degree of segregation in nursing jobs than in teaching (Table 10.2). Women have a primary sector of their own, the *Women's Primary Sector*, which is a sexually segregated sector on the whole. it has two divisions within it, the non-manual occupations of clerical, nursing and intermediate non-manual, and the manual occupations of skilled and semi-skilled factory. All are full-time jobs. On the whole, there is little movement between occupations in each sub-group; clerical workers tend to stay in clerical work; for example, and semi-skilled factory workers stay in semi-skilled factory work. When mobility does occur, the movement is largely out of full-time occupations, either non-manual or manual, into the part-time areas of the *Women's Secondary Sector*. Some return mobility takes place, and these women return to their former occupations in the women's primary sector; it is by no means all women who recover their status after a move into the part-time secondary sector.

The *Women's Secondary Sector* contains the occupations which constitute the semi-skilled profile: selling; childcare; semi-skilled domestic; other semi-skilled; unskilled and some cases of semi-skilled factory and low-level clerical work. It is a sexually segregated sector with two divisions; one is a sub-sector of full-time jobs and the other a sector of part-time jobs. Part-time jobs are not necessarily higher turnover jobs however, particularly when in service industries. The part-time and full-time jobs are largely in the same occupations with similar amounts of sexual segregation although, again, the sub-sectors are distinguishable because the part-time jobs have lower rates of pay, worse conditions of service and fewer benefits than the full-time jobs. Movement occurs between the full-time and part-time sectors; most of the movement is into part-time largely over women's break from work for childbirth. In this way, the part-time sector is one which is formed to coincide with life-cycle variations in women's employment.

The broad outlines of labour market segmentation for women's employment have been documented above. On the basis of women's work histories, it has been possible to identify sectors and sub-sectors and the mobility channels between them, although this schema may well be able to be refined with better data. It is also worth noting that women seem to be aware of a ranking of these sectors which puts primary non-manual at the top of the list and women's secondary sector jobs at the bottom. Their choices from leaving school onwards reflect this ranking, and the occupational profiles identified result largely when women are successful in the pursuit of their preferences. Semi-skilled profiles probably result more from the failure to successfully achieve their occupational choices than from a positive choice.

Men and women differ considerably from each other both at the point of entry into the labour market and in their subsequent experiences. They exhibit the greatest degree of similarity when they enter the primary non-manual sector. The greatest degree of dissimilarity can be seen in the development of the part-time women's secondary sector. In this respect, a sexually divided labour market has emerged in Britain built around a sexual division of labour and responsibility within the home. (There have been state inducements for this growth, primarily through employers' insurance contributions.) Women and men might both expect to experience upward vertical occupational mobility over their lifetime. For men, the moves would be expected to be cumulative and consolidating, whereas for women upward moves are more likely to be the recovery of lost status.

The study of women's social mobility needs to have a clear understanding of their life-cycle mobility patterns if it is to avoid confusing different types of mobility. Of course, the objectives of any study will be important for directing data collection and subsequent analyses. It is important to remember that women employed over their family formation period, or shortly after returning to work, are likely to be in jobs which under-represent their potential and their lifetime career preferences. That they may have experienced temporary downward social mobility will be important in studies concerned with current household income, poverty, lifestyle and consumption patterns. However, such mobility will probably not be important in the socialization process, as operated through the family, or its property transmission over generations etc. In the case of these latter interests, women's position may best be represented either by their 'best' lifetime social class, their education, or in some cases (the small group of married women who are and intend to stay permanently out of the labour market) their husband's or father's class position. If the interest is in women's class formation and potential for class action, based on the extent of their social mobility, one would need to extend the traditional studies in a number of ways. As well as comparing father's class position with the women's own best class, the amount of class formation for women would also be likely to be influenced by the extent to which they had deviated from their 'best' class position and also whether the best position had been recovered, if it had been lost. In the light of the occupational mobility documented in this paper, one might predict that class formation amongst women would be greatest where a number of circumstances converge; where women's fathers were in semi-skilled or skilled manual employment, where women's best occupation was in the same groups, and where women had not experienced any downward occupational mobility, or part-time work; class formation and action amongst higher grade semi-professional women is also conceivable, given the same relationships and constraints.

Notes

The details of the occupational categories are as follows:

1 *Professional occupations*
   Barristers, solicitors, chartered and certified accountants, university teachers, doctors, dentists, physicists, chemists, social scientists, pharmacists, dispensing opticians, qualified engineers, architects, town planners, civil servants — Assistant Secretary level and above.

2 *Teachers*
   Primary and secondary school teachers, teachers in further and higher education (not universities), head teachers, nursery teachers, vocational and industrial trainers.

3 *Nursing, medical and social occupations*
   SRN, SEN, nursing auxilliary, midwife, health visitor, children's nurse, matron/superintendent, dental nurse, dietician, radiographer, physiotherapist, chiropodist, dispenser, medical technician, houseparents, welfare occupations (including social workers), occupational therapist.

4 *Other intermediate non-manual occupations*
   Civil Servants — Executive Officer to Senior Principal level and equivalent in central and local government, computer programmer, systems analyst, O & M analyst, librarian, surveyor, personnel officer, managers, self-employed farmers, shopkeepers, publicans, hoteliers, buyers, company secretary, author, writer, journalist, artist, designer, window dresser, entertainer, musician, actress.

5 *Clerical occupations*
   Typist, secretary, shorthand writer, clerk, receptionist, personal assistant, cashier, (not retail), telephonist receptionist, office machine operator, computer operator, punch card operator, data processor, draughtswoman, tracer, market research interviewer, debt collector.

6 *Shop assistant and related sales occupations*
   People selling goods in wholesale or retail establishments, cashiers, in retail shops, check out and cash and wrap operators, petrol pump attendant, sales representative, demonstrator, theatre/cinema usherette, programme seller, insurance agent.

7 *Skilled occupations*
   Hairdresser, manicurist, beautician, make-up artist, cook, domestic and institution housekeeper, nursery nurse, travel stewardess, ambulance woman, van driver and deliveries, baker, weaver, knitter, mender, darner, tailoress and dressmaker (whole garment), clothing cutter, milliner, upholsterer, bookbinder, precision instrument maker and repairer, instrument assemblers, laboratory assistant, driving instructor, policewoman.

8 *Childcare occupations*
   Childminder, school meals and playgroup supervisor or leader, nanny, au pair, people doing housework in addition to childcare (NB exclude nursing and teaching).

9 *Semi-skilled factory work*
   Assembler, packer, labeller, grader, sorter, inspector, machinist, machine operator, paper wrapping, filling or sealing containers, spinner, doubler, twister, winder, reeler.

10   *Semi-skilled domestic work*
     Waitress, barmaid, canteen assistant, people serving food at tables or counters, serving school meals, home help, care attendant, ward orderly, housemaid, domestic worker.

11   *Other semi-skilled occupations*
     Agricultural workers, groom, kennel maid, shelf filler, bus conductress, ticket collector, post woman, mail sorter, laundress, dry cleaner, presser, mail order and catalogue agent, market and street trader, collector saleswoman, traffic warden, telephone operator, photographer.

12   *Unskilled occupations*
     Cleaner, char woman, kitchen hand, labourer, messenger.

Chapter 11

Stratification over the Life-course: Gender Differences within the Household

Angela Dale

This chapter argues for a widening of the definition of stratification (and therefore, by implication, of mobility) to incorporate 'all aspects of structured inequality' (Blackburn, 1980) rather than the much narrower definition used by Lockwood (1986) which limits stratification to a concern with traditional class analysis.[1] There is nothing very new in making this argument: Newby (1982 p. 18), in his report on the state of research into social stratification, endorses both Townsend and Pahl in suggesting the need to incorporate into stratification research alternative 'resource systems', such as household economies, and to examine the extent to which the costs of the 1979/81 recession were borne by different 'minority groups'. This is not to deny the importance of class analysis but to argue that, by following Pahl in taking the household as a social and economic unit, it becomes possible to widen the area of analysis to incorporate all members of society and to examine levels of resources and the system of distribution (both within and between households), as well as that of production. Pahl (1988 p. 253) goes on to suggest that 'This emphasis on the *household* as the salient social and economic unit, rather than the individual, has important implications for contemporary social structure', leading to a move away from the hierarchically structured pyramid based on individual jobs.

This is not, however, to argue for retaining the conventional approach to class anlaysis (eg., Goldthorpe, 1983) whereby all household members are allocated the class position of the main earner, but instead, to argue for an approach which locates *the individual within the household context*. Such an approach recognizes that there may be neither consensus nor equality between household members, and that individuals within the same household may differ markedly in the level of resources at their disposal. Nonetheless, by locating the individual *within* the household context, it recognizes the importance of interactions between household members (e.g., husband/wife; mother/child) and also the way in which household assets (total income; car ownership) may set the parameters which constrain the assets available to an individual. The reasons for this approach will be developed in the following pages.

It is also important to develop a concept of stratification and mobility which can locate individuals within a longitudinal or life-course perspective. Such a conceptualization is greatly facilitated by taking a more holistic view of stratification, as suggested above, and also by using a two level approach in which the individual is located within the household context. This then brings into play the tension in most stratification research between the individual and the family/household as the unit of analysis.

By recognizing the household as the unit of productive capacity, one can incorporate into the analysis both paid and unpaid work and bridge the gap between the productive and domestic spheres (Finch, 1983). By also taking a life-course perspective one becomes forced to recognize the importance of household composition, the changing relationship of household members to the labour market, the way in which this affects the generation of income and assets over time and how this creates successive states within a mobility pattern. Thus the employment relationships of husband and wife over the life-course are seen to have an effect both on the level of household affluence and also on the earning capacity of the individuals involved. Gender relations within the household, the distribution of resources, and the way in which this is linked to labour market position, then become key topics of analysis.

However, this perspective does not assume that there is consensus amongst household members or that families always make rational decisions about dividing up work (Beechey, 1988). It does, however, highlight the gender-based inequalities that may arise within the household over time. The dissolution and reconstitution of households over the life-course (Burgoyne and Clark, 1981) also highlight the effect for the individual of the traditional sexual division of labour within the household and also in the labour market.

The Household as the Unit of Productive Capacity

While contracts of employment are offered to individuals, not households, it is increasingly recognized that the household is the most appropriate unit for an analysis of production and reproduction. There is ample evidence that people's employment decisions are influenced by the employment status or earning capacity of other household members (Hunt, 1980; Porter, 1983; Pahl, 1984) or by the care requirements of children or other dependants, and that unemployment tends to be concentrated within households (Payne, 1987). All adult members of the household are likely to contribute to the productive capacity of the household, whether by directly participating in paid work or in servicing the needs of other members in paid work. Pahl (1988) argues that it is the characteristics of all household members which combine to distinguish households as either rich or poor of wage labourers. Pahl's polarization thesis is also supported by evidence from the British General Household Survey (Dale and Bamford, 1989) which shows that, over the period 1973–82 there was an increasing tendency for either both or neither spouses in a household to be in paid work. There was a steady decrease in the proportion of households in which only the husband was in paid work. There are, therefore, strong theoretical reasons for conceptualizing the household as the unit of production and for conceptualizing as 'household' resources, the income and other assets which accrue through the relationship of household members to the sphere of production.

In order to gain an adequate understanding of the individual within the household context, we need to know much more about the effects of intra-household relationships and changes in household structure through time. We need a better understanding of the respective roles of household members, particularly spouses, in generating household assets, the relationship of inputs to outcomes, and the effects of changes in household composition and earning power, both over the life-course and through marital dissolution and reconstitution. As Bechhofer (1986 p. 229) has argued, research on gender and stratification needs to be aware of processes which vary over the life-cycle. While the importance of an occupational trajectory (Stewart *et al.*, 1980) has been accepted within class analysis and social policy has long been concerned with the association between poverty and life-cycle (Rowntree, 1902; Townsend, 1979; O'Higgins *et al.*, 1988) there has been much less concern with the effects of life-course within stratification research, except in terms of conventional social mobility.

Intra-household employment relationships should be located within a life-course perspective. We can then examine the way in which the traditional sexual division of labour within the home (in conjuction with labour market practices and social policy) may appear to be functionally beneficial to the household — in terms of its location within the social structure — but at the level of the individual, may lead to a widening of gender-based inequalities through the life-course. Because of the dearth of longitudinal data, many of the empirical examples used here are drawn from cross-sectional data. It is important to emphasize that one cannot distinguish cohort, life-cycle and period effects using cross-sectional data; neither can one establish causality.

The Relationship Between the Individual and the Household

While we may conceptualize the household as the unit of productive capacity, nonetheless the majority of household income and assets are channelled into the household through the direct relationship of one or more individuals to the labour market. While the work of an unwaged wife may make a very substantial contribution to the ability of her husband to fulfil his job effectively (Pahl and Pahl, 1971; Finch 1983), nonetheless wages or salaries are only paid to those with a formal attachment to the labour market. The wife of a clergyman or the wife of a business executive gets no formal acknowledgment of the contribution which she makes to her husband's job. Through the institution of the 'family wage' there is no direct recompense for time spent in producing labour power (but see Land, 1980 and Barrett and McIntosh, 1980). Thus income from employment is formally attached to an individual, not to a household. One effect of this, which will be discussed in more detail later, is that when a household splits into two separate units, the income from employment remains attached to the individual who holds that employment, rather than being shared with those responsible for the production of labour power.

It is well established that those households with the highest levels of affluence are likely to contain at least two-earners — typically a husband and wife both in paid work and perhaps also an adult 'child'. Such 'multi-earner' households pave the way to an upward spiral of material mobility, enabling the acquisition of assets which are likely to have major implications for improving current or future life-style (Pahl 1988). Especially amongst those households with low paid jobs, women's earnings are important not only in providing a supplement to the 'family wage' but also in lifting a considerable proportion of households out of poverty (Layard, 1978; Pahl 1988).

Figure 11.1 shows the way in which 'two + earner' households have increased their access to home ownership at a much faster rate than the population as a whole.[2]

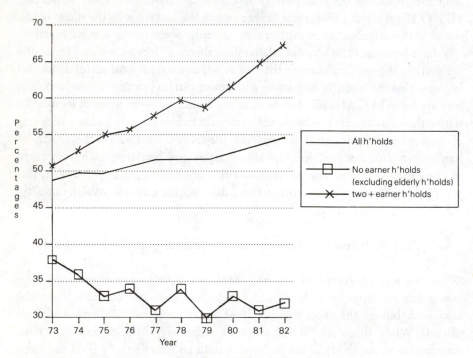

Figure 11.1 Levels of owner occupation: 1973 to 1982
Source: GHS 1973–82

The value of home ownership, not only as a means of capital accumulation but also in providing the basis for cash borrowing (Lowe, 1988), has been widely acknowledged. However, multi-earner households are associated with particular stages of the life-course and particular types of household structure (Table 11.1). Not only does a working wife raise considerably the household's level of total net weekly income (Table 11.2), but the extent of this varies by stage of life-course. Table 11.2 shows that amongst couples at a 'pre-family' stage (household category 3), total net weekly income is 81 per cent higher in households where both spouses work than households where only the husband is in paid work. However, for couples with a dependent child (category 4), there is only an increase of 22 per cent in the total net weekly income in households where the wife also works.

Within a particular category of household, husband's earnings from employment also vary by whether a wife works full-time or not (Table 11.3). Amongst households comprising a married couple and one or more dependent children, men whose wives are in full-time work earn less than men whose wives are in part-time work or not in employment. While we have considerable knowledge of the factors which influence the production of household assets (with employment status and class location having prime importance) we have only very limited empirical evidence on the basis upon which assets are distributed *within* households.

Although the productive efforts of all household members may determine the

Table 11.1 Number of people in paid work by type of household

Household type	No-one	One person	Two +	Total %	N
1 One person <35	26	74	0	100	350
2 Two or more non-married adults	19	24	57	100	357
3 Couple under 35	3	17	80	100	479
4 Couple + child(ren)	10	45	45	100	2349
5 One parent h'hold	63	37	0	100	323
6 One parent + other adults	27	39	34	100	119
7 Couple + child(ren) + elderly person(s)	6	38	56	100	69
8 Couple + child + single adult	4	14	83	100	507
9 Non-elderly adult + elderly person	26	52	22	100	442
10 Couple + single adult	4	14	82	100	690
11 One person > 35	38	62	0	100	540
12 Couple 35 and over	22	36	41	100	1015
13 Elderly couple	88	11	2	100	1039
14 One elderly person	94	6	0	100	1516

Source: GHS 1984
See Appendix for details of household categories

Table 11.2 Median net weekly income of household, for selected household types, by employment status of spouses

H'Hold type:	Both spouses in paid work	Husband in paid work; wife not	Wife in paid work; husband not	Neither spouse in paid work
3. Couple <35	£183	£101	£90	£48
Valid n	(309)	(46)	(14)	(11)
4. Couple + dep. child(ren)	£173	£137	£97	£74
Valid n	(750)	(743)	(41)	(205)
8.* Couple + dep. child(ren) + single adult(s)	£240	£196	£160	£121
Valid n	(155)	(68)	(23)	(32)
10* Couple + single adult(s)	£240	£196	£160	£137
Valid n	(202)	(83)	(27)	(48)
12. Couple > 34	£166	£118	£132	£78
Valid n	(279)	(190)	(57)	(173)

Source: GHS 1984

*In household categories 8 and 10 the total net weekly income of the household may contain income from other household members as well as spouses.

degree of affluence of the household (measured in terms of total income, home ownership, cars etc.) and enable the household to be allocated a location in the social structure, it is not so easy to draw inferences about the outcomes for individual household members (although Lazear and Michael (1988) attempt this). The work of Land (1983), J. Pahl (1983; 1988; 1989) and Graham (1987) has shown that we cannot assume that there is equality of distribution within the household, or consensus over the division of labour within the household; indeed, it has been demonstrated that there is not. This means that, despite being able to allocate a household to a position within the social stratification system, this will not necessarily provide an accurate representation for the individual members of that household.

Despite the pioneering work of Land, Pahl, Graham and others there remains very little national level quantification of the extent of inequality within households. Most large scale government surveys, (the General Household Survey, the Family Expenditure Survey), which form the basis for much secondary analysis within the academic community, do not concern themselves with distribution within the household. In part this reflects the policy assumptions of government (i.e., that within household distribution is not a legitimate concern of government) but it also reflects

Table 11.3 Relationship between husband's income from main job and wife's employment status and income

Married couple with one or more dependent children; no other household members; husband in paid work (HHSTRUCT = 4)

Income: Usual gross weekly income from main job, including any over-time pay and bonuses

Wife working full-time:					
Husbands's income	25% quartile £109	median £142	75% quartile £193	Valid n 87	Missing n 22
Wife's income	£69	£106	£156	96	13
Wife working part-time:					
Husband's income	25% quartile £128	median £170	75% quartile £221	Valid n 304	Missing n 63
Wife's income	£17	£29	£46	338	29
Wife not in paid work:					
Husband's income	25% quartile £129	median £167	75% quartile £228	Valid n 525	Missing n 98

Source: GHS 1984

the acknowledged difficulty of collecting such information in survey form. However, recognition of this shortcoming has led to the inclusion of some questions on household allocation within both the Social Change and Economic Life Initiative and the British Household Panel Study.

If the household and its members are to form the basis of a sustained analysis, then it is vital that we understand not just the sources of household affluence (the paid and unpaid work of individual members) but also the way in which assets are distributed, both in the short term in expenditure, use of goods, space etc., and also in the long term through inheritance (Delphy and Leonard, 1986). We also need to know what role paid work plays in determining patterns of distribution. For example, does increased power outside the home feed back into the domestic power structures? What is the relationship between the division of labour within the family and in the wider economy? Recent work (Pahl, 1989; Vogler, 1990) is starting to provide some of the evidence needed to establish these relationships.

Employment-Related Benefits

However, paid employment brings more benefits than just a wage or salary. As Titmuss pointed out in his 1955 Eleanor Rathbone Lecture 'there has occurred a great expansion of occupational welfare benefits in cash and in kind' (1963 p. 50). Among these he lists pensions; health and welfare services; personal expenses for travel, entertainment; meal vouchers; cars and season tickets; residential accommodation; school fees; sickness benefits; medical expenses; education and training grants; cheap meals; unemployment benefits. The value of these non-wage benefits from employment has increased dramatically over time. Townsend (1979) calculated fringe benefits at about 13 per cent of the household income of the wealthiest quintile in 1969. It is estimated that, in the late 1980s, fringe benefits form about 30 per cent of total remuneration of employees in the finance sector, and the gas, water and electricity industries (Smail, 1988). As many as 1.5 million directors and employees have a company car while employers' superannuation contributions are estimated at £1,500 per annum for the average full-time employee.

Not only does employment bring income but a whole series of other benefits which may be available to all household members but which, ultimately, are attached to an individual household member. (The most dramatic example is probably tied housing). For the self-employed, tax deductible business expenses and under-declaration of true earnings provide extra sources of income. In the case of many skilled manual workers, it is the tools and skills acquired through paid employment that can be put to good use in evenings and weekends (Pahl, 1984). Thus although living standards may be enhanced by self-provisioning it is a firm attachment to the labour market that is the necessary pre-requisite for affluence within households. However, while the value of employment-related benefits may filter through to all household members, they are, nonetheless, firmly tied to those with an employment contract — usually a full-time permanent contract. While 85 per cent of men in employment are in permanent full-time jobs, only 53 per cent of women fall into this category and as few as 40 per cent of married women (Dale and Bamford, 1988). In this way, occupational mobility may seem similar for men and women, when in fact it can be sharply different in terms of the fringe benefits attaching to jobs.

Survey data provides some empirical evidence of gender-based differences in entitlement to sick-pay and occupational pensions. Evidence of the distribution of other benefits is much more difficult to obtain. In 1980, only 51 per cent of women part-timers were entitled to receive sick-pay from their employer and only 9 per cent of part-timers were members of an occupational pension scheme (Martin and Roberts, 1984). About two-thirds of women working part-time fall below the National Insurance threshold and therefore do not qualify for unemployment benefit or a state retirement pension in their own right. Table 11.4 shows the extent to which contributions to an occupational pension scheme vary by gender, marital status and full or part-time working. Only 18 per cent of men working part-time and 15 per cent of women working part-time reported making contributions to an occupational pension scheme in 1984. This compares with 60 per cent of men working full-time and 49 per cent of women working full-time. (There are, of course, also large class-based

Table 11.4 Contribution to an occupational pension scheme among those in paid employment, 1984

a. By full-time/part-time working and sex:

	Male			Female		
	Full-time	Part-time	All	Full-time	Part-time	All
% in occup. pension scheme	60	18	59	49	15	38
Valid n	2652	72	2729	1371	697	2072

b. By marital status and sex:

	Male				
	Married	Single	Widow	Divorced	Separated
% in occup. pension scheme	65	40	40	57	70
Valid n	1922	623	30	61	23

	Female				
	Married	Single	Widow	Divorced	Separated
% in occup. pension scheme	38	36	27	52	41
Valid n	1325	514	82	105	46

Source: GHS: 1984

differences among both men and women.) These figures are based on reported payment of contributions and do not, therefore, include those in non-contributory pension schemes. This may under-represent the different level of occupational pensions between full and part-time workers. Among employed women, a much higher proportion of those who are divorced are contributing to an occupational pension compared with either single or married women.

The implications of a failure to contribute to an occupational pensions scheme are evident from research into income levels in later life (Laczko *et al.*, 1988; Gilbert *et al.*, 1989). Occupational pensions play an important role in raising the income of elderly people above the level of income support i.e. preventing downward mobility in income terms; they are also largely responsible for the observed income difference between elderly men and elderly women living alone. In order to understand the reasons for this large gender differential in earnings-related benefits it is necessary to look at the way in which men's and women's attachment to the labour market and occupational level change over the life-course.

Women's Employment Over the Life-Course

Women are now slightly more likely than men to hold an educational qualification on leaving school (EOC, 1986) and to go into full-time further or higher education (DES, 1986). At a pre-family formation stage, their occupational distribution, although different from that of men, is not dramatically lower — for example, approximately equal proportions of men and women under 35 and without children can be roughly classified as in semi and unskilled work (including shop work) as Table 11.5 shows. However, the very considerable degree of gender segregation leads to significant differences between men and women in the promotion prospects available within their jobs and the levels of pay attached to them.

The position of women within the labour market is affected by two major influences — the sexual divisions and barriers within the labour market and the sexual division of labour within the home. The former tend to channel young women into sex stereotyped occupations with few promotion prospects (Cockburn, 1987), while the latter result in women's downward mobility during family formation (Martin and Roberts, 1984; Dex, 1987; Dale, 1987a). Using cross-sectional data it is apparent that the occupations held by married women with children are markedly lower by comparison with younger childless women, while those of married men with children are higher by comparison with younger men without children (Table 11.5). Thus married women appear to be downwardly mobile across the occupational structure while married men are upwardly mobile. (With the cross-sectional data shown here, it is not, of course, possible to establish whether this is a life-course rather than a cohort effect.)

However, the Women and Employment Survey (Martin and Roberts, 1984) has been able to provide longitudinal evidence of women's labour force behaviour over the life-course. It has confirmed women's downward occupational mobility and shown how it is linked to a break from the labour market during family formation and a return to part-time work. In Britain (but not in most other western countries) it is still usual to leave the labour market at child-bearing, although the length of time before women return to paid work is getting progressively shorter (Martin and Roberts, 1984). Women still hold prime responsibility for domestic work and child-care and, with very little child-care provision available, the majority of women return to part-time work after child-birth, usually in a lower level occupation (see Chapter 10).

Despite the fact that the period away from paid work has decreased, in the twenty years from 1955–59 to 1975–79 there had been *no* increase in the proportion of women who returned to full-time work within six months of a first birth — i.e. women who retain their jobs, usually through taking statutory maternity leave. Martin and Roberts (1984; Table 9.11) show that, of women with a first birth in 1955–59, 10 per cent returned to work full-time within the six month period and 4 per cent returned part-time. Of those with a first birth in 1975–79, 8 per cent returned full-time and 9

Table 11.5 Occupational distribution by life-cycle and sex

	Under 35, no children		Married with dep. children		35 and over, no dep. child	
	Female	Male	Female	Male	Female	Male
Professional	2	6	1	7	1	5
Teaching and nursing	12	3	14	4	12	4
Intermediate	7	14	8	21	9	21
Clerical	42	10	22	5	27	7
Skilled manual	9	39	8	41	9	37
Shop	12	5	10	3	9	3
Semi- and unskilled manual	18	23	38	18	34	24
Total	100 (11667)	100 (14603)	100 (14251)	100 (23791)	100 (10600)	100 (12656)

Source: Labour Force Survey 1981 in Dale, 1987a

per cent part-time. While there are increasing numbers of young women gaining professional qualifications (see Chapter 8 above), many of whom are delaying child-bearing, we do not yet know whether they will manage to retain their occupational status during family formation and how this will effect their life-course mobility as a whole. At present, schemes by some employers (e.g. the major clearing banks) to retain 'high-flying' women employees are having very little impact on the majority of women who still face occupational down-grading after a break from the labour market. Demographic changes are, however, beginning to impact upon the labour market with some evidence that employers are trying to retain their skilled women employees through the provision of workplace nurseries.

Not only are part-time jobs principally found in lower level occupations, they are also less well paid, proportionately, than full-time jobs. Ermisch and Wright (1988), using WES data, show that part-time jobs reward human capital less than full-time jobs, while Main (1988), calculates that if women part-timers experienced continuous full-time employment with the same employer since leaving full-time education, their earnings would rise by 35 per cent. Extensive quantification of the effects on women's earnings of part-time work and family responsibilities has been carried out by Joshi and colleagues (Joshi, 1987; Joshi *et al.*, 1985) which suggests that the lifetime income of an illustrative mother is 54 per cent that of a comparable childless woman, who would herself get 37 per cent more had she been a man.

Work based on the Panel Study for Income Dynamics in the US has used annual income data over a 13-year period to show that, in the US also, a break from employment followed by part-time working leads to a fall in income that is not recovered on return to full-time work (Corcoran *et al.*, 1983). By contrast, women who return to work full-time after a break show a considerable wage 'rebound', although, at the end of a 10-year period they still experience lower wage rates than women who remained in continuous work (op.cit.).

However, in neither the US nor Britain can male-female income differentials be entirely accounted for by differences in work experience or in continuity associated with the sexual division of labour within the family. Some of these income differentials can only be explained by the well-documented inequalities within the labour market that systematically disadvantage women (Walby, 1986; Beechey, 1988; Cockburn, 1987).

Part-Time Jobs and Intra-Household Employment Relationships

Almost all the increase in women's employment in recent years has been in part-time work and this has provided a ready channel for women returning to work after child-bearing (Dale, 1987a). There has been very little increase in full-time employee jobs. Table 11.6 taken from Joshi *et al.* (1985) shows that, since 1951, there has been a steady

Table 11.6 Full- and part-time work among women aged 20–64 (%)

	Full-time workers	Part-time workers	Unemployed	All active
1951	30.3	5.2	0.8	36.3
1961	29.8	10.2	1.0	41.0
1966	31.7	15.2	1.4	48.3
1971	29.0	20.2	2.3	51.5
1981	31.6	22.4	3.7	57.7

Data drawn from Census reports for Great Britain; full-time means more than 30 hours, except teachers with over 24 hours.
Source: Joshi, Layard and Owen (1985)

increase in the percentage of women aged 20–64 in part-time work, but no sustained increase in full-time working, although there has, since 1983, been a recovery in some of the full-time jobs lost between 1979–81. Thus while women have steadily increased their labour market activity, and have thereby contributed to the affluence of the household, this has largely happened through part-time working in jobs which fail to provide an adequate reward for the skills and experience which women hold. There is little evidence yet of a significant increase in women's attachment, over the life-course, to secure career jobs carrying occupational benefits.

The expansion of part-time jobs is also associated with a more extensive expansion of the service sector and a dichotomization of the labour market between those 'core' jobs located within internal labour markets and carrying occupational welfare benefits and jobs which are 'peripheral' in the sense that they are only loosely attached to an employer and do not have associated fringe benefits. This expansion of the service sector, together with a move towards deregulation in the labour market, is likely to accentuate this division in the foreseeable future. This provides a clear example of the way in which domestic responsibilities and the household division of labour structure employment (Siltanen, 1986). Employers' demand for low-paid, flexible part-time jobs is met by a supply of component wage-earners, constrained in their access to paid work by domestic commitments, yet able to accept these low paid jobs because of the presence of a full-wage earner (or other source of income) in the household.

Case studies show that many employers are constructing these jobs precisely to avoid the cost of extra benefits associated with employment: paid meal-breaks, over-time working, National Insurance contributions, occupational pensions, and redundancy payments (Hurstfield, 1987). In some cases this means that employees are simply re-engaged as 'self-employed' workers who are no longer the responsibility of the employer and who have to bear their own occupational welfare costs. Coyle (1985) has described the way in which privatization has led to a loss of employment protection and basic benefits such as a paid holiday for many women.

By contrast, many of those jobs loosely designated 'core' may be subject to more fringe benefits than previously — e.g. low interest mortgages, membership of a private health scheme and a compnay car. As Pahl (1988 p. 251) has suggested

> some — but certainly not all — households with 'core' workers and other members of the household also in employment (either full or part-time) are able to achieve and to maintain high household incomes and substantial affluence, despite the individually weak labour market position of some of their members.

Thus, while multi-earner households are generating affluence in income and assets at the level of the household, this is often achieved through a sexual division of labour whereby many men hold higher paid and more secure 'core' jobs to which are attached occupational welfare benefits and the majority of wives, at least for a substantial part of their working lives, hold part-time jobs without such benefits. Thus it appears that, while women are mobile down the occupational hierarchy at the stage of family formation, this is exactly the time when many men are upwardly mobile into jobs with secure long-term employment and benefits which carry though into old age, thereby leading to widening inequality between spouses over the life course.

In a consensual model of the household, where income and assets are shared equally and where partnerships are for life, this arrangement may well provide a rational way to improve life-style and living standards. It is in line with the new 'home economics' which argues that there should be specialization within the household in paid work and unpaid work (Becker 1985). However, Owen (1987 p.167) points out that 'complete market specialisation by fathers and complete or part specialisation in home time by mothers may not be the best strategy'. Using WES data she shows that, for economic *efficiency*, both partners should work part-time during family formation. As Owen makes clear, this argument is located within an economist's framework and is concerned simply with achieving efficiency — the maximizing of output from a given set of inputs — and leaves on one side considerations of justice and equity.

Household Dissolution and Reconstitution

Further problems arise because the specialization recommended by the new home economics is only effective if households are permanent arrangements in which consumption and allocation of goods is equitable. Becker (1985 p. S34) indeed suggests that 'Married women may participate more as a protection against the financial adversity of subsequent divorce'. While it is clear that assumptions of permanency in marriage cannot be made, nonetheless most married women do not follow employment profiles that maximize their earnings potential, and therefore do not participate fully in the 'mobility stakes'. On the basis of present trends, one in three of all first marriages will end in divorce (Haskey, 1986) and, when this happens, the level of affluence of female headed households is likely to be considerably reduced: in financial terms, this is a form of downward mobility to which women in particular are exposed.

Longitudinal data from the Michigan Panel Study of Income Dynamics reveals that by the seventh year of the study fewer than one-third of the families in the sample had the same compostion as in the first year and over one-third were headed by someone who had not been the head of the 'same' family seven years before (Duncan and Morgan, 1981). (We might add that the notion of a coherent family of origin class in mobility studies must therefore be called into question). Further evidence shows that 'One-third of the initially married women living in families with income above the poverty line who became divorced and did not remarry were in poverty by the seventh year of the study'. (Duncan and Morgan, 1981 p. 13). Available evidence from Britain (Eeklaar and Maclean, 1986) suggests that, here, women also experience a considerable drop in household income in relation to Supplementary Benefit (now Income Support) on divorce or separation and a sharp rise on re-marriage.[3] Table 11.7 shows cross-sectional data on household income for male and female headed households. It is evident that female headed lone parent households have considerably lower levels of net weekly income than male headed lone parent households.

Table 11.7 Current net weekly income for male and female headed households of selected types

	Number	25% Quartile	£ Median	75% Quartile
Household type 5. One parent + one or more dependent children				
Male headed	24	49	94	113
Female headed	299	50	69	88
Household type 14. One elderly person				
Male headed	317	42	53	63
Female headed	1199	31	43	55

Source: GHS 1984

While one-parent households may constitute only a small proportion of the whole population (see Appendix), longitudinal data shows the extent to which this is a transitory stage through which many women pass. Table 11.8, using marital history data from the General Household Survey for women aged 18–49, shows that almost 17 per cent of women in this age group have experienced at least one marriage breakdown, either through divorce, separation or widowhood. However, over a half of these women report that they are currently married. Rimmer and Popay (1983) estimate that more than one in six children born today will see their parents divorced during their childhood.

Table 11.8 Marital history of women aged 18–49 (or 16–49 if married)

Marital history	(1) % women	(2) % of (1) who are currently 'married'
Single, not cohabiting	18.6	—
Single, co-habiting	2.5	59
Legally married	62.3	100
Widowed/separated/divorced: not cohabiting	7.0	0
Widowed/separated/divorced: cohabiting	1.5	77
2 legal marriages	7.8	90
3 + legal marriages	0.3	78
Total	100.0 (5255)	72

Source: GHS 1984
Of women in this table, 16.6% have experienced at least one marriage break-down.

While maintenance payments have been the traditional answer to the gender-inequalities left by divorce, this, in fact, accounts for a very small proportion of the income of divorced mothers (Millar, 1987). Additionally, the 1984 Matrimonial Proceedings Act removes the notion of dependency when a marriage breaks up by no longer making settlements for long-term maintenance. Millar suggests that this policy fails to recognize the continued existence of dependency within marriage and the extent to which women's earning capacity has been weakened by their role as housewife and mother.

However, dissolution and reconstitution of families and households is not solely a feature of marital breakup. As a woman progresses through the life course she is likely to experience a number of changes to her household composition — if only following the stereotype family formation pattern of marriage, child-bearing, children leaving home and death of spouse. Each of these stages is associated with different levels of attachment to paid work and quite different levels of household income, even using a standardized measure of income relative to needs (Dale, 1987b).

In reality, there is, of course, a much greater diversity in household composition than these traditional patterns suggest. It is readily apparent that households containing two or more members of working age are likely to be more affluent than one person households or households containing retired people. Also, the greater range of incomes within the former groups bears witness to the power of occupational position in creating diversity. The low income levels of one-parent families and elderly one-person households is well documented within the social policy literature (Glendinning and Millar, 1987). This reflects not only the fact that over 80 per cent of these households are female-headed but that single parents have sole responsibility for child care and that most elderly widowed or divorced women are suffering the consequences of their lack of earning capacity at an earlier age and the inadequacy of non-contributory state benefits in maintaining a comfortable standard of living. As Walker (1980) has pointed out, the inequalities of the labour market are perpetuated into old age.

Conclusion

By locating individuals within a household context, it is possible to incorporate all members into the stratificatory system, whether in paid work or not. However, it is also necessary to examine inequalities within the household, and avoid the assumption that all household members share the same life-chances and therefore the same stratificatory location. This is facilitated by taking an individual-based, life-course perspective which makes visible inequalities between household members, and the way in which their impact changes over time. A life-course perspective also draws attention to the gender differences in the effect of household dissolution and formation. In the absence of such a perspective we run the risk of extrapolating from cross-sectional data as though it were fixed across time. To apply simple male based models of social mobility to this complex of life-course and household processes is to leave more unexplained and unilluminated than is revealed.

Notes

1   I am very grateful to members of the Cambridge Stratification Group, Janet Siltanen, Bob Michael and Bart Bakker for comments on an earlier draft of this paper. I would also like to thank OPCS for allowing the use of the General Household Survey and the ESRC Data Archive for supplying the data. This work forms part of an ESRC research project, grant number G00232299.

2   Because this uses cross-sectional data we cannot be certain of the direction of causality. However, it is likely that having several earners in a household is more important in facilitating house purchase than the converse.

3   However we cannot establish with certainty the way in which women as individuals experience this drop in household income. Graham (1987) has suggested that, because of the inequitable distribution of money before divorce, some women have more money at their disposal without a male spouse, despite the considerably lower household income.

Appendix

A categorization of households General Household Survey: 1984

Household structure	% all households	Description
1 One person household, age < 35	3.6 (350)	59% male; 83% single
2 Two or more non-married adults in h'hold	3.6 (357)	14% co-habiting couples 41% single adults sharing
3 Couple under 35, no children	4.9 (479)	Couples at pre-family stage 10% co-habiting
4 Couple with one or more dependent children	24.0 (2349)	
5 One parent + child; no other adults in the household	3.3 (323)	93% are female: the majority aged 23–40; 60% are divorced or separated
6 One parent + child, with other adult	1.2 (119)	The other adult may be a co-habitee (10%), an adult child (54%) or a widowed or divorced mother
7 Couple with dependent children + elderly person(s)	0.7 (69)	The elderly person is typically the wife's widowed mother
8 Couple + dependent children + non-dependent 'children'	5.2 (507)	In 86% h'holds this is one nuclear family; 14% contain other relatives or lodgers
9 Non-elderly adults, single or married + elderly person	4.5 (442)	Most contain an elderly couple or widow with an adult 'child' living at home
10 Couple with non-dependent 'child(ren)'	7.0 (690)	In 7% h'holds there are other relatives or lodgers
11 One person household, 35 and over but not elderly	5.5 (540)	59% men; Of women — 49% are widowed; men — 48% single; 30% divorced or separated

12 Couple 35 and over, no children in the household	10.4 (1015)	Non-elderly couples whose children have left home or who are childless
13 Elderly couple	10.6 (1039)	Includes some elderly not married (9%)
14 One elderly person	15.5 (1516)	79% are female; 80% are widowed
Total all households	100.0 (9,795)	

Definitions

Couple   The term couple is used for those describing themselves as married.

Parent   A parent always has a dependent child

Elderly   Elderly is defined as 60 or over for a woman and 65 or over for a man. A couple is defined as elderly where the husband is 65 or over.

Couple 35 and over   The age is that of the woman; the couple is not elderly

Dependent child   A dependent child is under 16, or under 19 if still in full-time education.

Household   In the GHS 1984 a household was defined as 'a group of people who have their accommodation as their only or main residence AND either share at least one meal each day or share the living accommodation'.

Chapter 12

Beyond Male Mobility Models

Geoff Payne and Pamela Abbott

Modelling the social mobility of women involves taking one step back for every two steps forward. In the early chapters of this book we began to describe and account for female mobility, using the conceptual tools of contemporary mobility analysis. However, no sooner had we set these broad macro-level patterns in place than we started to raise doubts about their adequacy, as the chapters about qualifications, careers, marriage, part-time employment and household structures began to challenge the underlying analytical paradigm derived from the study of male mobility. This is not to argue that the earlier chapters are wrong or unnecessary. Rather, we need to learn everything we can at this stage of our intellectual development, in order to test the limits of our concepts, and to operate at a variety of levels which give complementary perspectives on what has hitherto been an under-researched topic.

For example, it remains a valid question — at least as a starting point — to ask how many women experience upward (or downward) mobility. Within the limits of a cross-sectional survey, and without fully seeking to explain our results, we can then compare males and females on the same measurements, to provide answers as in Chapters 2 and 3. Furthermore, if the answers leave us feeling uncomfortable — as, say, the consequences for 'the three theses' argument in Chapter 4 may do — then we can move on to the next issue, namely what the implications are for ideas about class behaviour if we define women as being mobile or immobile in their own right. It *may* be that married women derive their class behaviour (as distinct from their subjective experience of class position or relations) from their partners, but, first, this has yet to be firmly demonstrated from empirical data, and second, if it is true then this seems an admirable sociological question to research. Such research would be unthinkable without a more adequate grasp of female social mobility than we have at present. In particular we would need to examine the gender-based processes of both the supply and demand sides of the labour market, and how these intermesh with women's career and household arrangements. We would need to *explain mobility*, before *mobility can explain* class behaviour.

With that in mind, this final chapter is organized around two connected themes.

We offer some synthesizing and elaborating comments on some of the work of our colleagues, with a view to drawing the threads of the arguments together. This is intended to assist any reader who, having assiduously read every chapter so far, may be feeling a little pressured by the detail and density of the text. Secondly, we draw attention to the limitations of the traditional paradigm and begin to indicate what a new one might be like. This is a developmental exercise, and we suspect that until a major empirical study of female social mobility is undertaken, the rigorous testing and codification of a new perspective may not be possible.

Intergenerational Mobility

Conventionally, mobility from family of origin to current class position has been operationalized, with minor variation, by comparing the occupation of the father with the paid job of the son at time of interview. This method is problematic for both males and females, because it removes the effects of the mother from the origin. It is also problematic for both genders in the sense that it either ignores the processes and individual experiences that actually connect origins and destinations or tends to treat the male version of these as typical, i.e. the norm from which female mobility deviates (if female mobility is considered at all). Thirdly, as Crompton, Dex and Dale show (above), women's experience of household and employment changes over time. The focus of their chapters was on *destination* experience, but the same point applies to *origin* households as well. It is true that the conventional operationalization standardizes this to some extent, by taking the position when the respondent was at the end of compulsory schooling. However, being an eldest child means that the mother in particular may not have fully resumed labour market participation (with its consequent effects for household income and roles), whereas being a youngest child could mean that the household has reached a new phase in its collective life-course. In short, both origin and destination locations are in constant states of flux.

We can link this to the broader context of historical change. The majority of today's working population grew up in an era where full-time male employment was the norm (even if the norm was not achieved in the 1930s and 1980s). However, during this period, attitudes towards women taking full-time paid employment, and their actual participation rates in both full-time and part-time work, have changed sharply (see Chapter 2 above). Taken together with the 1944 Education Act and changes in attitudes towards the desirability of schooling for women, mothers today have different profiles of work and qualification than, say, before the Second World War. They show more extensive changes in this respect than do fathers.

It follows that in future intergenerational mobility research, greater attention should be paid to the operationalization of origins and destinations. How much sophistication can be brought to the analysis will depend partly on the purpose of the research and therefore the level at which it is cast, and partly on practicalities. Obtaining good information on fathers' employment and education is difficult enough; reliable data on mothers, given the under-valuing of female employment and schooling, may prove almost impossible to collect by conventional retrospective survey methods. Some measure of work and education must nonetheless be obtained, and the Irish Study (Chapter 6) shows this to be possible.

Of course, the picture will be complicated if mother and father come from different social classes, but it does not matter for present purposes whether her marriage has been class-homogamous or cross-class, or only 'superficially' cross-class (Chapter 9) — although it is not unreasonable to suggest that complex female mobility profiles are likely to have some effect on the way woman influence their children and perceive their children's mobility. However, the more basic point is that the mother must have an influence on the children's mobility potential, *via* standard of living or by influencing attitudes and values (see e.g. Jackson and Marsden, 1966), and one of the easiest ways of indexing this is to use her occupation and educational qualifications.

It has already been suggested that women's labour market participation modifies the lives of their families of marriage (Chaper 6: see also Hindess, 1981; Heath, 1981; Beck, 1983). The additional income raises the quality of life, which can be measured in terms of better housing (e.g. owner-occupation in the British case), better diet and better family health. Improved living conditions and health in early life would seem to have a plausible connection with future upward mobility potential. The key mechanism here is likely to be education: good living conditions permit home study, while lack of chronic illness means fewer days of schooling lost (and one of the major sources of childhood illness is respiratory disease associated with poor housing). Enhanced household income means greater disposable income, some of which is likely to feed into cultural enrichment. Again, in the British case this may take the form of paying for fringe educational activities such as trips, or extra books, or even the payment of fees for schooling as a whole. We say 'may take' because we know of no empirical evidence that explicitly addresses any of these issues.

This approach draws on the work of the Irish Mobility Study, both in Chapter 6 and elsewhere. Hayes (1987), in an analysis of the Irish survey data, argues that mother's social class is more important than father's in dictating the destination class of daughters and that this finding is significant in relation to the category 'housewife'. In a later paper (Hayes, forthcoming) she demonstrates that mother's social class contributes more to the occupational distribution of Northern and Southern Irish women than father's social class or the educational achievements of either parent. The examination of the predictors of social class of employed brothers and sisters in Northern Ireland in Chapter 6 establishes that mother's occupation is a significant determinant of the educational level of both brothers and sisters independent of the effects of father's occupation, and that the advantage of having a mother with high educational attainment applies more strongly to daughters than to sons. Educational attainment is also strongly associated with occupational attainment. Sisters attain less than brothers — this is a gender effect and not due to family background or personal educational attainment. Given the strong independent influence of mother's occupation on educational attainment and the strong relationship between that and class distribution, this analysis suggests a strong effect of mother's class on sons'/daughters' destinations. However, mothers have a much stronger influence on daughters' education than on sons' and consequently on their class destination.

The picture is also complicated by the usual problem of mobility studies as historical analyses. When we look at employment/class now, we look back at careers and beyond to the parents' careers. Certainly in Britain this takes us into an era in which married women not only had low labour market participation and also when few women (as well as men) gained educational credentials. The rapid change over time in labour-market participation particularly affects the mother's occupation and education, and that of older respondents. Closer scrutiny of more contemporary patterns is another important item for the research agenda. The concentration of women in routine non-manual work helps to obscure the separate effects of education and employment (see Jones, 1986; Abbott and Sapsford, 1987; Marshall *et al.*, 1988), so a detailed scrutiny is required, rather than a broad-brush approach.

Intragenerational Mobility

In the previous section we left the issue of the gendered labour market virtually unstated, because it now goes almost without saying that comparing male (fathers') occupational classes with those of females (daughters) necessarily colours the picture of mobility which emerges. Similarly, there is a danger that one might labour this point in the current section, on career mobility. Nevertheless, any discussion of careers can take place only against a background of employment structures — structures which are not merely passive but interact actively with individual and household lives.

One illustration of this is the point made above about education and employment among women, which applies to both inter and intragenerational movements. Jones (1986), examining the social mobility of 16–29 year old men and women without children, found that class of origin and level of educational qualification were important factors for both boys and girls, but for women this effect was more difficult to see because so many women end up in routine non-manual work. Similarly, Abbott and Sapsford (1987) suggest a strong relationship between father's occupational class, education and destination class for women, pointing out, however, that the possession of educational credentials does not fully protect women from falling into a low-status occupation. Comparing men and women, Marshall *et al.* (1988) argue that the relationship (correlation) between educational qualifications and class is much stronger for men than for women. They conclude that men get a much higher return on credentials than women — a high percentage of women with educational credentials end up in routine non-manual work, while few men do so. Conversely, women are more likely than men to have credentials if they are in Social Classes I or II. Indeed, the higher the social class, the more likely that women will be better qualifed than men. It may also be that women's occupations are concentrated in the newer service industries, where credentials are the determinant of placement and thus of the pacucity of upward mobility, while men also find employment in more traditional industrial sectors where it is still possible to obtain upward mobility by promotion on the basis of work experience alone (Payne, 1987a,b).

Before leaving the question of education, it is worth stressing how things continue to be in a state of flux. Even a cursory look at DES statistics shows rapidly changing female participation (as do the several longitudinal studies of child development). Crompton also makes this point about professional qualifications in Chapter 8. We do not know, at this stage, how qualifications are altering the work *aspirations* of young women, nor how their life strategies will be able to cope with organizational cultures. These have to be set against structural industrial shifts in the demand for employment, and an increase in employment practices geared to casualization and part-time work, with the consequences highlighted by Dale in the previous chapter.

What we can be sure of is the historically-created concentration of women into a narrow range of jobs and into the lower ranks of each of the occupational classes they occupy. The connections — or rather, the lack of them — between these classes creates distinctive career/mobility profiles. As Dex shows in Chapter 10, these labour-market conditions mesh with women's household needs, shaping and being shaped by them. Most women experience downward mobility at some stage of their lives. The most typical case of this is the period after childbirth, although in material terms leaving work to start a family is a form of downward mobility experienced in advance of this. Suspecting what we do about gender and power imbalance in household economies, this effect is likely to impinge more on wives than husbands. Even if this were not so, it would still remain true that downward mobility is the most widely shared experience of women's lives. This is not true of men. Recovery from downward mobility may be possible, but the key point is that women and men do not share the same mobility profiles.

Mobility Profiles

We know that male and female mobility patterns are different, both inter and intragenerationally. Given most women's intermittent labour market participation, necessitated by domestic responsibilities, this is perhaps not surprising. However, as with intergenerational mobility, when we look at women who have not had career breaks or are unlikely to do so we find that the pattern remains dissimilar to men's. While the male mobility studies indicate that men have either stable or upward mobility during their working lives, the pattern for women is quite different. Women are less likely than men to experience upward mobility after entry to the labour market, and this is also true, though to a lesser extent, of women with no children (Chapman, Chapter 7; Greenhalgh and Stewart, 1982; Abbott and Sapsford, 1987). A more complex picture emerges when women's experiences of paid employment are studied over the life-course, as both Dex and Dale demonstrate. While a high proportion of women do have a labour market commitment (they remain in the same occupation despite movement in and out of the labour market and having part-time as well as full-time employment), this is not true of all women. There is in fact a tendency for women to move class when returning to employment after having a break to care for children, and for this to be a move down. There is a subsequent trend for some of this downward mobility to be 'made up'.

It also follows from gendered occupational distributions that when women marry they cannot all marry within their own class, because there is a shortage of class-homogamous mates. Not only must most women marry some-one from a different class, but they will on average marry someone from a higher class. We have already observed that even *within* a class, men are likely to be in a 'superior' position (Tables 2.1 and 2.2). We have also noted that about half of all marriages are cross-class unless we equate female routine non-manual work with male skilled manual work: of the 46 per cent in the Scottish data, two out of three were females marrying hypergamously. As we might expect, the large male occupational classes are the most common source of higher-class marriage mates. If for the moment it is granted that marriage is some kind of mobility experience (a point to be debated below in connection with cross-class marriage and dominance theories), then we have gone some way towards identifying certain characteristics of the female mobility profile. While of course there is great variety in the range of patterns, we can suggest the following core model: In Figure 12.1 the heavy line shows the 'core model', with typical mobility experiences being initial *downward* mobility at the start of work, followed possibly by *upward* mobility through the early career, into hypergamous marriage (marrying a man from a higher class); a break in paid employment during child-bearing and child-rearing or due to partner-led geographical mobility; and then resumption of work at a *lower* point, followed by some small-scale *upward* mobility late in the career. The broken lines show the main variants. These are (a) no early career mobility, followed by either homogamous or hypergamous marriage, (b) homogamous marriage, (c) relatively advantageous re-entry into the labour market after child-bearing or partner's geographical mobility, or (d) no career progression in late career. Variants (a) and (b) are statistically important, given the high levels of homogamy. The argument for downward mobility after family building is based on the evidence of Dex's chapter

Origin: father's class	First destination own first employment	Second destination own pre-marriage career	Third destination marriage	Family building: no paid employment	Fourth destination return to work: own employment	Fifth destination own post-marriage career

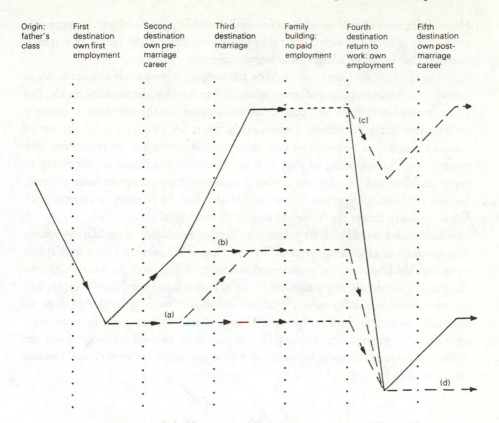

Figure 12.1 Female mobility profiles

that re-entry is on average part-time and at a lower skill level. (The idea of marriage as mobility is developed below).

The first observation to be made about the core model is that it contains both upward and downward mobility, and that continuity of status, let alone monotonic career progression, is *not* the typical experience of women. *Our fundamental conception of mobility should therefore be not a move from one origin to one destination, but a profile.* Further more, we should note that the typical experience of the female half of the population probably includes mobility, so that *a state of high social fluidity should be seen as* **normal** *in contemporary society.* In one step, therefore, we have recast mobility into a totally different problem, in which the ideas of a largely static society, and coherent career progression, are seen to be a false starting point.

This conclusion also necessitates making a connection between objective and subjective mobility. Relatively little is know about the extent to which people *feel* mobile, even when sociologists define them as such. Our core model contains upward and downward movements which are comparatively 'short': is the move from one

Hope-Goldthorpe class to an adjacent one really 'mobility', or is subjective experience of mobility restricted to moves, say, in or out of the service class? This is an empirical question that has to be added to the research agenda.

The fact that we have to re-confront this forgotten question is a direct result of considering female mobility and recognizing the variability in the mobility profile. In a more conventional, male and class dominated, paradigm the question is not only unimportant but a distraction. Goldthorpe's focus, for example, is on the use of mobility analysis to demonstrate demographic class formation, as an interim step towards the understanding of class as a socio-political phenomenon. Variability of career mobility and its subjective meaning makes such an enterprise more difficult, because it is seen to represent 'noise' within the data. In contrast, a concern with female mobility shows the 'noise' to be part of the 'signal'.

Indeed, we should also ask whether subjective experience of mobility is equally occasioned by all kinds of movement. To what extent is a woman's (or a man's) first entry into the labour market experienced as a form of mobility? At what point does she escape from the identity attributed to her as a member of her father's family, into her own social and class *persona*? While as sociologists we may be able to draw an analytical distinction between 'pre-work' and 'work' position, this operates more effectively for young men, because of the prevailing cultural attitudes about the different significance of work for males, as well as notions of 'protectiveness' towards young women.

Cross-Class Marriage and 'Marriage Mobility'

This question of the subjective meaning of mobility is also central to the cross-class marriage, which, as we have seen above, is a phenomenon affecting, by some definitions, half of all women, and which has been one of the main issues in the debate about how to measure a women's class position. However, we would not wish to restrict our observations to cross-class marriages: all marriages involve a kind of mobility. Ninety per cent of women marry or cohabit at some stage of their lives, most of whom have children and experience disruption of their labour market participation. It is this typicality of marriage that led to our inclusion of it (above) in the female mobility profile, and which now also needs to be explored more fully.

Marriage is a mobility process in two quite separate ways. In the first place it involves a change of social identity which in conventional culture is defined as an improvement in status. To be married is to escape from the junior status as a member of the parental family: together with child-birth it is seen as the achievement of 'adulthood', of fulfilment as a female person. In the sense that married women occupy this culturally-defined enhanced status, marriage represents a kind of non-class upward mobility.

For many women, as well as men, marriage also represents upward mobility in a financial sense. Young couples with two incomes and no children have more disposable income than they did as two single people. Their quality of life is improved, and new developments in 'life style' become possible. This further marks off married life from the previous social existence. In class terms, the former socio-political class identity is challenged by greater affluence, new non-work focuses of interest and a loosening of previous interactional ties. This is not to assert that all newly-weds immediately change their class behaviour, but rather to point to marriage as one of the locations in the life cycle where people experience more acutely those factors which class analysis has identified as relevant to class action (or inaction). Paradoxically, even those who are class homogamous in their marriage are upwardly mobile through marriage because of these factors.

Research has also shown that in cross-class marriages, class-related behaviour is modified. Britten and Heath (1983b), in arguing for a household class scale, show that voting and fertility patterns of cross-class couples differ from those where both partners are in the same class. Examples are given in Table 12.1. However, as with the Essex Class Project, the man's class on its own is a better indicator of the wife's voting behaviour than is the woman's class (as defined by current occupation) on its own. Marshall *et al.* (1988) contrast this with the situation for a woman's qualifications and occupational class, which are more strongly associated than are her class and husband's class, or her qualifications and husband's class. This is taken by Marshall *et al.* as evidence that a woman's class position in a demographic sense is independent, whereas her position for class action purposes is modified by marriage itself (as, indeed, a man's may be).

What we do not know is why we have this data pattern. It may be a matter of measurement error: occupation at time of survey may be a poor indicator of women's occupation-based class sentiments, given the lifetime pattern of women's occupational mobility and that these are women who have formed their families already. It may be, however, that more subtle processes are at work. For instance, it may be that women

Table 12.1 Class of marriage partners and class-relevant behaviour

Class of partners		% women voting Labour in 1979	% families with > 2 children
Man	Woman		
Professional/managerial	Professional/managerial	21	36
Professional/managerial	Routine white collar	15	24
Manual	Routine white collar	40	29
Manual	Manual	50	45

Note: class is defined in terms of the Registrar General's scale.
Source: Britten and Heath, 1983b, pp. 57–8.

who 'marry up' are those who have experienced downward intergenerational mobility, so that their class value systems owe more to their parental family than to their own occupational experience. In that case, it could be claimed that it is the latter that is less important. Alternatively, the evidence in Table 2.2 above shows that each class contains a *range* of occupations, while the lack of precision in occupational classification for 'female jobs' has been well demonstrated (e.g. Abbott and Sapsford, 1987, pp. 22–8). It would follow from this that a woman 'near the top' of one class, marrying a man 'near the bottom' of a higher class, may not so much change her class in socio-political terms as confirm it by selecting a mate with similar values. Both of these latter explanations (which are elaborations of Jones' argument in Chapter 9) point not to individual-level value changes but to a structural process of class formation in which there is a kind of 'tidying up' of classes by the progressive re-assortment of class members into their 'proper' classes. There is clearly an item for the research agenda here: what are the processes, both interpersonal and socio-economic, which bring about changes in a *person's* class values connected with marriage, and why do male occupations seem to have stronger predictive power in this respect? It seems to us that this is a more fruitful line of investigation than to take cross-class marriage as a given and to proceed direct to arguments about classification schemes. To put it another way, we may know something about mobility *rates* but we do not yet know enough about mobility *processes*.

Class and Mobility

The foregoing review and reconceptualization of mobility shows how the inclusion of women recasts the problem. We can ask how this view of mobility feeds into class analysis, to replace our previous view. Class analysts are concerned with class formation — both in the extent to which classes are self-recruiting (i.e. members display high levels of homogeneity) and in the extent to which classes pursue their own class interests. The two are seen as related; to the extent that classes are self-recruiting they are thought to be more likely to exhibit class consciousness and undertake class action. To return to the example in Chapter 4, in operationalizing class formation Goldthorpe set out to test three hypotheses: the social closure, buffer zone and counterbalance theses. On the basis of his findings about men he rejects all three, whereas female data, while supporting the prevalence of long-range mobility, suggests stronger support for the buffer-zone model and for class closure against women. These findings have at least to be taken into account when making statements about the class structure of modern Britain and the extent and type of mobility within it. It could well be that women's jobs are less important than men's, that married women take on the class attitudes of their households (or rather, of their head of household), that women's own work experience has little or no effect on their class attitudes or action. It could be that a 'white blouse' worker married to a manual worker exhibits his attitudes and values and is little influenced by her own work-place experiences and the women with whom she works (many of whom may well come from a middle-class background). It could be that women's own educational experiences or class background have little significant effect on their own attitudes and values. These are contingent statements, however, subject to empirical investigation, and not matters to be taken for granted. We agree with Goldthorpe and Payne (1986, p. 550) that we need 'to bring forward systematic evidence in support of the assumption that married women's own employment can be reliably taken as a major determinant of their class identity', but we dispute their statement that studies which have concentrated on men and excluded women from consideration have not 'seriously limited or disorted our understanding of class mobility'.

Also, as Marshall *et al*. (1988) and Abbott and Sapsford (1987) pointed out, the distribution of people between occupational slots over time is powerfully conditioned by gender, so that the inter and intragenerational mobility chances of men are not understandable without reference to the ways in which and the conditions under which women also participate in paid employment. Abbott and Sapsford demonstrate this by examining changes in the occupational structure for men and women during this century. In Table 12.2, for example, the first three columns give the percentages in various kinds of employment in 1921 and 1971, with the third column showing the percentage change over the period, for *men*; the next three columns give similar figures for *women*. In columns c and f a figure of 1.0 would represent 'no change'; a figure greater than 1.0 indicates a relative increase in the proportional size of the category, and a figure less than 1.0 a relative decrease. Each set of figures is interesting in its own right. If we want to look at changes in the labour market, however, we should study columns g–i — the distribution of occupations, and changes in distribution, for both genders combined. The final column summarizes changes in gender balance over the period, with a figure greater than 1.0 indicating an increase in female participation over male participation. What we find is that male jobs have increased substantially more than female ones in the 'professional' categories and decreased far less in the 'skilled manual' category, and that there are similar but less dramatic trends for 'administrators and managers' and 'semi-skilled workers'. Women's participation has increased more than men's, on the other hand, in the areas of clerical work, unskilled work, shop work and 'inspectors, supervisors and foremen'. In other words, with the exception of the last of these categories it appears that women have migrated to the bottom of both the manual and the non-manual groups, making space for men further up. There appears to be a zero-sum game at work in the figures, with men's apparent overall upward mobility bought at the price of downward mobility for women.

Marshall *et al*. (1988) argue that sexual segregation, which is an influence on the structure of class positions, should be a legitimate concern of class analysis:

Table 12.2 Changes in occupational mobility, 1921–1971

Socio-economic group	Males 1921 (a) %	1971 (b) %	ratio b/a (c)	Females 1921 (d) %	1971 (e) %	ratio e/d (f)	Total 1921 (g) %	1971 (h) %	ratio h/g (i)	Ratio f/c (j)
— Self-employed and higher-grade salaried professionals	1.6	6.1	3.8	0.9	1.4	1.6	1.4	4.4	3.1	0.4
— Employers and proprietors	7.7	5.2	0.7	4.7	2.9	0.6	6.8	4.4	0.6	0.9
— Administrators and managers	4.3	9.9	2.3	2.1	3.3	1.6	3.7	7.5	2.1	0.7
— Lower-grade salaried professionals and technicians	1.8	5.5	3.1	6.3	10.8	1.7	3.1	7.4	2.4	0.5
— Inspectors, supervisors and foremen	1.9	4.5	2.4	0.3	1.2	4.0	1.4	3.3	2.3	1.7
— Clerical workers	5.1	6.1	1.2	9.8	28.0	2.9	6.5	14.0	2.2	2.4
— Sales personnel and shop assistants	4.1	3.9	1.0	7.5	9.4	1.3	5.1	5.9	1.2	1.3
— Skilled manual	32.3	29.4	0.9	20.3	9.3	0.5	28.8	22.2	0.8	0.5
— Semi-skilled	24.5	21.2	0.9	40.0	27.3	0.7	29.1	23.4	0.8	0.8
— Unskilled	16.7	8.2	0.5	8.1	6.4	0.8	14.2	7.6	0.5	1.6

Source: Abbott and Sapsford (1987) Table 70, on p. 180

an interest in demographic class formation embraces the study of the various mechanisms that generate and stabilise the demographic collectivities themselves. Not to ask how it is that places become available in the structure across time is to assume (wrongly) that class processes are wholly independent of the social division of labour (pp. 83–4)

They go on to point out that

class structures, and the market processes behind them, are (to use the current terminology) 'gendered'. It is not 'social actors' that are distributed via the market through the places of the structure: it is men and women. Their different experiences are interdependent, so that the distribution and situations of men are powerfully influenced by those of women as well as vice versa. The fact that women are vocationally constrained in this way serves only to highlight the obverse side of the situation: namely, that the collective effect of women's employment on the occupational system would seem to be one of privileging men (p. 84)

In this sense, at least, women do make a difference to demographic class formation — the opportunities that are available for men are strongly conditioned by the labour market postion of women. Even if (and this remains an area of considerable dispute) women's class identity and action are conditioned by the occupations of their husbands, there would still be a strong argument for including women in mainstream mobility studies (see Abbott and Sapsford, 1987; Marshall *et al.*, 1988).

However, we would argue that there are good reasons for studying women's occupational mobility in its own right: that not to do so is not just to ignore the experiences of half the population but to act as if they did not exist. To reiterate, it is also important to recognize that there is no 'normal' pattern of social mobility — that men's patterns are not a norm against which women's have to be measured and thereby seen as deviant or somehow wrong (although the comparison does raise interesting questions about the ways in which the labour market works systematically to disadvantage women and advantage men in terms of access to high-status, well paid jobs). Finally (and we take this up in the final section of the chapter), we want to suggest that by analyzing and reflecting on the problems of undertaking research on women's social mobility new questions and areas of concern become evident that are equally as important for research into male mobility as female mobility.

Confronting Traditional Mobility Research

We want to argue not only that it is necessary to incorporate women in social mobility research and class theory, which in itself necessitates recognizing that our methodologies and theories need to be radically re-thought, but also that there are questions that need to be asked which have not yet been raised in conventional mobility research. Furthermore, we want to suggest that the need to ask these questions has arisen out of our consideration of women's social mobility. We do not deal with them in any order of priority here — indeed, we do not think there is such an order — nor do we suggest that the ideas are totally original to us.

First there is the question of the fluidity of the occupational structure itself — that is, the extent to which occupational categories as opposed to individuals are upwardly or downwardly mobile. While conventional mobility theorists are aware that occupational categories are mobile, they tend to assume a static model when they compare father-son mobility. A case in point is clerical work; whether or not clerical workers have been proletarianized, it is clearly the case that their relative status and pay has declined during this century. This is true even if we omit female 'white blouse' workers from our analysis. (Conversely, if it is the case that the relative pay and status of clerical work has declined, then has the clerk son of a skilled manual worker 'really' been upwardly mobile?) It becomes quite legitimate to ask, therefore, whether a school-teacher son of 60 years has been upwardly mobile as compared with his father who was a clerk forty-six years ago. This problem is more sharply delineated when we are concerned with father-daughter mobility because women tend to occupy the lower-status, low paid jobs within each occupational sector and because of the concentration of women in routine non-manual work.

Second, there is the question of segments within occupational classes. Occupational classes cover and are comprised of people with a wide range of occupations, pay levels, status positions and career prospects. It can therefore be asked whether fathers in certain occupational categories *within* classes are able to promote their sons and/or daughters, and also what occupational categories upwardly mobile sons and daughters enter and how far up the career ladder they reach.

This becomes more sharply focused when we are concerned with female social mobility because fathers are less able to promote their daughters than their sons, and it would be interesting to know which fathers are most able to promote their children. Delamont (1989b) suggests that it is possible that it is the intelligentsia families (father and/or mother in professional employment and mother with a career) whose daughters become Class I professionals, while the daughters of the old bourgeoisie enter the feminine semi-professions. It is also the case that even in occupations that have a career structure women are less likely to move up the ladder than men. This raises the question of whether there are differences in the class backgrounds of both men and women who do or do not move up the career ladder.

Third, male mobility studies have assumed that men (people) either have a career or are stable in a class, and that occupation is the determinant of the class position — also that class attitudes, beliefs and behaviours are primarily determined by the workplace experience of those in employment. Thus, taking the father's occupation when the son was 14 years old as the basis of his class and comparing it with the son's class when the survey was undertaken is seen as a 'good' measure of origin and destination class. Studying women's mobility patterns suggests much more fluidity than is assumed for men, together with the need to include household structures and changes, and this is seen as a problem if women are to be included in such studies. It raises the general question (which we cannot go into here) not only of how we measure social class, but also more narrowly of which occupation determines social class (especially class attitudes, values and behaviours). Is it the highest level of occupation that someone has had, or what they regard as their normal occupation, or their current occupation? This raises the question of how useful it is to regard occupation as a straightforward index of social class, a question which arises initially with women but may be relevant to men if career change and/or periodic unemployment becomes a norm. Indeed, it could be argued that using occupation as an index is at best of historically and regionally circumscribed use even for men. It is only in this century — probably since the Second World War — that permanent, life-long employment has been seen as the norm for men, and then probably only in some regions of the United Kingdom (see Kumar, 1984). Furthermore, even at times and in regions were reasonably full employment obtains, the extent of changes between occupational classes over time by men as well as women may be far greater and far less patterned than is generally assumed in social mobility studies and class theory in general (see Gilbert, 1985).

Fourth, there is the question of the influence of mothers' social class on sons' and daughters' destination class. The influence of mother's class has not been considered by conventional mobility research, which has looked at movement between father and son and considered the other possible factors to be father's and son's education (Heath, 1981). However, if we reject the view that the household is the unit for class analysis and argue for individuals, then mothers as well as fathers have a class in their own right, and it becomes possible to consider the influence of mothers' class on sons' as well as daughters' mobility. It is also important to recognize, as Chapman has pointed out, that a wife's social class may be important in enabling a man to be intragenerationally mobile; her ability to take on the lifestyle of a higher class may be crucial in his ability to be upwardly mobile. Also, the fact that married women tend 'to be employed' rather than 'to have a career' is crucial in explaining male mobility. Genuine dual-career families are a rarity; generally one partner (the male) has a career while the other (the wife) has at best a good steady job.

Fifth, class theorists have generally not been interested in the meaning of mobility for individuals. They have been concerned with the objective clas structure and failed to ask questions about when individuals think they are upwardly or downwardly mobile and the meaning it has for them. Once we seriously consider women these become seen as releveant and important issues. Do women consider themselves upwardly/downwardly mobile when they marry a man from a higher/lower class than their father's, or indeed *vice versa*? (If mobility can be *via* marriage for women, then presumably the same is true for men; if a married woman can be assumed to have a derived class position, then it is equally plausible to argue that a married man may have one.) More important, perhaps, is what *counts* as mobility for women and for men. What do they measure mobility against — their father's occupational class, or their mother's, or some view of their home background? Do women compare their occupational backgrounds and class positions with some neutral scale, or do they compare themselves with men or with other women? Indeed, how do people actually identify what social class they are in, and what counts for them as mobility? These are questions asked not out of idle curiosity, but ones which relate to class identity and action and to a sense of well-being which may reduce class-based action. If these are important questions for women, they are equally important for men.

Finally there is the question of credentials as class determinants. Women need credentials to get managerial or professional jobs, but it is also true that whatever credentials they have seem to 'buy less' than men's. This raises the question of the exact relationship between credentials and destination — is it just gender that articulates with credentials, or can other factors do so, and if so then what are they? In other words, it raises a question about the *residuals* in class prediction models — what other factors influence social mobility? Gender is obviously just one of the factors that have been ignored.

In sum, we are suggesting that the problems that we experience in attempting to incorporate women into mobility studies, or indeed to study the social mobility of women at all, are not restricted to women. They are problems that also arise in studying men, but their importance has either been less obvious when research has been confined to men or they have been disregarded as 'minor issues'. While we have not necessarily identified all of these issues, the ones we have raised are: the need to examine occupational categories rather than social class as a whole; the flexibility of the occupational structure itself; the questionable assumption that every individual has a career or a steady place in the labour market; the influence of mother's and partner's social class via household dynamics; the meaning of social mobility to those who experience it; and the need to look more carefully into alternative factors that have been ignored in explaining social mobility.

We want to conclude by stressing that while we feel that women's social mobility is an area of sociological interest in its own right, in practice we can only make sense of women's and men's social reality when we study both together. Class theory can be developed fully only when methodologies and theories are developed which enable us to incorporate men *and* women into our research and to develop adequate theories to explain all our results.

Bibliography

ABBOTT, P. and SAPSFORD, R. (1987), *Women and Social Class*, London, Tavistock.

ABBOTT, P. and WALLACE, C. (1990), *An Introduction to Sociology: feminist perspectives*, London, Routledge.

ACKER, J. (1973), 'Women and Social Stratification: a case of intellectual sexism', *American Journal of Sociology*, 78, 4, pp. 936–45.

ALLEN, S. (1983), 'Gender Inequality and Class Formation', in, Giddens, A. and Mackenzie, G. (Eds) *Social Class and the Division of Labour*, Cambridge, Cambridge University Press.

ARBER, S. (1987), 'Social Class, Non-Employment and Chronic Illness: continuing the inequalities in health debate', *British Medical Journal*, 25 April.

ARBER, S., DALE, A. and GILBERT, N. (1984), 'Evaluating Alternative Measures of Social Class: Does gender make a Difference?', Paper presented to the 1984 BSA Conference, Bradford University.

ARMSTRONG, P. (1982), 'If It's Only Women It Doesn't Matter So Much', in West, J. (Ed) *Work, Women and the Labour Market*, London, Routledge & Kegan Paul.

ASHER, H. (1976), *Causal Modelling*, London, Sage.

ATKINSON, J. (1984), 'New Patterns of Working Relationships', Paper for the Conference of the Manpower Society, mimeo.

ATTWOOD, M. and HATTON, F. (1983), 'Getting On. Gender Differences in Career Development: A case study from the hairdressing industry', in Gamarnikow, E., Morgan, D., Purvis, J. and Taylerson, D. (Eds) *Gender, Class and Work*, London, Heinemann.

BARRETT, M. and MCINTOSH, M. (1980), 'The family wage: some problems for socialists and feminists', *Capital and Class*, 11, Summer.

BARRON, R. D. and NORRIS, G. M. (1976), 'Sexual Divisions and the Dual Labour Market', in Barker, D. L. and Allen, S. (Eds) *Dependence and Exploitation in Work and Marriage*, London, Longman.

BEAVIS, S. (1989), 'Ticking Demographic Time Bomb as Women await the Back to Work Call', *Guardian*, November 4th.

BECHHOFER, F. (1986), 'Gender and Stratification: some general remarks', in Crompton, R. and Mann, M. (Eds) *Gender and Stratification*, Cambridge, Polity Press.

BECK, S. (1983), 'The Role of the Other Family Members in Intergenerational Occupational Mobility', *Sociological Quarterly*, 24, 3, pp. 273–85.

BECKER, G. S. (1985), 'Human Capital, Effort and the Sexual Division of Labour', *Journal of Labor Economics*, 3, 1, pt 2, pp. S33–S58.

BEECHEY, V. (1978), 'Women and Production: a critical analysis of some sociological theories of women's work', in Kuhn, A. and Wolpe, A. M. (Eds) *Feminism and materialism: women and the modes of production*, London, Routledge & Kegan Paul.

BEECHEY, V. (1988), 'Rethinking the Definition of Work', in Jenson, J., Hagen, E. and Reddy, C. (Eds) *Feminization of the Labour Force*, Cambridge, Polity Press.

BLACKBURN, R. (1980), 'Social Stratification', Paper presented to the 1980 BSA Conference, Lancaster University.

Bibliography

BLACKBURN, R. and MANN, M. (1979), *The Working Class in the Labour Market*, London, Macmillan.

BLAU, P. M. and DUNCAN, O. D. (1967), *The American Occupational Structure*, New York, Wiley.

BONACICH, E. (1976), 'Advanced Capitalism and Black/White Race Relations in the United States: a split labour market interpretation', *American Sociological Reveiw*, 41, 1, pp. 34–51.

BOSANQUET, N. and DOERINGER, P. B. (1973), 'Is There a Dual Labour Market in Great Britain?', *Economic Journal*, 82, 2, pp. 421–435.

BOTTOMORE, T. (1964), *Elites and Society*, London, Watts.

BOTTOMORE, T. (1965), *Classes in Modern Society*, London, Allen and Unwin.

BOYD, M. (1982), 'Sex Differences in the Canadian Occupational Attainment Process', *Canadian Review of Sociology and Anthropology*, 14, 1, pp. 1–28.

BOYD, M. (1985), 'Immigration and Occupational Attainment in Canada', in Boyd, M. *et al*. (Eds) *Ascription and Achievement: studies in mobility and status attainment in Canada*, Ottowa, Carleton University Press.

BOYLE, J. (1976), 'Analysis of the Irish Occupational Index', Department of Social Studies, The Queen's University of Belfast, (Unpublished manuscript).

BRADLEY, H. (1989), *Men's Work, Women's Work*, Oxford, Polity Press.

BRANNEN, J. and WILSON, G. (1987), *Give and Take in Families*, London, Allen & Unwin.

BRAVERMAN, H. (1974), *Labour and Monopoly Capital*, London, Monthly Review Press.

BRITTEN, N. and HEATH, A. (1983), 'Women, Men and Social Class', in Gamarnikow, E., Morgan, D., Purvis, J. and Taylerson, D. (Eds) *Gender, Class and Work*, London, Heinemann.

BROWN, R. (1982), 'Work Histories, Career Strategies and Class Structure', in Giddens, A. and Mackenzie, G. (Eds) *Social Class and the Division of Labour*, Cambridge, Cambridge University Press.

BROWNING, H. and SINGLEMAN, J. (1978), 'The Transformation of the US Labour Force', *Politics and Society*, 8, 4, pp. 481–509.

BRUEGEL, I. (1978), 'Bourgeois economics and women's oppression', *m/f* 1, pp. 103–11.

BURGOYNE, J. and CLARK, D. (1981), 'Reconstituted Families', in Rapoport, R. N., Fogarty, M. and Rapopart, R., *Families in Britain*, London, Routledge & Kegan Paul.

CHANEY, J. (1981), *Social networks and job information: the situation of women who return to work*, Manchester, Equal Opportunities Commission.

CHAPMAN, A. (1984), *Patterns of Occupational Mobility amongst Men and Women in Scotland: 1930–1970*, Plymouth, Unpublished PhD Thesis, Plymouth Polytechnic.

CHAPMAN, A. (1987), *Men's Work, Women's Work*, Stoke-on-Trent, Information Education.

CHAPMAN, A. (1989), *Just the Ticket? Men and Women Graduates in the Labour Market Three Years after Leaving College*, Higher Education and the Labour Market Working Paper, 8, London, CNAA.

CHASE, I. D. (1975), 'A Comparison of Men's and Women's Intergenerational Mobility in the United States', *American Sociological Review*, 40, 4, pp. 483–505.

CHIPLIN, B. and SLOANE, P. (1982), *Tackling Discrimination at the Workplace*, Cambridge, Cambridge University Press.

CLARKE, E. (1957), *The Conditions of Economic Progress*, (3rd Edn), London, Macmillan.

COCKBURN, C. (1983), *Brothers: male dominance and technological change*, London, Pluto.

COCKBURN, C. (1987), *Two Track Training*, London, Macmillan.

COONEY, R., SOKOLOVE, A. and SALTO, J. (1982), 'Status Attainment of Young White Men and Women: two socioeconomic measures', in Powers, M. (Ed) *Measures of Socioeconomic Status*, New York, Westview Press.

CORCORAN, M., DUNCAN, G. and PONZA, M. (1983), 'A Longitudinal Analysis of White Women's Wages', *The Journal of Human Resources*, 18, 4, pp. 497–519.

COYLE, A. (1982), 'Sex and Skill in the Organisation of the Clothing Industry', in West, J. (Ed) *Work, Women and the Labour Market*, London, Routledge & Kegan Paul.

COYLE, A. (1985), 'Going Private: the implications of privatisation for women's work', *Feminist Review*, 21, 4, pp. 6–22.

CRAIG, C., GARNSEY, E. and RUBERY, J. (1985), *Pay in Small Firms: Women and Informal Payment Systems*, London, Research Paper No 48, Department of Employment.

CRAIG, C., RUBERY, J., TARLING, R. and WILKINSON, F. (1982), *Labour Market Structure, Industrial Organisation and Low Pay*, Cambridge, Cambridge University Press.

CRAIG, C. and WILKINSON, F. (1985), *Pay and Employment in Four Retail Trades*, London, Research Paper No 51, Department of Employment.

CROMPTON, R. (1984), 'Women and the "Service" Class', Paper presented at the ESRC Gender and Stratification Symposium, Cambridge.

CROMPTON, R. (1989), 'Class Theory and Gender' *British Journal of Sociology*, 40, 4, pp. 565–587.

CROMPTON, R. and JONES, G. (1984), *White Collar Proletariat: Deskilling and Gender in the Clerical Labour Process*, London, Macmillan.

CROMPTON, R. and MANN, M. (1986), *Gender and Stratification*, Cambridge, Polity Press.

CROMPTON, R. and SANDERSON, K. (1990), *Gendered Jobs and Social Change*, London, Unwin-Hyman.

DALE, A. (1985), 'Integrating Women into Class Theory', *Sociology*, 15, 3, pp. 407–34.

DALE, A. (1987a), 'Occupational Inequality, Gender and Life-Cycle', *Work, Employment and Society*, 1, pp. 326–351.

DALE, A. (1987b), 'The Effect of Life-Cycle on Three Measures of Stratification', in Bryman, A., *et al.*, (Eds) *Rethinking the Life Cycle,* London, Macmillan.

DALE, A. and BAMFORD, C. (1988), *Flexibility and the Peripheral Workforce*, Occasional papers in Sociology and Social Policy, 11, Department of Sociology, University of Surrey.

DALE, A. and BAMFORD, C. (1989), 'Social Polarization in Britain, 1973–1982: evidence from the GHS — a comment on Pahl', *International Journal of Urban and Regional Research*, 13, 3, pp. 481–500.

DALE, A. and GILBERT, N. (1984), 'Labour Market Structure in the UK: a consideration of some theories of segmentation', mimeo, Department of Sociology, University of Surrey.

DELAMONT, S. (1989a), 'Citation and Social Mobility Research: self-defeating behaviour', *Sociological Review*, 37, 2, pp. 333–37.

DELAMONT, S. (1989b), *Knowledgeable Women: Structuralism and the Reproduction of Elites*, London, Routledge.

DELPHY, C. and LEONARD, D. (1986), 'Class Analysis, Gender Analysis, and the Family', in Crompton, R. and Mann, M. (Eds) *Gender and Stratification*, Cambridge, Polity Press.

DEPARTMENT OF EDUCATION AND SCIENCE (1986), *Statistical Bulletin*, 4/86, February.

DEX, S. (1984a), *Women's Work Histories: an analysis of the Women and Employment Survey*, London, Research Paper No 46, Department of Employment.

DEX, S. (1984b), 'Work History Analysis, Women and Large-Scale Data Sets', *The Sociological Review*, 32, 4, pp. 637–61.

DEX, S. (1985), *The Sexual Division of Work*, Brighton, Wheatsheaf.

DEX, S. (1987), *Women's Occupational Mobility*, London, Macmillan.

DEX, S. (1990), 'Goldthorpe on Gender and Class — the case against it', in Clark, J., Modgil, C. and Modgil, S. (Eds) *John H. Goldthorpe: Consensus and Controversy*, London, Falmer Press.

DEX, S. and PERRY, S. M. (1984), 'Women's employment changes in the 1970s', *Employment Gazette*, 92, 4, pp. 151–64.

DUNCAN, B. and DUNCAN, O. D. (1978), *Sex Typing and Social Roles*, New York, Seminar Press.

DUNCAN, G. J. and MORGAN, J. N. (1981), 'Persistence and Change in Economic Status and the Role of Changing Family Composition', in Hill, M. S. *et al.* (Eds), *Five Thousand American Families — Patterns of Economic Progress*, 12, Ann Arbor, University of Michigan, Survey Research Center.

DUNCAN, O. D., FEATHERMAN, D. and DUNCAN, B. (1972), *Socioeconomic Background and Achievement*, New York, Seminar Press.

EDWARDS, R. C. (1979), *Contested Terrain*, New York, Basic Books.

EEKELAAR, J. and MACLEAN, M. (1986), *Maintenance After Divorce*, Oxford, Clarendon Press.

ELIAS, P. and MAIN, B. (1982), *Women's Working Lives*, Institute for Employment Research, University of Warwick.

ENGLAND, P. (1981), 'Assessing Trends in Occupational Segregation, 1900–1976', in Berg, J. (Ed) *Sociological Perspectives on Labour Markets*, New York, Academic Press.

EQUAL OPPORTUNITIES COMMISSION (EOC) (1986), *Men and Women in Britain: a statistical profile*, London, HMSO.

177

ERIKSON, R. (1984), 'Social Class of Men, Women and Families', *Sociology*, 18, 4, pp. 500–14.

ERIKSON, R. and GOLDTHORPE, J. (1985), *Commonality and Variation in Social Fluidity in Industrial Nations: some preliminary results*, Mannheim, CASMIN, Working Paper No 4.1.

ERIKSON, R. and PONTINEN, S. (1985), 'Social mobility in Finland and Sweden: a comparision of men and women', in Alapuro, R., *et al.* (Eds), *Small States in Comparative Perspective*, Oslo, Norwegian University Press.

ERMISCH, J. and WRIGHT, R. E. (1988), *Women's Wages in Full and Part Time Jobs in Great Britain*, London, CEPR Discussion Paper No 234.

FEATHERMAN, D. and HAUSER, R. M. (1976), 'Sexual Inequalities and Socioeconomic Achievement in the US, 1962–1973', *American Sociological Review*, 41, 4, pp. 462–83.

FINCH, J. (1983), *Married to the Job*, London, Allen & Unwin.

FLOUD, J. and HALSEY, A. (1961), 'Introduction', in Halsey, A., Floud, J. and Anderson, C. (Eds) *Education, Economy and Society*, London, Collier-Macmillan.

FOGARTY, M., ALLEN, A., ALLEN, I. and WALTERS, P. (1971), *Women in Top Jobs*, London, Allen and Unwin.

GIDDENS, A. (1973), *The Class Structure of the Advanced Societies*, London, Hutchinson.

GILBERT, N. (1985), 'Occupational Class and Inter-class Mobility', *British Journal of Sociology*, 37, 3, pp. 370–91.

GILBERT, G., DALE, A., ARBER, S., EVANDROU, M. and LACZKO, F. (1989), 'Resources in Old Age: Ageing and the life course', in Jeffreys, M. (Ed) *Growing Old in the Twentieth Century*, London, Routledge & Kegan Paul.

GLASS, D. V. (Ed) (1954), *Social Mobility in Britain*, London, Routledge & Kegan Paul.

GLENDINNING, C. and MILLAR, J. (Eds) (1987), *Women and Poverty in Britain*, Brighton, Wheatsheaf.

GLENN, N., ROSS, A. and TULLY, J. (1974), 'Patterns of Intergenerational Mobility of Females through Marriage', *American Sociological Review*, 39, 4, pp. 683–99.

GOLDTHORPE, J. H. (1983), 'Women and Class Analysis: in defence of the conventional view', *Sociology*, 17, 4, pp. 465–88.

GOLDTHORPE, J. H. (1984), 'Women and Class Analysis: a reply to the replies'. *Sociology*, 18, 4, pp. 491–9.

GOLDTHORPE, J. H., with LLEWELLYN, C. and PAYNE, C. (1980, 1987), *Social Mobility and Class Structure in Modern Britain*, Oxford, Clarendon Press.

GOLDTHORPE, J. H. and PAYNE, C. (1986), 'On the Class Mobility of Women: results from different approaches to the analysis of recent British data'. *Sociology*, 20, 4, pp. 531–55.

GRAHAM, H. (1987), 'Women's Poverty and Caring' in Glendinning, C. and Millar, J. (Eds) *Women and Poverty in Britain*, Brighton, Wheatsheaf.

GREENHALGH, C. and STEWART, M. B. (1982), *Occupational Status and Mobility of Men and Women*, Warwick, University of Warwick, Warwick Economic Papers, 211.

HAKIM, C. (1979), *Occupational Segregation*, London, Research Paper No 9, Department of Employment.

HARRIS, A. and CLAUSEN, R. (1967), *Labour Mobility in Great Britain*, London, HMSO.

HARTMANN, H. (1976), 'Capitalism, patriarchy and job segregation by sex', *Signs*, 1, 2.

HASKEY, J. (1986), 'One-parent Families in Britain', *Population Trends*, 45, pp. 5–13.

HAUSER, R. M. and FEATHERMAN, D. (1977), *The Process of Stratification: trends and analyses*, New York, Academic Press.

HAUSER, R. M., FEATHERMAN, D. and HOGAN, D. (1974), *Race and Sex in the Structure of Occupational Mobility in the US, 1962*, Working Paper, Center for Demography and Ecology, University of Wisconsin.

HAUSER, R., KOFFEL, J., TRAVIS, H. and DICKINSON, P. (1975a), 'Temporal change in occupational mobility', *American Sociological Review*, 40, 3, pp. 279–97.

HAUSER, R., DICKINSON, P., TRAVIS, H. and KOFFEL, J. (1975b), 'Structural Change in Occupational Mobility Among Men in the United States', *American Sociological Review*, 40, 5, pp. 585–98.

HAYES, B. C. (1987), 'Female Intergenerational occupational Mobility within Northern Ireland and the Republic of Ireland: the importance of maternal occupational status', *British Journal of Sociology*, 38, 1, pp. 66–76.

HAYES, B. C. (forthcoming). 'Female Intergenerational Occupational Mobility within Northern Ireland: do parental background characteristics matter?', in Maguire, M. (Ed) *Unequal Labour: Women and Work in Northern Ireland*, Belfast Policy Research Institute, Northern Ireland.

HAYES, B. C. and MILLER, R. L. (1989), 'Intergenerational Occupational Mobility within the Republic of Ireland: the ignored female dimension. *Women's Studies International Forum*, 12, pp. 439–45.

HEARN, J. (1977), 'Towards the concept of non-career', *Sociological Review*, 25, 2, pp. 273–88.

HEATH, A. (1981), *Social Mobility*, London, Fontana.

HEATH, A. and BRITTEN, N. (1984), 'Women's jobs do make a difference', *Sociology*, 18, 1, pp. 475–90.

HEATH, A., JOWELL, R. and CURTICE, J. (1985), *How Britain Votes*, Oxford, Pergamon.

HERITAGE, J. (1983), 'Feminisation and Unionisation', in Gamarnikow, E., Morgan, D., Purvis, J. and Taylerson, D., (Eds) *Gender, Class and Work*, London, Heinemann.

HIBBERT, V. (1988a), 'Childcare Provision I: employers head for the nursery', *Industrial Relations Review and Report*, 425, October 4th, pp. 2–7.

HIBBERT, V. (1988b), 'Childcare Provision II: allowances and other benefits', *Industrial Relations Review and Report*, 428, November 15th, pp. 7–9.

HIBBERT, V. (1989), 'Bridging the career break', *Industrial Relations Services Employment Trends*, 431, January 10th, pp. 6–9.

HINDESS, B. (1981), 'The Politics of Social Mobility', *Economy and Society*, 10, 2, pp. 184–202.

HOLLAND, L. (1989), 'Career break schemes', *Women in Management Review and Abstracts*, 4, 2, pp. 5–9.

HOPE, K. and GOLDTHORPE, J. H. (1974), *The Social Grading of Occupations: a new approach and scale*, Oxford, Oxford University Press.

HUNT, P. (1980), *Gender and Class Consciousness*, London, Macmillan.

HURSTFIELD, J. (1987), *Part-timers Under Pressure*, London, Low Pay Unit.

JACKSON, B. and MARSDEN, D. (1966), *Education and the Working Class*, Harmondsworth, Penguin.

JACKSON, J. A. (1975), 'A Survey of Social and Occupational Mobility in Ireland: Report on progress', in *Proceedings of the Second Annual Conference*, Belfast, Sociological Association of Ireland, pp. 93–101.

JOHN, A. V. (Ed) (1986), *Unequal Opportunities: women's employment in England 1800–1918*, Oxford, Blackwell.

JOHNSON, T. (1972), *Professions and Power*, London, Macmillan.

JONES, G. (1986), 'Youth in the Social Structure: Transitions to adulthood and their stratification by class and gender', unpublished PhD thesis, University of Surrey.

JONES, G. (1987a), 'Young Workers in the Class Structure', *Work, Employment and Society*, 1, 4, pp. 486–507.

JONES, G. (1987b), 'Leaving the Parental Home: an analysis of early housing careers', *Journal of Social Policy*, 16, 1, pp. 49–74.

JOSEPH, G. (1983), *Women at Work*, Oxford, Phillip Allan.

JOSHI, H. E. (1984), *Women's Participation in Paid Work: further analysis of the women and employment survey*, Research Paper No 45, Department of Employment.

JOSHI, H. (1987), 'The Cost of Caring', in Glendinning, C. and Millar, J. (Eds) *Women and Poverty*, Brighton, Wheatsheaf.

JOSHI, H., LAYARD, R. and OWEN, S. J. (1985), 'Why Are More Women Working in Britain?' *Journal of Labor Economics*, 3, 1, Part 2, pp. S147-S176.

KELLY, J. (1990), 'The Failure of a Paradigm: log linear models of social mobility', in Clarke, J., Modgil, C. and Modgil, S. (Eds) *John H. Goldthorpe: Consensus and Controversy*, London, Falmer.

KENDRICK, S., BECHHOFER, F. and McCRONE, D. (1982), *Industrial and Occupational Structure*, Edinburgh, Social Structure of Modern Scotland Project Working Paper No 2, University of Edinburgh.

KUMAR, K. (1984), 'Unemployment as a Problem in the Development of Industrial Societies', *Sociological Review*, 23, 2, pp. 185–233.

LACZKO, F., DALE, A., GILBERT, N. and ARBER, S. (1988), 'Early Retirement in a Period of High Unemployment', *Journal of Social Policy*, 17, 3, pp. 313–33.

LAND, H. (1980), *The Family Wage*, The Eleanor Rathbone Memorial Lecture, 1979, Liverpool, Liverpool Free Press.

LAND, H. (1983), 'Poverty and Gender: the distribution of resources within the family', in Brown, M. (Ed) *The Structure of Disadvantage*, London, Heinemann.

LAYARD, R., PIACHAUD, D. and STEWART, M. (1979), *The Causes of Poverty*, Royal Commission on the Distribution of Income and Wealth, Background Paper, 5, London, HMSO.

LAZEAR, E. P. and MICHAEL, R. T. (1988), *Allocation of Income within the Household*, Chicago, University of Chicago Press.

LEE, D. (1981), 'Skill Craft and Class', *Sociology*, 15, 1. pp. 56–78.

LLEWELLYN, C. (1981), 'Occupational Mobility and the use of the comparative method', in Roberts, H. (Ed) *Doing Feminist Research*, London, Routledge & Kegan Paul.

LOCKWOOD, D. (1986), 'Class, Status and Gender' in Crompton, R. and Mann, M. (Eds) *Gender and Stratification*, Cambridge, Polity Press.

LOETHER, H. and McTAVISH, D. (1980), *Descriptive and Inferential Statistics: an introduction*. London, Allyn & Bacon.

LOVERIDGE, R. and MOK, A. (1979), *Theories of Labour Market Segmentation*, The Hague, Martinus Nijhoff.

LOWE, S. (1988), 'New Patterns of Wealth: The growth of owner occupation', in Parker, G. and Walker, R. (Eds) *Money matters*, London, Sage.

McCLENDON, J. (1976), 'The Occupational Status Attainment Process of Males and females', *American Sociological Review*, 41, 1, pp. 52–64.

McNALLY, F. (1979), *Women for Hire*, London, Macmillan.

McRAE, S. (1986), *Cross-Class Families*, Oxford, Clarendon Press.

MAIN, B. (1988), 'Women's Hourly Earnings: the influence of work histories on rates of pay', in Hunt, A. (Ed) *Women and Paid Work*, Warwick Studies in Employment, Basingstoke, Macmillan.

MARINI, M. (1980), 'Sex Difference in the Process of Occupational Attainment: a closer look', *Social Science Research*, 9, 3, pp. 307–61.

MARSHALL, G., ROSE, D., NEWBY, H. and VOGLER, C. (1988), *Social Class in Modern Britain*, London, Unwin-Hyman.

MARTIN, J. and ROBERTS, C. (1984), *Women and Employment: A lifetime perspective*, London, HMSO.

MILIBAND, R. (1969), *The State in Capitalist Society*, London, Weidenfeld and Nicolson.

MILLAR, J. (1987), 'Lone Mothers', in Glendinning, C. and Millar, J. (Eds) *Women and Poverty in Britain*, Brighton, Wheatsheaf.

MILLER, R. L. (1979), 'A Model of Social Mobility in Northern Ireland', in Compton, P. (Ed) *Religion, Education and Employment*, Belfast, Institute of Irish Studies, Queen's University of Belfast.

MILLER, R. L. (1981), 'A Model of Social Mobility in Northern Ireland', in Compton, P. A. (Ed) *The Contemporary Population of Northern Ireland and Population-Related Issues*, Belfast, Institute of Irish Studies, the Queen's University of Belfast.

MILLER, P. L. (1983), 'Religion and Occupational Mobility', in Cormack, R. J. and Osborne, R. D. (Eds) *Aspects of equal opportunity in Northern Ireland*, Belfast, Appletree Press.

MILLER, R. and HAYES, B. (unpublished), *Gender and Intergenerational Mobility in Northern Ireland*.

MÜLLER, W., KARLE, W., KONIG, W. and LUTTINGER, P. (1988), 'Education and Class Mobility', Mannheim, CASMIN Working Paper No 14.

NEWBY, H. (1982), *The State of Research into Social Stratification in Britain*, London, SSRC.

O'HIGGINS, M., BRADSHAW, J. and WALKER, R. (1988), 'Income Distribution over the Life Cycle' in Parker, G. and Walker, R. (Eds) *Money Matters*, London, Sage.

OPCS (1979), *General Household Survey, 1971*, London, HMSO.

OPCS (1980a), *General Household Survey, 1980*, London, HM SO.

OPCS (1980b), *Classification of Occupations, 1980*, London, HMSO.

OPCS (1984), *Population Census, 1981*, London, HMSO.

OPPENHEIMER, V. K. (1977), 'The Sociology of Women's Economic Role in the Family', *American Sociological Review*, 42, 3, pp. 387–405.

OSBORNE, R. D. (1986), 'Segregated Schools and Examination Results in Northern Ireland: some preliminary research', *Educational Research*, 28, 1, pp. 43–50.

OWEN, S. (1987), 'Household Production and Economic Efficiency: arguments for and against domestic specialisation', *Work, Employment and Society*, 1, 2, pp. 157–78.

PAHL, J. (1983), 'The Allocation of Money and the Structuring of Inequality within Marriage', *Sociological Review*, 31, 2, pp. 237–62.

PAHL, J. (1988), 'Earning, Sharing, Spending: married couples and their money', in Parker, G. and Walker, R. (Eds) *Money Matters*, London, Sage.

PAHL, J. (1989), *Money and Marriage*, London, Macmillan.

PAHL, J. and PAHL, R. (1971), *Managers and their Wives*, Harmondsworth, Penguin.

PAHL, R. (1984), *Divisions of Labour*, Oxford, Blackwell.

PAHL, R. (1988), 'Some Remarks on Informal Work, Social Polarisation and the Social Structure', *International Journal of Urban and Regional Research*, 12, 2, pp.247–67.

PAHL, R. and WALLACE, C. (1985), 'Household Work Strategies in Economic Recession', in Mingione, E. and Redlift, N. (Eds) *Beyond Employment*, Oxford, Blackwell.

PARKIN, F. (1972), *Class Inequality and the Political Order: social stratification in capitalist and communist countries*, St Albans, Paladin.

PARKIN, F. (1979), *Marxism and Class Theory*, London, Tavistock.

PAYNE, G. (1987a), *Employment and Opportunity*, London, Macmillan.

PAYNE, G. (1987b), *Mobility and Change in Modern Society*, London, Macmillan.

PAYNE, G. (1989a), 'Social Mobility', in Burgess, R., (Ed) *Investigating Society*, London, Longman.

PAYNE, G. (1989b), 'Social Mobility', *British Journal of Sociology*, 40, 3, pp. 471–92.

PAYNE, G. (1990), 'Social Divisions, Social Change and Social Mobility', paper read at the BSA Annual Conference, Guildford, Surrey.

PAYNE, G., FORD, R., and ROBERTSON, C. (1976), 'Changes in occupational mobility in Scotland: some preliminary findings of the 1975 Scottish Mobility Study', *Scottish Journal of Sociology*, 1, 1, pp. 57–79.

PAYNE, G., FORD, G. and ULAS, M. (1979), *Education and Social Mobility*, SIP Occasional Papers No 8, Edinburgh, SIP.

PAYNE, G., FORD, G. and ULAS, M. (1981), 'Occupational and Social Mobility in Scotland', in Gaskin, M. (Ed) *The Political Economy of Tolerable Survival*, Beckenham, Croom Helm.

PAYNE, G. and PAYNE, J. (1981), 'Social Mobility and the Labour Market', paper read at the BSA Annual Conference, Aberystwyth.

PAYNE, G., PAYNE, J. and CHAPMAN, T. (1983), 'Trends in Female Social Mobility', in Gamarnikow, E., Morgan, D., Purvis, J. and Taylerson, D., (Eds) *Gender, Class and Work*, London, Heinemann.

PAYNE, J. (1987), 'Does Unemployment Run in Families?', *Sociology*, 21, 2, pp. 199–214.

PEARSON, J. (1983), 'Mothers and Daughters: measuring occupational inheritance', *Sociology and Social Research*, 67, 2, pp. 204–17.

PEARSON, R., PIKE, G., GORDON, A. and WEYMAN, C. (1989), *How Many Graduates in the 21st Century? The Choice is Yours*, Brighton, IMS.

PEDHAZUR, E. (1982), *Multiple Regression in Behavioural Research*, New York, Holt, Rinehart & Winston.

PIORE, M. J. (1975), 'Notes for A Theory of Labor Market Stratification', in Edwards, R., Reich, M. and Gordon, D. (Eds) *Labour Market Segmentation*, Lexington, D.C. Heath.

PORTER, M. (1983), *Home, Work, Class Consciousness*, Manchester, Manchester University Press.

POWELL, B. and JACOBS, J. (1984), 'Gender Differences in the Evaluation of Prestige', *Sociological Quarterly*, 25, 2, pp.173–90.

POWERS, M. G. (1982), 'Measures of Socioeconomic Status: an introduction', in Powers, M. (Ed) *Measure of Socioeconomic Status*, New York, Westview Press.

PSACHAROPOULOS, G. (1978), 'Labour Market Duality and Income Distribution: the case of the UK', in Krelle, W. and Shorrocks, A. F. (Eds) *Personal Income Distribution*, North-Holland.

RAFFE, D. (1979), 'The "Alternative Route" Reconsidered: part-time further education and social mobility in England and Wales', *Sociology*, 13, 1, pp. 47–73.

RILEY, D. (1980), 'The Free Mothers: pronatalisation and working women in industry at the end of the last war in Britain, *History Workshop*, 11, Spring, pp. 59–118.

RIMMER, L. and POPAY, J. (1983), *Employment Trends and the Family*, London, Study Commission on the Family.

ROBERTS, K. (1975), 'The Developmental Theory of Occupational Choice: a critique and an alternative', in Esland, R., Salaman, G. and Speakman, M. (Eds) *People and Work*, Edinburgh, Holmes-MacDougall.

ROSENFELD, R. (1978), 'Women's Intergenerational Occupational Mobility', *American Sociological Review*, 43, 1, pp. 36–46.

ROSSI, A. (1971), 'Women in Science: why so few?' in Epstein, C. and Goode, W. J. (Eds) *The Other Half*, Englewood Cliffs N.J., Prentice-Hall.

ROWNTREE, B. S. (1902), *Poverty: a study of town life*, 2nd Ed, London, Macmillan.

RUBERY, J. (1978), 'Structured Labour Markets, Worker Organization and Low Pay', *Cambridge Journal of Economics*, 2, 1, pp. 17–36.

RUBERY, J. and WILKINSON, F. (1980), 'Notes on the Nature of the Labour Process in the Secondary Sector', *Low Pay and Labour Markets Segmentation*, Conference Papers, Cambridge, 1979.

RUTTER, K. and HARGEN, L. (1975), 'Occupational Positions and Class Identifications of Married Working Women', *American Journal of Sociology*, 86, 3, pp. 934–48.

SAUNDERS, P. (1989), 'Left Write in Sociology', *Network*, 44, pp. 4–5.

SAUNDERS, P. (1990), *Social Class and Stratification*, London, Routledge.

SEWELL, W., HAUSER, R. and WOLF, W. (1980), 'Sex, Schooling and Occupational Status', *American Journal of Sociology*, 86, 3, pp. 551–83.

SHEPHERD, P. (1985), *The National Child Development Study: an introduction to the background of the study and the methods of data collection*, London, Working Paper 1, NCDS User Support Group, City University.

SILTANEN, J. (1986), 'Domestic Responsibilities and the Structuring of Employment', in Crompton, R. and Mann, M. *Gender and Stratification*, Cambridge, Polity Press.

SILVERSTONE, R. (1980), 'Accountancy', in Silverstone, R. and Ward, A. (Eds) *Careers of Professional Women*, London, Croom Helm.

SMAIL, R. (1988), 'Non-wage Benefits from Employment', in Parker, G. and Walker, R. (Eds) *Money Matters*, London, Sage.

SOROKIN, P. A. (1927), *Social Mobility*, New York, Harper & Brothers.

SPAETH, J. (1977), 'Differences in the Occupational Achievement Process between Male and Female College Graduates', *Sociology of Education*, 50, 7, pp. 206–17.

SPEAKMAN, M. (1980), 'Occupational Choice and Placement', in Esland, G. and Salaman, G. (Eds) *People and Work*, Milton Keynes, Open University Press.

STANWORTH, M. (1984), 'Women and Class Analysis: a reply to Goldthorpe', *Sociology*, 18, 2, pp. 159–70.

STEVENS, G. and BOYD, M. (1980), 'The Importance of Mother: labour force participation and intergenerational mobility of women', *Social Forces*, 59, 1, pp. 186–99.

STEWART, A., PRANDY, K. and BLACKBURN, R. (1980), *Social Stratification and Occupations*, London, Macmillan.

TITMUSS, R. (1963), *Essays on 'The Welfare State'*, London, Unwin University Books.

TOWNSEND, P. (1979), *Poverty in the United Kingdom*, Harmondsworth, Penguin.

TREAS, J. and TYREE, A. (1979), 'Prestige versus Socioeconomic Status in the Attainment Process of American Men and Women', *Social Science Research*, 8, pp. 201–21.

TYREE, A. and TREAS, J. (1974), 'The Occupational and Marital Mobility of Women', *American Sociological Review*, 39, 3, pp. 293–302.

VOGLER, C. (1990), *Labour Market Change and Patterns of Financial Allocation within Households*, London, SCELI Working Paper No 12, ESRC.

WALBY, S. (1986), *Patriarchy at Work*, Cambridge, Polity Press.

WALKER, A. (1980), 'The Social Creation of Poverty and Dependency in Old Age', *Journal of Social Policy*, 9, 1, pp. 49–75.

WEBSTER, J. (1986), 'Word Processing and the Secretarial Labour Process', in Purcell, K., Wood, S., Waton, A. and Allen, S. (Eds) *The Changing Experience of Employment: restructuring and recession*, London, Macmillan.

WEDDERBURN, D. and CRAIG, C. (1974), 'Relative Deprivation in Work', in Wedderburn, D. (Ed) *Poverty, Inequality and Class Structure*, London, Cambridge University Press.

WEST, J. (1978), 'Women, sex and class', in Kuhn, A. and Wolpe, A. (Eds) *Feminism and Materialism: women and modes of production*, London, Routledge & Kegan Paul.

WEST, J. (1982), 'New Technology and Women's Office Work', in West, J. (Ed) *Women, Work and the Labour Market*, London, Routledge & Kegan Paul.

WESTERGAARD, J. (1972), 'The Myth of Classlessness', in Blackburn, R. (Ed) *Ideology in Social Science: Readings in critical social theory*, London, Fontana.

WESTERGAARD, J. and LITTLE, A. (1967), 'Educational Opportunity and Social Selection in England and Wales: Trends and implications', in *Social Objectives in Educational Planning*, Paris, OECD.

WESTERGAARD, J. and RESLER, H. (1975/1977), *Class in Capitalist Society: a study of contemporary Britain*, London, Heinemann/Harmondsworth, Penguin.

WIGGINS, R. and O'MUIRCHEARTAIGH, C. (1977), 'Sample Design and Evaluation for an Occupational Mobility Study', *The Economic and Social Review*, 8, 2, pp. 102–16.

WRIGHT, E. O. (Ed) (1978), *Class, Crisis and the State*, 1979, New York, Verso.

YEANDLE, S. (1984), *Women's Working Lives*, London, Tavistock.

Notes on Contributors

Pamela Abbott is Principal Lecturer in Sociology and Social Policy at Polytechnic South West, Plymouth. She has contributed to Open University units, and has written *Women and Social Class* (with Roger Sapsford, 1987, Tavistock) and *Introducing Sociology: a feminist perspective* (with Claire Wallace, 1990, Routledge). She has also co-edited several books on health, the caring professions, and gender.

Tony Chapman is Senior Lecturer in Sociology at Teesside Polytechnic. After completing doctoral work on women and social mobility at Plymouth Polytechnic he taught sociology at Staffordshire Polytechnic where he researched the careers of women and men graduates funded by the CNAA. He is currently engaged in research on equal opportunities policies.

Rosemary Crompton is Senior Lecturer in Sociology at the University of Kent. She has edited (with Michael Mann) *Gender and Stratification* (Polity, 1986) and her most recent book is *Gendered Jobs and Social Change* (Unwin Hyman, 1990).

Angela Dale is Deputy Director of the Social Statistics Research Unit, City University. She has a long-standing interest in women's employment issues and stratification generally. Most of her work has used secondary analysis of large scale government surveys: she is joint author of *Doing Secondary Analysis* (Unwin Hyman, 1988).

Shirley Dex is Senior Lecturer in Economics at the University of Keele. She is the author of *The Sexual Division of Work*, (Wheatsheaf, 1985). *British and American Women at Work*, (Macmillan, 1986) with Lois Shaw, *Women's Occupational Mobility*, (Macmillan, 1987) and *Women's Attitudes Towards Work*, (Macmillan, 1988).

Bernadette C. Hayes is a Research Fellow at the Australian National University. She has written a number of articles on social, stratification and gender relations in Ireland and is currently investigating the social mobility experiences of Australian women.

Gill Jones is a Research Fellow at the Centre for Educational Sociology, University of Edinburgh. Her overall research interest is in inequalities in youth, and she is currently researching family and household formation, and the economic basis of the transitions to adulthood.

Robert L. Miller studied at Duke and the University of Florida (Gainesville) before joining Queen's University of Belfast where he completed his PhD and became a Lecturer in Sociology. He has written on social mobility, and equal opportunity in Northern Ireland, some of the latter work leading directly to reforms in the Northern Ireland Civil Service.

Geoff Payne is Dean of Human Sciences at Polytechnic South West, Plymouth. Formerly Director of the Scottish Mobility Study at Aberdeen University, he has written extensively on mobility and related topics, including *Mobility and Change in Modern Society* (1987, Macmillan) and *Employment and Opportunity* (1987, Macmillan).

Judy Payne has been a Lecturer in Sociology at Newcastle Polytechnic and a Research Officer in the Medical Sociology Unit at Aberdeen University, writing on social mobility, housing and fertility. She was occupationally mobile into a second career as a systems analyst, before recently beginning a third career. At the time of going to press she is in her final year of a Fine Art degree.

Kay Sanderson was a mature undergraduate and graduate student at University of Essex between 1979–1984 and until 1988 was as researcher for the 'Women's Careers' project at UEA. She is currently employed as co-ordinator of the Women's Employment Enterprise and Training Unit, based in Norwich.

Subject Index

Aberdeen 5, 6, 25
accountants 9, 17, 74, 89–94, 98, 99, 105
'alternative route' 111
America: *see* United States
armed forces 52
autonomy 17–18
banking 9, 92, 95, 98, 99, 150
British General Election Survey 38
British Household Panel Study 145
British Sociological Association ix, x
brothers 8, 18, 62, 65, 161–2
buffer zone 7, 37–9, 41, 44–5, 168
Building Societies Institute 94
capital 51
career (*see also* Mobility) 4, 7, 8, 9, 18, 85,
  86–100, 118, 119, 159, 164, 172
casmin 65, 70
catering 88
census 17, 24, 41, 52, 78, 80, 81, 104, 151
Chartered Association of Certified
  Accountants 93
Chartered Building Societies Institute 89
Chartered Institute of Public Finance and
  Accountancy 89–90, 93, 94–5
Chartered Insurance Institute 89, 93, 94
child bearing *see* child birth
child birth 9, 10, 11, 83, 84, 87, 119, 126–9, 131,
  133, 134, 135, 148, 150, 154, 155, 163, 164
child care 10, 81, 88, 134, 148
class analysis 6, 121, 139
  definition of women's ix, 4, 15, 47–9, 61–2,
    84, 101–3, 159, 168–74
  endogamy 3, 106–12, 117–8
  exogamy 10
  manual 41, 44–5, 49, 50ff, 62, 103, 106, 167
  middle 43, 109, 111, 114–8, 169
  mobility ix, 4, 11, 14, 15, 16, 47

non-manual 41, 44–5, 49, 50ff, 62, 78, 103
occupational (*see* occupations)
  service 6, 17, 166
  structure 7, 15, 21, 37, 54, 101
  working 41, 50, 53, 62, 87, 109, 114–8
cohort 24, 73, 74, 78, 83, 148
Council for Legal Education 94
counter-balance 37–8, 41, 44, 168
counter-mobility 7, 10, 41–4, 114–6, 117–8
cross-class marriage, *see* marriage

daughters 5, 6, 17, 22, 40, 41, 42, 43, 44, 52–3,
  62–71, 162, 172
decision-making 17–8
demand-side factors 7, 85, 159
demobilization 52
dentistry 89, 93, 94
Depression 7, 51
Department of Education 100, 163
Department of Employment 83, 123
destination 4, 5, 6, 21, 47, 48, 53, 62, 64, 160
division of labour 140, 144, 145, 150, 151, 152,
  171
divorce 10–11, 87, 141, 147, 148, 152, 153, 154,
  156
doctors *see* medicine

education (*see also*) qualifications) 2, 5, 7, 8, 9,
  10, 38, 41–3, 44, 58, 61, 63, 65, 66–71, 105,
  111, 114–8, 136, 160, 161, 162–3, 167, 169,
  174
Education Act 7, 160
élites 37
ESRC 119, 155
Essex Class Study 4, 5, 6, 13, 14, 17, 18–20, 24,
  39, 167

Family Expenditure Survey 144
fathers 6, 8, 15, 18, 20, 26, 28, 29, 34, 38, 39,
    41, 42, 43, 44, 51, 62, 63, 65, 68, 70, 71,
    101, 103, 107–10, 119, 136, 152, 159, 160,
    162, 166, 172, 173, 174
feminists 1–2, 12, 122

GCE 'A' levels 86, 90
    'O' levels 90
gender (as a variable in regression) 66–8
General Household Survey (GHS) 9, 13, 104,
    105, 106, 108, 110, 112–3, 114, 115, 119,
    141, 142–5, 147, 153, 154, 155, 156–7
graduates 81

hairdressing 91, 124
home ownership 142–4, 161
household 3, 4, 10–11, 13–14, 48, 84, 101, 104,
    136, 139, 140, 141, 142–6, 152, 153, 154,
    155, 156–7, 159, 160, 161, 162, 163, 173,
    174
human capital 84–5, 150
husbands 2, 8, 9, 14, 15, 47, 49, 101, 103, 107,
    108, 109, 114–6, 136, 139, 140, 141, 142,
    144–5, 163, 167

immobility 28, 34, 54, 114–8, 159, 164
income (*see also* pay) 11, 101, 136, 139, 140–2,
    144–7, 148, 150, 152–4, 160, 161, 167
industry, manufacturing 7, 51, 54–7, 59, 123, 124
    old staple 51
    sectors 7, 54–60
    secondary (*see* manufacturing)
    service 7, 54, 60, 122, 151, 163
    tertiary (*see* service industry)
    primary 54, 58
Institute of Banking 88, 89, 94
Institute of Chartered Accountants 94
Institute of Cost and Management
    Accountants 90, 94, 95
Institute of Purchasing 89
Ireland, Republic of 63, 64, 70
Irish Mobility Study 5, 7, 13, 24, 63–71

job *see* occupation
    aspirations 48

Labour Force Survey 149
labour market 2, 3, 5, 7, 9, 10, 11, 14, 15,
    16–21, 22, 26, 28, 34, 38, 42, 59, 66, 73, 74,
    78, 80, 81, 84, 87, 101, 102, 121, 122, 134,
    135, 136, 140, 141, 146, 147, 148, 149, 150,
    152, 159, 160, 161, 162, 163, 164, 166, 169

gender segregation 16–21, 22
Labour Mobility Study 12, 13
law 9, 89, 91
Law Society 94
lawyers 16, 74, 105
lecturers 17
librarians 16
life-course 11, 140, 143, 147, 148, 150–1, 152,
    154–5, 160, 164
life-cycle 10, 87, 121, 123, 129, 134, 136, 141,
    149, 167
life-style 48, 152, 167, 173
log-linear models 21, 24, 111, 119
London School of Economics 12, 25

managers *see* occupational categories
manual workers *see* occupational categories
manual class *see* class
market situation 17
marriage 9, 10, 53, 83, 101–119, 131, 152, 154,
    159, 168, 173–4
    cross-class 9, 14–5, 103, 113–4, 161, 164,
    166–8
    partners 3, 6, 11, 101–19
medicine 9, 10, 89, 91, 93–4, 105, 124–5
mobility (*see also* class mobility, immobility)
    absolute 15, 16, 21–4, 25, 28, 36, 114
    career 43, 47–60, 73–81, 162
    downward 8, 10, 11, 18, 28, 34, 41, 43–4, 62,
    74, 78, 91, 104, 107, 109, 111, 114–8, 126,
    127, 128, 129–131, 133, 134, 136–7, 147,
    148, 153, 159, 163, 164–5, 172–3
    geographical 91
    gross 18
    inflow 6, 19, 25, 29–32, 36, 39, 40
    intergenerational 15, 37, 41–5, 71, 74, 80,
    162, 169
    intergenerational 6, 7, 37, 62, 71, 74, 81, 107,
    162, 169
    long-range 20, 37, 39, 41, 44–5, 168
    marital 101, 102–3, 106–12, 118
    outflow 6, 20, 25, 29–32, 36, 39, 40
    rates 7
    relative 15, 16, 21–4, 25, 32, 34, 114
    short-range 37, 39, 41, 44
    structural 21, 52–3
    upward 6, 7, 8, 9, 11, 17, 18, 20, 21, 28–9, 32,
    34, 41–4, 50ff, 74, 78, 80, 87, 92, 101, 105,
    107, 113, 117–8, 122, 126, 127, 128, 129–31,
    133, 142, 148, 152, 159, 161, 163, 164–5,
    167, 172–3
mothers 5, 7, 8, 47, 48, 62–3, 64, 66–8, 70, 71,
    139, 152, 154, 160, 161, 162, 171, 173, 174

National Child Development Study   43, 112
National Canadian Mobility Study   62–3
National Examinations Board for Supervisory
    Studies   89
National Insurance   146, 151
National Survey of Health and Development   84
National Training Survey   85
Non-manual workers *see* occupational categories
    or class
non-manual class *see* class
Northern Ireland   8, 24, 63–4, 65, 66, 68–70
Northern Ireland Education Act, 1947   70
Nuffield Study   *ix*, 4–5, 12, 25, 37, 39, 41, 44
nurses   10, 16, 74, 83, 86, 88, 90, 92, 105, 124–6,
    131, 132–3, 134–5, 149

occupational attainment   62, 63–4, 70, 101
occupational categories (*see also* class, 'women's
    jobs', etc)
  clerical   10, 22–3, 49, 91, 103, 124–6, 132–3,
      134–5, 149, 169–70, 172
  employers/proprietors   16, 23, 26, 40, 68–9
  farming   16, 26, 69
  intermediate non-manual   10, 16, 124–5, 131,
      132–3, 134–5, 149
  junior non-manual   16, 41, 68–9, 105, 107
  managers   16, 22–3, 39, 40, 41, 53, 68–9, 85,
      88, 105, 167, 169–70, 174
  personal service   16, 68–9
  professional   6, 8, 9, 16, 22–3, 26, 28, 29, 32,
      39, 40, 41, 53, 62, 69, 73, 74–81, 84, 89, 91,
      93, 105, 124, 126, 131, 132, 149, 167,
      169–70, 172
  routine non-manual   6, 7, 22–3, 26, 28–9, 41,
      42, 44–5, 49, 53, 59, 68, 73, 78–81, 162,
      163, 167, 172
  self-employed   16, 22, 26, 53, 69, 105, 146
  semi-skilled manual   6, 10, 22–3, 26, 42, 69,
      73, 78–81, 83, 105, 124–6, 131, 132–3,
      134–5, 149, 169–70
  self-employed   16, 22, 26, 53, 69, 105, 146
  semi-skilled manual   6, 10, 22–3, 26, 42, 69,
      73, 78–81, 83, 105, 124–6, 131, 132–3,
      134–5, 149, 169–70
  skilled manual   6, 22–3, 26, 28, 29, 32, 41, 42,
      68–9, 73, 78–81, 105, 124–6, 132–3, 134–5,
      146, 149, 169–70, 172, 174
  supervisory   16, 22–3, 26, 28, 29, 32, 53,
      68–9, 73, 78–81, 89, 105, 126, 128–9, 169,
      170
  technical   22–3, 26, 28, 29, 32, 78–81
  unskilled manual   22–3, 26, 42, 68–9, 73,
      78–81, 83, 105, 124–6, 132, 135, 149, 169–70

occupational classification and scales   12, 14, 17,
    26, 40, 42, 49, 65, 73, 80, 104–6, 112–3, 125
  distribution   6, 16, 34, 44, 78–9, 149
  prestige   61, 63, 83, 84, 99, 150
  status *see* occupational prestige
  structure   68, 22, 78, 83, 93, 122, 169, 172
  transition   7, 53, 58
office work   17, 49, 57, 59
OPCS   93, 104, 119, 123
Open University (*see* People in Society)
optics   93–4
origins   4, 5, 6, 10, 21, 47, 48, 61, 62, 66, 70, 71,
    73, 75–7, 105, 107, 109, 111, 112, 118
Oxford *see* Nuffield

Panel Study for Income Dynamics
    (Michigan)   150, 153
part time work   10, 11, 14, 41, 44, 71, 83–5, 90,
    95–100, 121, 122, 125, 131, 133, 134–5,
    146–7, 148, 150, 151, 159, 165
participation rates   9, 11, 14, 22, 66,78, 81, 83,
    84, 134, 135, 160, 161, 162, 163, 166
path analysis   8, 64–5, 68
pay (*see also* income)   10, 78, 80, 81
People in Society Survey   13, 37, 38–9, 40–2, 44
pension   11, 146, 147, 151
pharmacy   92–8
Pharmaceutical Society   95–7
Polytechnic South West   *x*
poverty   141, 153
professionals, *see* professional/managerial classes
    occupations
professors   17
programmers   90
proletarianization   45
property   48, 136
public finance   9

qualifications (*see also* education)   9, 10, 54, 60,
    64, 84–100, 148, 150, 159

race   62
regression   64, 66–9, 71
religion   66–70
reserve army   91, 100
role-modelling   63
routine non-manual *see* occupations
RSA   89

Sales work   17, 23, 49, 59, 83, 105, 124–5, 132,
    135, 149, 169
Scotland   26–31, 51
Scottish Mobility Study (*see also* Aberdeen)   2, 7,
    12–3, 14, 17, 18, 25–6, 39, 43, 49, 73

secretaries 22–3, 88, 89, 105
sisters 8, 18, 64, 65, 66, 161–2
skilled manual *see* occupational categories
Social Change and Economic Life Initiative 145
social closure 7, 32, 37–40, 44–5, 51, 168
social fluidity 21
social mobility, defined 2
 schools of thought 3–5
socialization 63
socio-economic groups 16, 104–5
Sociology ix, x
sons 6, 17, 22, 39, 41, 43, 44, 63, 150, 162,
 172–3
status attainment 63, 64, 68, 71
supervision in work 17–8
supervisory *see* occupational categories
Supplementary Benefit 153
Supply side factors 4–5, 159

teachers 10, 16, 74, 83, 88, 90, 92, 95, 105,
 124–6, 131, 132–3, 134, 149, 172
tightening link 60

trade unions 81, 122

UCCA 93
United States 25, 38, 44, 62–3, 102–3, 123, 150
unemployment 140, 173

voting behaviour 11, 167

War 48, 127
 First World 7
 Second World 2, 7, 51–2, 53, 56–7, 84, 159,
 173
welfare benefits 146
wives 14, 25, 66, 108, 118, 139, 140, 141, 152,
 163
women, and class position (*see* class)
Women and Employment Survey (WES) 10–11,
 13, 43, 45, 83, 84, 86, 87, 88, 123, 125, 134,
 135, 148, 150, 152
women, excluded from mobility studies 12–16
'women's jobs' (*see* by name) 137–8, 168
Work situation 17

Author Index

Abbott, P. 4, 7, 13, 14, 17, 18, 22, 23, 38, 39, 41, 43, 45, 61, 62, 162, 164, 168, 169, 170, 171
Acker, J. 47
Allen, A., see Fogarty, M.
Allen, I., see Fogarty, M.
Allen, S. 104, 111
Arber, S. 13, 119
Armstrong, P. 122
Asher, H. 64
Atkinson, J. 100

Bamford, C., see Dale, A.
Barrett, M. 142
Barron, R. D. 122
Bechhofer, F. 141, see also Kendrick, S.
Beck, S. 161
Becker, G. S. 152
Becker, H. 87
Bechey, V. 122, 140, 150
Blackburn, R. 122, 139, see also Stewart, A.
Blau, P. M. 64
Bonacich, E. 122
Bosanquet, N. 122
Bottomore, T. 37, 38
Boyd, M. 63, see also Stevens, G.
Boyle, T. 65
Bradley, H. 81
Brannen, J. 101, 104, 119
Braverman, H. 84
Britten, N. 14, 47, 167
Brown, R. 9, 90, 122
Browning, H. 58
Bruegel, I. 84
Burgoyne, J. 140

Chaney, J. 129
Chapman, A. 6, 8, 9, 25, 26, 28, 34, 38, 39, 80, 81, 164, 173, see also Payne, G.

Chase, I. D. 102
Chiplin, B. 84
Clarke, D., see Burgoyne, J.
Clarke, E. 58
Clausen, R., see Harris, A.
Cockburn, C. 81, 148, 150
Cooney, R. 63
Corcoran, M. 150
Coyle, A. 122, 151
Craig, C. 122, see also Wedderburn, D.
Crompton, R. 9, 14, 29, 81, 84, 85, 88, 91, 98, 100, 101, 111, 160, 163
Curtis, J., see Heath, A.

Dale, A. 10, 11, 25, 122, 141, 146, 148, 154, 160, 163, 164, see also Arber, S.
Delamont, S. 13, 172
Delphy, C. 145
Dex, S. 5, 10, 13, 25, 28, 44, 61, 83, 84, 87, 104, 121, 122, 123, 125, 148, 160, 163, 164, 165
Dickinson, P., see Hauser, R.
Doeringer, P. B., see Bosanquet, N.
Duncan, B. 65, see also Duncan, O. D.
Duncan, G. J. 153, see also Corcoran, M.
Duncan, O. D. 25, 65, see also Blau, P. M. and Duncan, B.
Edwards, R. C. 84, 122
Eckelaar, J. 153
Elias, P. 85, 86, 95
England, P. 61
Erickson, R. 14, 24, 38, 70
Ermisch, J. 150
Featherman, D. 61, see also Duncan, O. D. and Featherman, D.
Finch, J. 141
Floud, J. 58

Fogarty, M. 87
Ford, G., *see* Payne, G.

Garnsey, E., *see* Craig, C.
Giddens, A. 4, 37, 38
Gilbert, N. 173, *see also* Arber, S. and Dale, A.
Glass, D. V. 2, 12, 25, 58
Glendinning, C. 154
Glenn, N. 103
Goldthorpe, J. 2, 3, 4, 6, 7, 8, 12, 13, 14, 15, 16,
  22, 25, 26, 32, 37, 38, 39, 44, 49, 61, 62, 84,
  85, 101, 121, 139, 166, 168, 169, *see also*
  Erikson, R. and Hope, K.
Gordon, A., *see* Pearson, R.
Graham, H. 144, 155
Greenhalgh, C. 43, 164

Hakim, C. 16, 49, 83, 124
Halsey, A., *see* Floud, J.
Hargen, L. 47
Harris, A. 12
Hartmann, H. 84
Haskey, J. 152
Hauser, R. M. 21, 24, 38, 61, 65, *see also* Rutter,
  K., Featherman, D. and Sewell, W.
Hayes, B. C. 5, 7, 13, 61, 63, 65, 70, 161
Hearn, J. 87, 88
Heath, A. 1, 14, 32, 61, 62, 84, 102, 103, 105,
  161, *see also* Britten, N.
Heritage, J. 98
Hibbert, V. 81
Hindess, B. 161
Holland, L. 81
Hope, K. 12, 26, 49
Hoyan, D., *see* Hauser, R. M.
Hunt, P. 140
Hurstfield, J. 151

Jacobs, J., *see* Powell, B.
Jackson, B. 161
Jackson, J. A. 64
John, A. V. 81
Johnson, T. 58
Jones, G., *see* Crompton, R.
Jones, G. 9, 10, 42, 43, 107, 111, 112, 117, 162,
  168
Joseph, G. 124
Jopshi, H R. 126, 150
Jowell, R., *see* Heath, A.

Kelly, J. 24
Kendrick, S. 78

Kaffel, J., *see* Hauser, R.
Kumar, K. 173

Laczko, F. 147
Land, H. 142, 144
Layard, R. 142
Lazear, E. P. 144
Lee, D. 52
Leonard, F., *see* Delphy, C.
Little, A., *see* Westergaard, J.
Llewellyn, C. 91, 98, *see also* Goldthorpe, J. H.
Lockwood, D. 139
Loether, H. 64
Loveridge, R. 122, 179
Lowe, S. 143

McClendon, J. 61
McCrone, D., *see* Kendrick, S.
McIntosh, M., *see* Barratt, M.
Maclean, M., *see* Eekelaar, J.
McNally, F. 29
McRae, S. 101, 103, 107, 113, 114
McTavish, J., *see* Loether, H.
Main, B. 150, *see also* Elias, P.
Mann, M., *see* Crompton, R.
Marini, M. 61, 65
Marsden, D., *see* Jackson, B.
Marshall, G. 2, 14, 17, 18, 19–20, 21, 22, 38, 39,
  103, 162, 167, 169, 171
Martin, J. 12, 13, 14, 16, 28, 45, 73, 80, 81, 83,
  104, 123, 124, 146, 148
Michael, R. J., *see* Lazear, R. P.
Miliband, R. 37
Millar, J. 154, *see also* Glendinning, C.
Miller, R. L. 5, 7, 13, 64, 70, *see also* Hayes, B. C.
Mok, A., *see* Loveridge, R.
Morgan, J. N., *see* Duncan, G. J.
Muller, W. 65

Newby, H. 139, *see also* Marshall, G.
Norris, G. M., *see* Barron, R. D.

O'Higgins, 141
Oppenheimer, U. K. l47
Osborne, R. 11
Owen, S. 152

Pahl, J. 101, 104, 139, 141, 144, 145, 146
Pahl, R. 14, 73, 101, 140, 141, 142, 152
Parkin, F. 4, 38, 45, 47, 58
Payne, C. 17, *see also* Goldthorpe, J. H.
Payne, G. 1, 2, 3, 4, 14, 16, 21, 25, 26, 34, 49, 51,
  53, 54, 58, 59, 61, 62, 121, 140, 163

Payne, J., 140
Payne, J. M., see Payne, G.
Pearson, J., 62
Pearson, R., 81
Pedhazur, E., 64
Perry, S. M., see Dex, S.
Piachard, D., see Layard, D.
Pike, G., see Pearson, R.
Piore, M. J., 122
Porter, M., 140
Popay, J., see Rimmer, L.
Powell, B., 61
Powers, M. G., 61
Prandy, K., see Stewart, A.
Psacharopoulos, G., 122

Raffe, D., 111
Resler, H., see Westergaard, J.
Riley, D., 81
Rimmer, L., 153
Roberts, C., see Martin, J.
Roberts, K., 87
Robertson, C., see Payne, G.
Rose, D., see Marshall, G.
Rosenfield, R., 62
Ross, A., see Glenn, N.
Rossi, 102
Rowntree, B. S., 141
Rubery, J., 122, see also Craig, C.
Rutter, K., 47

Salto, T., see Cooney, R.
Saunders, P., 16, 21, 22
Sanderson, H. see Crompton, R.
Sapsford, R., see Abbott, P.
Sewell, W., see Rutter, K.
Siltanen, J., 151
Silverstone, R. 98
Singleman, J., see Browning, H.
Sloane, P., see Chiplin, B.

Small, R. 145
Sokolove, A., see Cooney, R.
Sorokin, P. A. 102
Speakman, M. 87
Speath, S. 61
Stanworth, M. 15
Stewart, A. 141
Stewart, M., see Layard, R.
Stewart, M. B., see Greenhalgh, C.
Stevens, G. 62, 63

Tarling, R., see Craig, C.
Titmuss, R. 145
Tolly, J., see Glenn, N.
Townsend, P. 141, 146
Travis, H., see Hauser, R.
Treas, J. 38, 61
Tyree, A. 38, 61, see also Treas, J.

Ulas, M., see Payne, G.

Vogler, C. 145, see also Marshall, G.

Walby, S. 150
Walker, A. 155
Wallace, C., see Abbott, P. and Pahl, R.
Walters, P., see Fogarty, M.
Webster, J. 29
Wedderburn, D. 49
West, J. 29, 45
Westergaard, J. 14, 38, 49
Weyman, C., see Pearson, R.
Wiggins, 64
Wilkinson, F., see Craig, C. and Rubery, J.
Wilson, G., see Brannen, J.
Wolf, W., see Sewell, W.
Wright, E. O. 112
Wright, R. E., see Ermisch, J.

Yeandle, S. 80